HE]
MAGIC

HERMETIC
MAGIC

The Postmodern
Magical Papyrus
of Abaris

Edited and Introduced by
Stephen Edred Flowers, Ph.D.

WEISER BOOKS
Boston, MA/York Beach, ME

First published in 1995 by
Red Wheel/Weiser, LLC
York Beach, ME
With offices at
368 Congress Street
Boston, MA 02210
www.redwheelweiser.com

Library of Congress Cataloging-in-Publication Data

Flowers, Stephen E.
    Hermetic Magic : the postmodern magical papyrus of Abaris /
Stephen Edred Flowers.
        p.   cm.
        1. Hermetism.   2. Magic.   3. Rites and ceremonies.
    1. Title.
    BF1611.F57   1995
    135'.4—dc20   95-38494
    ISBN 0-87728-828-3   CIP
08 07 06 05 04 03
14 13 12 11 10 9 8 7 6

TS

Typeset in 11 point Garamond

Printed in the United States of America

07   06   05   04   03
10   9   8   7   6   5   4   3

The paper used in this publication meets the minimum requirements of the
American National Standard for Information Sciences—Permanence of Paper for
Printed Library Materials Z39.48-1984.

This work is dedicated to my Teachers, my Students, and most especially to Pη–εν–Σηθ, whose Word guided my hand, and to Σετνακτ, whose Works show us further horizons.

It is also dedicated, in the deepest sense, to Κρυσταλλια, who is my Wisdom and my Power.

Table of Contents

PART I: A HISTORY OF HERMETIC MAGIC

PART II: THEORY

APPENDICES

Figures

Tables

Preface

"*Quod superius est sicut quod inferius et quod inferius est sicut quod superius ad perpetranda miracula rei unius*—That which is above is like that which is below and that which is below is like that which is above, to achieve the wonders of the One Thing." These words ring out from the wisdom of Hermês Trismegistos—the Thrice-Greatest, as recorded in the *Tabula Smaragdina*, or *Emerald Tablet*. As it was, so it might also be, applied to the Hermetic laws as far as the working of true Hermetic magical formulas is concerned. The Hermetic tradition of magic is one of the most often invoked of the so-called Western schools of magic. Its technical formulas have been well documented for nearly a hundred years. But even now they remain only barely known to the community of modern magicians—or theurgists—who would make use of them. The formulas have been "buried" out in the open—in academic books, many written in non-English languages. This book is intended to open the gate to the actual use of the real Hermetic formulas concealed in the magical papyri of Egypt.

These formulas are at least part of the basis of what later came to be known as the "Hermetic tradition." The most famous example of this is the "Hermetic Order of the Golden Dawn" in the late 1800s. The Victorian understanding of the formulas was, however, rather limited and sometimes misinformed. No doubt the magic contained in the papyri has great potency. It represents the first known attempt to bring together many traditions of magic in the world and to forge them into a unified eclectic system. The papyri themselves, the great repository of these formulas, required extensive research by experts over a period of several decades before they were truly ready to reveal their many secrets. Now is that time. These are their secrets.

I originally had the idea for this book when doing academic research for the Runic school of magic. I became aware of the fact that there were well over a hundred documents of original magical literature dating from the first four centuries C.E. which contained the roots of what was widely practiced out of occult books of our day. These documents were written in the Greek, Coptic, and Egyptian languages.

Further research, both scholarly and practical, revealed that the magic of the papyri was much more "down to earth" and pragmatic than the often complex forms of Renaissance and Victorian occultism derived from the practices outlined in the papyri. This pragmatic base became clear once a certain set of codes was cracked open.

This book also might have been titled "The Practical Greek Kabbalah." But this title would not be entirely accurate. It would, however, express the great debt we owe to the Hebrew tradition for having preserved intact a system of mystical speculation and cosmology. Without the Hebrew Kabbalah the reconstruction of the "Hellenistic Cosmograph" would have been impossible. However, the tradition expressed in this text is something *other* than the Hebrew Kabbalah. It is a *pagan* parallel and analog to that tradition.

The original papyri contain many formulas which call for animal sacrifice or the use of substances that must be obtained from dead animals. *None of the workings presented in this book do so.* But we must remember the time and place of the papyri—a largely agricultural world of some 1500 to 2000 years ago. When one of the old spells called for the "blood of a black ass," it was really no more a rare ingredient than, let's say, the crank case oil of a black Chevy pickup truck would be today. I would advise anyone who is going to use this book seriously to look into the originals behind the forms given here. (They can be found in English translation in *The Greek Magical Papyri in Translation,* edited by Professor Hans Dieter Betz, published by the University of Chicago Press in 1986.) In choosing the models for the workings given in the practical part of this book, I always chose ones that did not even originally require the use of practices or substances now repugnant to us. This, by the way, was not difficult since a great number of the workings rely almost totally on verbal and other symbolic acts.

In many ways this book is different from other modern manuals of magical practice. More details are given on how it is different in the introduction. If you find yourself *mystified* by the contents of the book, refer back to this preface for clarification.

This is a book of experimental and experiential philosophy and paleology—the study of ancient things. It is not enough to read about such things. We can learn something of the true essence of a teaching by experiencing its actions as much as by hearing or reading its words. Purely "academic" exploration is rarely transformative. The voyager must actually do, work, experience and thereby gain real results and real understanding. It is by such voyaging that the magician reaches the opposite shore of the river.

But as the Hermetic dictum is applied to a temporal model—as it was, so shall it be—by experiencing the sights, sounds, thoughts, actions, and all the dozens of other things that come with the performance of magical acts, we can not only become one with the ancients, but more importantly we can become one with the very models or "paradigms" they themselves were using.

It is my hope that the reader—the experimenter and explorer—will undertake this voyage of discovery along the path of the ancient Hermeticists. To know, to will, to dare, and to conceal what you learn in the depths of your hearts. For, in the end, no matter how much you try to say concerning what you will experience, the truth will only be audible in silence.

Stephen Edred Flowers, Ph.D.
Μαγος Μυστηιου
Austin, Texas

Abbreviations

Notes on Pronunciation

Sometimes approximate phonetic representations of shorter vocal formulas are placed in square brackets immediately after the formulas, for example: ABLANATHANALBA [ah-blahn-ah-t'ahn-AHLB-ah]. A complete guide to the pronunciation of the Greek letters, or *elements*, is provided in Appendix F.

Also, in the original Greek of the period (100–500 C.E.) the *theta* and *phi* were not pronounced as modern English "th" and "ph" ("f"), but rather as strongly aspirated "t" and "p" respectively, which are rendered here phonetically as t' and p'.

Acknowledgments

Special thanks go to Ronald L. Barrett, Robert Menschel, Robertt Neilly, Don and Rosemary Webb, and Robert Zoller for their thoughtful reading of the manuscript and helpful commentaries.

Introduction

This book consists of four main parts or sections. Each is necessary, each completes the other. The history, theory, practice, and actual examples of experimental operations must each be explored, worked through and realized before a true quintessence can be reached. The history of the ancient Hermetic tradition must be understood today in order for us to grasp, even in some small way, the place it held in the matrix of world cultures. As Hermeticism is essentially a synthetic tradition, that is, it brings together diverse elements and harmonizes them into a whole, the various elements need to be understood so that a new synthesis can be reached by each individual Hermetic in this postmodern era. What was done in ancient times can be done again. But we must understand *how* it was done.

Theory is not dry, cognitive wool-gathering. On the contrary, it is the process of vivifying internal models of thought which gives life and vitality to magical practice. Practice without a basis in sound theory usually ends in the muddle-headed mumbo-jumbo so often too typical of "okkultnik" culture. The Greek word θεορεια (*theoreia*) means contemplation—from the verb *theoreô*. A true theory must be based on thought deeper than what is normally used in everyday life; the things observed must be more profound than everyday occurrences. A truly Hermetic theory can only be developed in conjunction with practice—*praxis*.

Practice is the actual exercise or enacting of the theoretical base, each operation of which, if contemplated, will perhaps in some way modify the theory until some true, Hermetic understanding is gained. The postmodern papyrus of Abaris is a collection of authentic ancient operational formulas specially translated and edited for this work. The fact that each is closely based on a formula originating in ancient times is essential to grasp. By re-enacting the ancient formulas, you undertake a higher form of magic than may seem to be the case with each individual operation. On one level you may be calling forth a lover of flesh and blood, but on another you are call-

ing forth the spirit of the time of the ancient papyri—you are bend-
ing time to your will, you are shifting paradigms by magic.

What lies before you is a postmodern experiment in opening
the mouths of the ancient Hermetic magicians. With this work their
methods and symbolism are allowed to speak to the reader directly,
as they spoke to the writer as the work was being put together. The
gods and goddesses standing at the gateways to this kind of knowledge have long been silent. Many have tried to make them speak in
the past century and a half. But the God of the old papyri does not
demand worship, but rather study and work. If this work is filled
with an exacting combination of passion and precision, the methods
of the Hermetic magicians can again yield a harvest of wondrous
powers.

This harvest can not be enjoyed by the multitude. Results of
successful work can not be transferred easily from one magician to
others. An attempt at work of this nature is witnessed by the life of
Jesus the Naassarene (the Serpentine). The subsequent and immediate betrayal of the work of that *magos* by his would-be followers is a
testimony to the impossibility of the results of work by one magician
being transferred to others. Methods of initiation, of μαγεια, and
even "salvation" can be taught, but all true magicians must ultimately
find the secret, the mystery of their own existences, from within.

The contents of this book, this new papyrus, describe many examples and clues to the unlocking of certain secrets hidden within
the souls of seventy-two men and women who will read its pages.
Many more will read the pages, of course, but only those seventy-two
will truly understand the mystery contained in them.

Within the idea of mystery there is the possibility of ultimate
understanding. On every leaf of this book there is a mystery. Readers
must look beyond appearances to the hidden, unmanifest reality
from which the appearances come, and which the appearances in
turn conceal from the eye of the seeker. This, at least in part, is how
the power of the *Mystêrion*, or as the Egyptians would have said it,
the *shtat*, works in the mind of magicians to give direction and impetus to their initiations. The papyrus which lies before you is an exercise in this principle or *archê* of existence, and comes from the *aiôn*
of the original Mystery.

How to Use this Book

This is not a typical manual of contemporary magical practice. Its purpose is not to indoctrinate the reader in a certain set form of cosmology and theology—although the generation of these things is essential to development of the individual magician. Rather, this book is intended as a *guide* for the creation of a new and *original synthesis* by the individual magician based on the same constituent parts that would have faced developing Hermetic magicians around 2000 years ago. The very *process* put forward by the book is an alchemical one. Elements are analyzed and recombined into a unique new synthesis—*solve et coagula.*

Early readers of the unpublished manuscript of this book were sometimes baffled by its structure. This was perhaps because its approach is so novel, or perhaps because they had not been exposed to the necessary *preliminary discourse* which I hope this preface will provide.

The book is divided into four parts: History, Theory, Practice, and Operation in the form of the text of the "Magical Papyrus of Abaris." In fact there are within these four divisions, three phenomena which can and should take place in someone who *studies* the contents of the book. The first phase is that of *theoria* (θεορεια), which encompasses the first two parts of the book. "Theory" is *thinking.* The reader is challenged to work through the contents of the first two parts of the book carefully and thoughtfully. Success in the first phase is the beginning of the second—*praxis* (πραξις). Practice comes from actual enactment of the objective data the reader has absorbed into his or her subjective universe. Practice is work. From work comes the actual experience of theory—which leads to real understanding. The operations which make up the last part of the text are the result of the author's active explorations of both *theoria* and *praxis.* This experience, if profound, will lead inevitably to the emergence of a Teaching (δοξα). The Teaching of the author is embedded in the whole of the book, but is especially to be found in this preface, in the synthetic "epistles" of Abaris, and in the editions of the operations themselves. The implicit exhortation is for the one-time student to evolve his or her own Teaching. Then and only then will the final stage of real progress be possible.

The old Hermetic books make reference to the culmination of this process when the teacher charges the student to take what has been taught and "carve for yourself in hieroglyphics in turquoise in the temple at Memphis."

Too much has been made in recent years of the idea that "magic is for the millions," that it is *easy* to understand and therefore easy to practice. In fact *magia*, as described in this book, is the most challenging of human endeavors. *Magia* is the development of the self to a virtually *divine* level. It is ludicrous to undertake such a process lightly or to assume this aim is easily attained. To do so is to make the difficult impossible.

Magical knowledge is *mysterious* knowledge. Books which purport to *clarify* magic to you in the same way that Greek grammar or geometry might be explained or taught are doing you a disservice. Magical knowledge, or *gnôsis*, must come through a combination of theory and experience in such a way that the *gnôsis* comes as a genuine, unique and original *discovery* on your part of something which had been up to that moment *hidden* and outside your conscious mind. This is why real Mysteries can not be "revealed" in profane words, but only through extended metaphors and whole methodological discourses.

The Word, or Λογος, which guides this Work is *Mystêrion* (or Mystery)—also sometimes referred to as *Kryptôn*—that which is Hidden. The Egyptians called it *sht-at*, and the Hebrews referred to such things as *razim*. The "trick" is to focus on actual Mysteries and to avoid concentration on "pseudo-mysteries." False mysteries are things that are secret simply because someone decides not to inform you about them. Real Mysteries are those things which can only be revealed, or discovered, *mysteriously*.

To illustrate this last point, compare "atomic secrets," which are just technical formulas on how to split the atom with "secrets of the atom"—which are tantamount to cosmological mysteries which can only be grasped in moments of extreme intellectual lucidity informed by the theories of physics. The first example is secret because of circumstances in the outer or objective universe (national security, and what not) while the second example remains secret because of realities of the inner world of the mind, or the absolute subjective universe.

In the original Greek of the magical papyri themselves, the words "magic" (μαγεια) and "mystery" (μυστηριον) are often used synonymously. *Magia* is the technical practice, while *mysterium* is the theory or overall inner framework of the technology.

Paradoxically, this seemingly obfuscating or obscurant concept of the Mystery actually leads the Hermetic magician toward clarity and precision. This is why it is so essential to magical theory. The practice of seeking the Mysteries fills the magician with power (*dynamis*) and the understanding of the mysteries creates conditions for self-transformation. This latter is the case because, in the unknown space of the mysterious, the self of the magician finds space to grow.

The method of the use of Mystery must involve a high degree of intellectual precision combined with an equally high degree of enthusiasm or passion for what is being done. Real Mysteries must be explored and penetrated both objectively and subjectively. The best scientific knowledge (Gk. *epistêmê* or *dianoia*) must be combined with inspired leaps of faith to result in sublime *gnôsis*. The use of mysterious symbols and aesthetically inspirational models can have wondrous effects and provide tremendous energy to the process of transformation. But if there is no rational and objective basis, the ultimate results are likely to be inauthentic and vacuous.

In an absolute sense, the method of this book is based on the eighth precept of the *Emerald Tablet*, attributed to Hermês Trismegistus. It says:

> Use your mind to its full extent and rise from Earth to Heaven, and then descend to Earth and combine the powers of what is above with what is below. Thus you will win glory in the whole world, and obscurity will leave you at once.

This means that the alchemist is to oscillate between the subjective spiritual realms (those "above") wherein dwell the sublime forms of theory and the Mind, and the objective material realms (those "below") wherein the forms and theories can be tested and perfected as nowhere else in the cosmos. This bipolar path leads to the greatest states of accomplishment, the highest levels of power—and the clearest levels of understanding. In a pragmatic sense this process is reflected in my method: [objective analysis] → [subjective synthesis] → [enactment]. Objective analysis of the data prepares the Mind for its assent to the upper realms where the subjective (inner) synthesis takes place. The process is not complete, however, until the subject *returns* from the inner (or "upper") realm to test his or her transformations on the world through *enactment* of the vision.

Essential to full and authentic use of this book and the method it espouses is a thorough study of the *Corpus Hermeticum* and other genuinely Hermetic texts of antiquity. This also includes the *Greek Magical Papyri*, of course. These are the primary *objects* of the objective analysis phase of the method. This book is an *example* of what can be done, but each individual must undertake his or her own journey to gain the full benefit of the method. Primary focus must be on the *oldest* available material which mostly comes from the first five centuries of the Common Era. According to the theory behind this book, pragmatic works of *Hermetic magic* were often preludes to further more spiritual, or subjective, work with the same theories. But with a background in the practical and objective effects of magic, the emergent Hermetic master would have a more complete grasp of the principles at work than someone who dealt with the theories only subjectively.

When and if you find yourself *mystified* by the contents of this book, I invite you to return to this preface and consider its words again. All knowledge and all power begin with a Sense of Mystery.

Ζητει Μυστηρια!

Part I

A History
of
Hermetic
Magic

ORIGINS

The kind of magic and philosophy we now call "Hermetic" is most clearly seen in documents dating from the first four or five centuries C.E. The epicenter of Hermetic ideas was Alexandria in the Nile Delta. This is where the ancient Greek (or Hellenic) culture and that of Egypt were most completely and powerfully brought together. A secondary site of this activity was in the Fayyum. These are the places where the two cultures most easily mixed—in both ethos and ethnos.

Our most important source for the study of operative Hermetic magic is the body of text known as the "Greek magical papyri." These will be discussed in more detail below. For now it is important to clarify that this body of writings is not *entirely* "Hermetic" in the strict philosophical, or even "theological" definition of the term. Our thesis is that the Hermetic path was one of gradual *intellectualization* or *spiritualization* of initiation. As the Hermetic initiates came closer to their goal, the techniques became progressively more focused on purely *Hermetic* imagery and language, but in the earlier stages of the work, it was more eclectic in its tastes and more practical in its methods.

The complex Hermetic tradition has a dual heritage. This is clear when we look into the origin of the name "Hermetic." The school is named after the Greek god Hermês (Gk.Ἑρμῆς), who is widely thought to be at least in part a Greek reinterpretation of the Egyptian god Thoth. The actual Egyptian form of his name is 𓅝 *dhwty* [jhuty]. This, the chief Hermetic god, was known in the tradition as Hermês Trismegistos—the Thrice-Greatest. In truth he is an amalgamation of the magicians' god of the Greeks and Egyptians—but also contains the seeds of all the other "gods of magic" from the Hebrews, Babylonians, and Persians as well.

If we look to the very deepest roots we can uncover the dual heritage of the Hermetic tradition. One of these roots underlies the Greek or Hellenic culture: the Indo-European. The other is that of the Semito-Hamitic or Egyptian culture. In the Hermetic magical system these two distinct, and usually distant, cultures have been

brought together in a pagan context. This original synthesis then becomes the model for any and all future amalgamations of magical traditions under the code name "Hermetic."

Ultimately all of these texts are Hermetic in the sense that they
are examples of operative magic, and Thoth-Hermês is *the* god of
magic *par excellence*. His patronage would have been understood as
being essential to the whole process in the time and place the papyri
were produced.

The Hellenic Root

We conveniently call "Indo-European" the descendants of that great
mass of folk speaking a related dialect and worshipping a certain pantheon of related gods and goddesses. The original homeland of these
people was somewhere in the region north of the Black and Caspian
Seas over 6000 years ago. One branch of this culture made its way
into the southern part of the Balkan peninsula (present-day Greece)
as early as 1900 B.C.E. Other independent groups of these folk later
formed the Germanic, Celtic, Slavic, and Italic peoples. The most
notable of the Italics were the Romans. These Indo-Europeans also
spread at an early date into central and southern Asia, where they
called themselves Irani and Aryans.

The ancient Indo-Europeans had a three-fold structure of the
divine. The pantheon was divided into three levels: the first of sovereign power, the second of physical power, and the third of productive
or generative power. The first of these was further refined into two
factors. One ruled the forces of law and order (among the Greeks this
was originally the purview of Zeus). Later some of Zeus' characteristics were absorbed by Apollo. The other factor was ruled by the forces
of magic and mantic activities of the mind. This was, at the oldest
stage, the realm of Hermês. Later his function was absorbed by other
gods and goddesses, including both Apollo and Dionysius. Hermês
was the inventor of writing and the great communicator.

Of course, like all peoples, the Indo-Europeans had their magical traditions. Some of these can be gleaned through comparative

study of the oldest levels of Celtic, Germanic, Roman, Greek, and Indo-Iranian magical practices.

The Hermês of the Greeks, the Mercury of the Romans, is the god of communication; the god who is in charge of transporting the souls of the dead to realms beyond the earth (a psychopomp); the god of inspired intellect and quick wit. The magic of Hermês is rooted in the intellectual faculty of humanity—in the part of the mind which understands the forms of symbols and can put them into inspired words of poetry. Hermês has the power to synthesize the contents of the right and left sides of the brain, and to put them into communicable forms, both verbal and nonverbal (signs, symbols, gestures, music, and so on).

The Hellenic spirit, exemplified in Hermês, is one which can take elements from a wide variety of sources and *synthesize* them into a *harmonious* whole. Since their early history, the Greeks had brought together elements from every exotic culture or civilization with which they had come into contact—the Aegean (Minoan), Anatolian, Persian, Hebraic/Canaanite, Mesopotamian, and Egyptian. This was made possible through the intellectual facility present in the genius of Hermês.

It was the intellectual spirit of Hermês that the Greeks brought to Egypt. This spirit confronted the Egyptian gods and goddesses and the kinds of magic done in their names, and from the synthesis of the two systems, Hellenic and Egyptian, the Hermetic tradition was born. Even in the latest phases of the Hermetic tradition, the Greek Hermês and the Egyptian Hermês were distinguished at a certain level. The Greek god was called Hermês Logios and was the focus of magical attention outside Egypt. Theurgically, his cult seems just as "Hermetic" as that of Trismegistus, "the Egyptian."

The Egyptian Root

The importance of Egyptian magic and philosophy in the origins of the Hermetic tradition can not be overestimated. One of the chief reasons for this is that probably most, if not all, of the actual authors of the magical papyri were *ethnic* Egyptians—although they were highly Hellenized. They had learned the Greek language and wrote and spoke it fluently; they had absorbed Greek philosophy and modalities of thought. One of the chief signs of this Hellenization is the enormous *eclecticism* of the technical Hermetic tradition. This is totally foreign to the purely Egyptian mentality, which is intrinsically highly xenophobic.

Hellenic culture began to influence Egypt strongly from about 660 B.C.E., when Gyges, the king of Lydia, sent mercenary troops to help secure the reign of Psammethichus I. After the war, the Greek soldiers were settled in Egypt. But the strongest Hellenistic influence is historically traced to the conquest of Egypt by Alexander the Great in 332 B.C.E. For several centuries, even millennia, preceding this date, however, there had been a long period of cultural exchange between the Greeks and Egyptians. Greek philosophers and magicians often cited Egypt as the ultimate source of their knowledge. The romantic allure of Egyptian origins has been an enduring motif in the history of western esoterica.

Egyptian thought and magical technology must be considered the basis of Hermetic, or actually, Thothian, philosophy and magic. Over this Egyptian base, Hellenistic philosophy and intellectual conceptions were laid to create a new synthesis which is the essence of the Hermetic tradition itself.

The Egyptian god commonly called Thoth was the patron of magic because he was the embodiment of Intelligence and the chief architect of the process of *communication.* These two elements are essential to the practice of *mageia.* Even the Greeks thought of the Egyptian Hermês as the exemplary model of *the magician,* and thought that the books of Thoth had been translated into Greek at an archaic period of time—"after the Flood."

In many ways the intellectual content of Egyptian philosophy remains obscure. The conceptual world of the ancient Egyptian and the modern European are sufficiently different to make substantial understanding difficult. The Hellenizing of Egyptian thought allows easier access to the intellectual world of Egypt as it existed in the Hellenistic and Roman periods—although it had by that time become significantly "westernized" or "Europeanized" in the process.

Egyptian magic is somewhat easier to comprehend because it conforms in most respects to the internal logic of magical operations throughout history. In the Egyptian religious tradition magic plays a large and often official role in the cult of the gods and goddesses.

The Hermetic Tradition

Many scholars would like to divide the Hermetic literary tradition into two distinct types: the philosophical (exemplified in the *Corpus Hermeticum*) and the technical or magical (one example of which is the Greek magical papyri). The philosophical tradition, they say, is worthy of serious attention, while the magical tradition is "rubbish." Attitudes such as this are merely indicative of the disease I call "modernosis." One who suffers from this disease believes that "magic" is a primitive stage of "religion," which has now given way to the new and improved way, to the true form of knowledge known as "science." In retrospect we can now see that magic is as much with us today as it was in ancient times, and that in fact some ancients were often every bit as "scientific" in their thought as moderns.

The magical tradition is merely the *operative* branch of the philosophy, which is more analytical or *illustrative*. In ancient times the two branches worked together in individuals and their schools of thought. Each had its place in the whole scheme of human endeavor—and so it should be again today in this post-modern world. In fact the very division between the two is an obviously modern invention. It has helped us to understand certain aspects of the tradition, but it has limited us in important ways too. Even scholars have begun to realize the limitations, and are coming to realize more and more that the "operative," "technical," and "philosophical" *genres* of Hermetic literature are really facets of a whole. A clarification of this problem is provided by Garth Fowden in his landmark study *The Egyptian Hermes*.

The operative tradition is mainly encoded in the magical papyri. These were recorded in Egypt and there are three major types of them linguistically: Greek, Demotic Egyptian, and Coptic. The technical tradition covers what appears to be a scientific field as this encompasses descriptions of natural phenomena in the context of the hidden sympathies which exist between and among them. The technical Hermetica include treatises on alchemy and astronomy (or astrology). The philosophical tradition is contained in a body of independent texts known as the *Corpus Hermeticum.*

Hermetic philosophy and operative technology is a combination of every major stream of thought present in the eastern Mediterranean region in the first few centuries after the birth of Jesus. It brings Gnosticism together with Neo-Platonism and Stoicism, and places them all in an Egyptian cultural matrix. It assimilates elements from the religious and philosophical systems of the Hebrews, Mesopotamians, and Persians. The concepts contained in Greco-Roman as well as Egyptian mystery schools were encompassed, as were some formulas and ideas taken from the fledgling Christian system. In the main, however, the genius of the Hermetic system was a dynamic and non-dogmatic assimilation of the two major esoteric cosmologies of the day: Gnosticism and Neo-Platonism.

Hermetic magic is in essence an operationalizing of the philosophy within the technical matrix. The same cultural and philosophical elements are assimilated and synthesized in the magical papyri as in the *Corpus Hermeticum.* But magic is something one *does,* or eventually which one *is,* not merely something one *contemplates.* But through a combination of action and thought the actual essence of a person can be raised qualitatively—and with that rise in quality true understanding can grow. A few of the ancients understood this— most modernists have forgotten it—but some post-modernists are beginning to remember.

The Ancient Phase

Development of the
Hermetic Tradition

Much of the development of the Hermetic tradition is lost in the relatively undocumented centuries before the birth of Jesus. It is clear that the tradition was being developed over these centuries, and that what we have in the oldest of the magical papyri is in fact a mature synthesis of the various magical and philosophical streams that had been crisscrossing the Nilotic culture for centuries.

The most significant development in the final stages of the history of ancient Egypt was its conquest by the Romans in 30 B.C.E. With this development, Hellenic and Egyptian cultures were forced together more than they had been before during the Hellenistic period—now both were subject peoples in the Roman Empire. In some respects the Hermetica could be considered philosophical reactions to cultural oppression.

By about 200 C.E. a well-documented combination of elements had come together which became the basis for the continuing development of the Hermetic tradition. This is the basis for the texts which serve as the original foundation for the magical operations presented in this book.

Early Development | During the period when our source texts were being recorded, there appears to have been a gradual development in the ideological content away from the ancient Egyptian models and more and more toward the Hellenistic models. This is simply because the old culture of Egypt was retreating increasingly into the background—knowledge of hieroglyphics and the cultic forms of the gods and goddesses of the Nile slowly gave way to more foreign features. Among these foreign influences was the growing presence of Christian material.

The vast majority of the magical papyri we have date from this period (200–400 C.E.). Their contents are certainly older, but the actual dates of most of the papyri themselves fall within this time frame. Technical Hermetica were being written perhaps as early as the middle of the second century B.C.E. These were for the most part "scientific" treatises on hidden sympathies between natural phenomena, and here too was the beginnings of alchemy, later to become a dominant aspect of Hermeticism.

The ideological content of the papyri form a relatively stable mixture of elements. The three main components of this mixture are the Egyptian, Greek, and Hebraic mythological and magical traditions. The Hermetic magician-philosophers used these elements in ways independent of any of the official traditions themselves. They were neither simply Egyptian or Greek pagans, nor were they Jews, and they were certainly not Christians. They had formed their own eclectic philosophical and operative religion and spiritual technology.

The magical traditions developed in three different strata of the written record: there were Demotic Egyptian magical papyri (whose contents are mostly Egyptian and, we must suppose, most representative of the ancient Egyptian magical technologies), Coptic magical papyri (beginning around 100 C.E. which come to embody a Hermeto-Christian synthesis) and the Greek magical papyri, which are essentially pagan and cosmopolitan.

Medieval Development   With the eventual development of dogmatic, institutionalized Christianity, the Hermetic tradition was increasingly suppressed in the geographical regions controlled by the church. Hermetic magic and philosophy, like that of all other "non-Christian" systems, was ruthlessly persecuted.

Curiously, however, the Hermetic tradition, at least the written form of it, was given a high level of respect and admiration by some of the early church leaders and writers. For example, Didymus the Blind (ca. 313–398) quotes from known Hermetic texts in his Christian treatise titled *On the Trinity*. Before him, Lactantius had praised Hermês Trismegistus as a "prophet of Christ," as did Cyril of Alexandria (died 444). These men and many others, were so impressed by Hermetic teachings that they incorporated many of them in their Christian doctrines—and simply "saw" in them the *true teachings of Christ.* Hermês came to be called by some "a Christian before Christ"!

Following the rise of Islam in the East, which conquered Egypt in 638 C.E., the Hermetic body of literature, as well as the ideas contained in it, was preserved better in the Islamic world. This is because Islam was more tolerant when it came to divergent ideas than were the Christians of the period. As long as the Muslim met his religious obligations to Allah, what he did in other fields was often more or less his own affair.

Islamic assimilation of magical technology in both the fields of operative magic as well as in the areas of alchemy and astrology—which were also part of the early Hermetic tradition—ensured its survival.

The church could not, however, prevent Hermetic ideas from penetrating into European culture even at the height of its power in the Middle Ages. For example, texts from the 1100s and 1200s which celebrate the mysteries of courtly love and the Grail legends often contain Gnostic and Hermetic ideas. The epic *Parzival* by Wolfram von Eschenbach is the crown of this creative achievement.[1]

At the same time many Hermetic and Gnostic ideas were absorbed into the esoteric tradition, or Kabbalah, of the medieval Jews throughout the world. These were mixed with their own theology and unique mystical insights and preserved in their remarkable books and schools of wisdom. Because they stood outside the stream of Christian dogma, these traditions were able to survive intact.

The Modern Phase

Renaissance and Enlightenment Philosophy

The modern world really began in northern Italy during the 15th century. Although modernism is characterized by the intellectual rejection of medieval Christian teachings based on faith in favor of objective knowledge, nevertheless it bore the legacy of the long shadow of the church in many ways. The new Hermeticists in the west would be men who still had a great deal of sentimental attachment to some ideas inherent in church teachings. They were therefore much more likely to see "Christian" things in the Hermetic tradition that were never actually there, or

---

[1]Wolfram von Eschenbach, *Parzival* (New York: Viking Penguin, 1980).

that were actually borrowed from Hermetic teachings by early Christians. From a Hermetic perspective, indeed, the teachings of the Thrice-Greatest were the root of all religions and all philosophies. Because Hermeticism is suited to account for all types of philosophies, it can be considered the root of all philosophies.

In fact, as we have seen, this "discovery" of Christian ideas in Hermetica was an old phenomenon at the time of the Renaissance. It had come so far by the 1400s in Italy that Hermês Trismegistus was honored as a quasi-saint in the art work of the cathedral at Siena, Italy, built around 1488. There we find a pavement mosaic with the inscription HERMIS MERCURIUS TRISMEGISTUS CONTEMPORANEUS MOYSI [Hermes-Mercury the Thrice-Greatest, contemporary of Moses].

Most of what the West had learned of the Hermetic tradition in the Middle Ages was fragmentary. But in 1460, the ruler of Florentine, Cosimo de Medici, acquired an original Greek manuscript of the *Corpus Hermeticum* and immediately commissioned the Florentine scholar and magician Marcilio Ficino to translate the entire text into Latin. This work was completed in 1463. In those days it was widely believed that the *corpus* contained the most ancient religious teaching available to humankind. By the way, most Renaissance philosophers and magicians believed they were being perfectly orthodox in their Christianity in their explorations of the Hermetic tradition, because they thought it represented the original theology—which found its culmination in Christ.

Throughout the Renaissance, more and more original Greek and Latin magical texts came to the attention of magicians and philosophers (both spiritual and natural). Also, Arabic texts based on the Hermetic tradition, especially in the field of alchemy, found their way into the increasingly free intellectual world of western Europe.

The role of magic—especially Hermetic magic—in the development of modern natural sciences remains generally unacknowledged. It is true, however, that many of the models of understanding, as well as fundamental theories used by, for example, Paracelsus (father of modern medicine) during the Renaissance, or Isaac Newton in the Enlightenment, had their origins in magical Hermetic philosophy. Chief among these ideas is the assumption that there is a direct correspondence between the larger world and the smaller one—between what would be called the macrocosm and the microcosm.

Romantic Occult Revival | Beginning in the 19th century the Hermetic tradition began to reassert itself as a truly *spiritual* methodology. This new beginning occurred during the Romantic period of European intellectual history. Interest in magic, and even the code-word "Hermetic," found a new level of enthusiasm.

The magical papyri were discovered in Egypt in the early part of the 19th century and transported to various western European libraries and museums. But these seminal magical texts made little or no impact on the practice of magic in the occult revival. The tradition they represented had undergone such a transformation through the centuries that the original essence could now hardly be recognized as being truly "Hermetic." So much elegant Victorian refinement and civilization had turned the vital and vibrant tradition of the papyri into the long-winded mutterings of a few old gentlemen.

It is ironic that the popularity of the idea of Hermeticism and the discovery of the actual papyri should come so close together historically. It would be another hundred years before the papyri were analyzed and published as a corpus. For many years the idea of Hermeticism was popular among practicing magicians, but the actual Hermetic tradition of magic remained secluded in the truly "arcane" world of academia. An early and somewhat inaccurate translation of one of the papyri by Charles Wycliffe Goodwin provided the "Bornless Ritual" used by the Hermetic Order of the Golden Dawn and subsequently by Aleister Crowley in his translation of the *Goêtia*, or "Lesser Key of Solomon."

The Postmodern Phase

Does anyone doubt that since the end of World War II we have been living on the brink of a new era in the history of the development of human ideas? At present we are in a rather confusing twilight zone for most people. But in the years to come, more and more people will begin to abandon the futile universalistic pipe dreams of the modernists, as they abandoned the catholic nightmares of the medievalists before them. For want of a better term, this new era is at present being called the post-modern period.

Postmodernism is characterized by a freedom from the pervasive modern myth of progress—the idea that as time goes on, by applying ever increasing rationality and scientific methodology, the problems of the world will be universally evaporated in the light of pure reason. The postmodernist realizes, as did the ancients, that such progress is only possible for *individuals*. Furthermore, the postmodernist is free of the constraints of modern progressivism: To the modern if it's not new, if it's not the *latest* thing, then it is "retrograde" or "reactionary" and hence unacceptable. Post-modernists are free to synthesize elements from all phases of human history—in any shape or form that suits their purposes. Therefore, the contents of texts such as the magical papyri gain a new relevance and potential for individual empowerment.

The Papyri in History

It is in the papyri, written down in the first few centuries of our era, that we have the most direct evidence of the nature and quality of the earliest form of the Hermetic school of magic. Without the survival of these physical objects, we would be able to *know* virtually nothing of the true tradition. Until recently the knowledge contained in these papyri has been obscured by ignorance and misunderstanding.

Papyrus is an early form of highly durable *paper* (a word derived from the Greek παπυρος, an Egyptian rush with triangular leaves). It was used in early Egyptian times, from about the Vth Dynasty, or 2500 B.C.E., but relatively few survive from that very ancient period.

Most of the original magical papyri adapted for this collection were written between the first and sixth centuries C.E.—that is, between the time of the historical Jesus and the year 500 C.E. The vast majority of the magical papyri are written with ink in the Greek language and using Greek letters. A few magical papyri were also written in Demotic Egyptian.

Time and intellectual tyrants have not been kind to the magical literary tradition. Early "Christian" church leaders were very anxious to destroy the magical texts (usually by burning)—and sometimes those who possessed such books were also burned along with them. In the Acts of the Apostles (19:19) we read that in Ephesus (an ancient city famous for magic located in what is now western Turkey) many magicians' books were burned as a part of the price of conversion to Christianity.

The early Muslims were no kinder to the old pagan learning. The destruction of the library of Alexandria in 641 is only the most famous example of the attempted programmatic destruction of the intellectual heritage of pagan antiquity by the orthodox religious forces of the day.

An extremely small fraction of these texts did survive. A number of them were collected by an unknown magician and scholar in the ancient city of Thebes (present-day Luxor). This unknown collector must have lived sometime before the year 500 C.E. He collected magical papyri in both the Greek and the Egyptian tongue, and was certainly a learned Egyptian, probably also of a philosophical type. Without doubt he was one of the last of the learned pagans—the keeper of a wisdom which was finally utterly extinguished by the coming of the Islamic conquest in the middle of the seventh century.

It was Egyptian tradition to bury sacred magical texts with the bodies of their owners. It was probably in such a tomb, the tomb of the unknown collector, that the papyri were discovered (or robbed) around 1300 years after the death and burial of the collector.

In the wake of Napoleon's conquest of parts of Egypt (in 1798) Europeans began looting, destroying, and in some cases saving, large amounts of the surviving Egyptian antiquities. One of these men was an ethnic Armenian calling himself Jean d'Anastasi (1780?–1857). He bought the bulk of the known magical papyri in a single purchase in Thebes and had the entire lot shipped to Europe where they were auctioned off to a variety of European museums, such as the British Museum, the Bibliothèque Nationale in Paris, the Staatliche Museum in Berlin and the Rijksmuseum in Leiden.

For several decades the papyri were unappreciated and virtually unknown. A few scholars began to give them some attention in the middle of the 19th century. In 1853 Goodwin published a translation of *PGM* V, which contains the misnamed "Bornless Ritual." Papyrology was in its infancy in Goodwin's day and there were a number of errors and question marks in his text that have been clarified in the meantime. Operation number 3 in the practical part of this book presents a more accurate version for those who wish to make use of it.

The papyri began to be most seriously studied in the early 20th century by German scholars. Professor Albrecht Dietrich planned to produce an edition of all the texts, but when he died in 1908, his students had to carry on. Unfortunately three of his students undertaking this task were killed in the First World War. It was not until 1928 that the first volume of the collected edition was brought out by another of Dietrich's students, Karl Preisendanz. In 1931 the second volume appeared. These were corrected and expanded in a two-volume edition of 1973–1974. These German editions contain the original Greek text along with an adjacent German translation. In 1986 Professor Hans Dieter Betz of the University of Chicago edited an English translation of the entire corpus.

The Hermetic tradition, when truly understood through theory and practice, through philosophy and operative work, is a synthetic blend of the precise and the passionate. It is at once based on exact and universal principles of mathematics and on approximate individualized forms at the active level. Hermeticism is a science and an art at the same time. To work with Hermetic principles authentically you must keep these two factors in balance—not by letting one negate the other but by positive indulgence in both extremes. By this practice you will hold a dynamic (moving) balance.

If a higher state of Being is the ultimate goal of the true magician, balance between the extremes is needed. But such a balance is soon lost and made unattainable when the focus on the magical work is transferred to the *state of being* rather than to the *process of becom-*

ing. Balance is relatively more possible on a moving object than on a stationary one. Try balancing yourself on a bicycle when you are standing still.

The Hermetic tradition has always been dynamic. So it is today. But what was called Hermeticism in late modern times was hardly in the spirit of the original Hermetics. It is to their spirit—to the spirit of fourth-century Alexandria—a spirit beyond the limits of time and space, that this postmodern papyrus seeks to take you.

THE HERMETIC SYNTHESIS

A number of cultural streams of influence can be seen to converge in the operative Hermetic tradition. The main ones are the Hellenic (or Greek) and the Egyptian, but the cultures of the ancient Hebrews and other Semites, the Persians and other Iranian peoples, the Mesopotamians (of various backgrounds), and the transcultural (or *anti*cultural) Gnostic and Christian traditions must all be considered for true insight into the human matrix in which the Hermetic synthesis took place in historical times. When speaking about a topic as elusive as "culture" might seem to be, four elements must be borne in mind: ethnic culture (who the people are physically), ethical or ideological culture (what the people think), material culture (what the people make), and linguistic culture (how the people communicate). Insight into these aspects is indispensable for any subsequent Hermetic synthesis of cultural features which individual Hermetics undertake today.

The history of magic is a history of the interactions of various major schools of magical practice throughout the world. Some of these are closely connected to ethnic or national religious traditions (such as those of the early Sumerians, Egyptians, or the early Indo-European peoples, such as the Indians, Iranians, Greeks, Celts, etc.) while others reach beyond national boundaries and are truly international schools. These tend to be of a later date, of course, and usually stem from the expansion of some national tradition. We see this with the Hellenistic expansion within the borders of the empire carved out by Alexander, or the expansion of Iranian magical traditions under the influence of the Seleucid Empire during the last three centuries B.C.E. The schools of magic expanded their theoretical bases to take in disparate elements from various national traditions. The process of absorbing elements from outside a system and synthesizing them so that they appear to have always been a part of the original system is called *syncretism.*

The Egyptian Stream

Khemet, the "Black Land," was a great cultural magnet for millennia. Historical civilization began on the Nile around 3000 B.C.E. The Egyptians themselves were an ethnic mixture from the beginning, as was their language. But in the earliest period they coalesced into an identifiable culture. In fact, Egypt was always a mosaic of local cultures, not a unified mass. Major features of Egyptian life were hardly ever exported—not until recently anyway! Others came to Egypt. Some came as invaders, or slaves, or traders—others came as students. As the Hellenic culture moved across the map like wildfire, the Egyptian culture remained along the Nile in its isolated splendor.

One of the chief aspects of ancient Egyptian culture which is sometimes overlooked is its extreme xenophobia. They hated and feared foreign things. Things Egyptian were good and holy, while things foreign were bad and corrupt—at least this was the attitude that an ancient Egyptian thought most proper. This makes the place of the magical papyri in Egyptian culture most curious. They are so obviously full of foreign elements that no "traditional" Egyptian would have found them to their taste. The obvious cultural conclusion is that the writers of the papyri were twilight figures—men and women caught between the Hellenic and Egyptian worlds.

"Philosophy" as understood by the Greeks, and by other Indo-European peoples such as the Brahmanic Indians, is difficult to separate out from the totality of the Egyptian culture. This is why it may be tempting to say the Egyptians had no "philosophy" at all. But the Greeks themselves were so impressed with what they felt the Egyptians had to teach that they often ascribed subjective elements of their own thought to what they had learned from the Egyptians.

The great advantage the Greek culture had over the Egyptian was its linguistic tradition. The hieratic writing systems of the Egyptians often baffled the Egyptians themselves. Ideas were lost or miscommunicated over time because the system was too cumbersome to teach quickly and easily. When the Greek system was made available to the Egyptians, at least some of them eventually adopted it and made it their own.

Even the Egyptian priesthoods, the last bastions of purely Egyptian culture, were largely Hellenized by the first century C.E. This according to the contemporary Egyptian philosopher-priest Chaeremon, who was a tutor of the Emperor Nero. By the fifth century C.E. all knowledge of the Egyptian writing systems had died out. But truly Egyptian traditions were nevertheless preserved in the Hellenized forms.

The importance of the Egyptian cultural stream to the development of the Hermetic tradition of magic is enormous. Most writers of the old magical papyri were ethnic Egyptians; the very material upon which the operations were recorded, the papyrus, was an Egyptian invention; material substances called for were often obtainable only along the Nile. Technical or procedural aspects of the magical operations in the ancient period were largely Egyptian in nature.

The Hellenic Stream

The culture of the Hellenes, or Greeks, as the Romans called them, was not geographically limited to the land called Greece today. Culturally, if not politically, the whole Mediterranean and Black Sea regions were Hellenic lakes. Greek language was *the* language of commerce and philosophy; the ideas carried by that language penetrated into all the cultures touched by it. The Greek cultural values of *synthesis, harmony,* and *moderation* were for centuries absorbed by neighboring nations and exported throughout the world through the pure prestige enjoyed by that culture. After the far-flung conquests of Alexander at the beginning of the fourth century B.C.E., Greek ways became more a part of the political establishment of many nations— those areas known as Egypt, Syria, Israel, Mesopotamia, and Persia. In the overall scheme of the Hermetic tradition, Greek culture brought many new sophisticated ideas, as well as the language needed to express those ideas clearly.

The earliest philosophers of Greece, the so-called Pre-Socratics, were mainly concerned with matters of cosmology and took for granted the existence of humanity and the human mind. They analyzed and categorized things such as the *Elements*—Fire, Air, Water, Earth, and Aether. Pythagoras developed a system of holistic science which saw the unity of the cosmos in all its manifold shapes. Some, such as the grandfather of Epicureanism, Demokritus (460–360 B.C.E.), held that all things were made up of material atoms (Gk. ατομοι). With Socrates and his student, Plato, and his student, Aristotle, the attention of the philosophers turned more toward the mind. The most important Greek thinker for the development of Hermeticism is Plato. But much of what Plato taught which is relevant to Hermeticism and *mageia* is inherited from the school of Pythagoras.

The later philosophical schools, such as Platonism, Neo-Platonism and Stoicism, accepted some of the premises of the Pythagorean system, but did not indulge heavily in the practical application of them. Legend has it that Pythagoras was an initiate of several Egyptian temples. This is certainly possible, although skeptics note that the way Pythagoras thought and theorized can not be found among the Egyptian traditions. It is most likely that he traveled in Egypt but that he brought with him a pre-existing tradition which was then syncretized with whatever he might have learned in the Egyptian temples.

This is confirmed by the basic cosmological scheme used by this school of magical thought, which might best be called a sort of "natural dualism." That is, there exists, as a matter of "nature," a difference between the world of nature and the world of "non-nature" or *psychê*. This same philosophy is found among the ancient Indians, lending credence to the theory that this is a common inheritance from the age of Indo-European unity (before 3000 B.C.E.). This cosmology can be contrasted with that of the Sumerians or Egyptians who held to a natural holism. The body/soul dichotomy was *natural* to the old Indo-Europeans, whereas it was not recognized by the Sumerians or Egyptians.

This gives the Pythagorean school an early role in the syncretizing of these two theories into a system which could be *operated* through the will of individual initiates. This school brings music to the level of what we might recognize today as "scientific thought."

These ideas were *remembered* and synthesized by Plato in a unique way which had enormous and long lasting effects on the world. Essential to Plato's philosophy is the duality between the realm of the Forms (eternal principles) and the world of Things, which are pale reflections or imprecise shadows of the real principles upon which they are modeled. The world of Things can be perceived with the five senses, but the realm of the Forms can only be perceived by Intelligence—the *nous*. The purpose of Plato's system was to discover a method for the education of the soul in order that it might know the eternal principles—and therefore act on that knowledge. Platonism was absorbed by many schools of magical philosophy—most notably by Hermeticism.

The Hermetic tradition is rich in personalities—some of them are historical, some mythic, and many of the historical ones have been recreated mythologically. But there is always something passionately human about the figures of the ancient Hermetic tradition. Memories of these personalities are constantly invoked in the texts of the magical papyri. Individual operations are ascribed to well-known teachers and magicians of the past. This tradition of attributing texts to respected figures of antiquity is not entirely "dishonest." It is also a way of honoring them and keeping their memories alive. On the Hellenic side of things these fathers include Apollonius of Tyana, Apuleius of Madaura and Plotinus the Egyptian of Rome.

Apollonius of Tyana | Born in the first century C.E., Apollonius of Tyana was a Greek philosopher and reputed worker of wonders. His life is mainly known to us through a biography written by Philostratus. Evidence shows he was essentially a Pythagorean in his philosophy. He was educated at Tarsus and at the temple of Aesculapius in Aegae.

After his basic education and initiation, he traveled to India, where it is said he studied with the priests (Brahmins). After his extended stay in the East, he returned to Greece, where he is reported to have worked wonders such as the removal of a plague from the people of Ephesus, the raising of a girl from the dead in Rome, and the exposure of the infamous "Bride of Corinth." In this latter episode, a Corinthian friend of Apollonius named Menippus was to marry a wealthy young and beautiful woman from Phoenicia. The young bride brought with her vast wealth as a dowry from Phoenicia. But Apollonius saw through the situation and caused all illusion to vanish—which exposed the bride as a lamia, or vampire, who made her wealth appear by magic.

When Apollonius is supposed to have died (sometime between 96 and 98 C.E.), he was almost a hundred years old. His followers, however, insist that he did not die at all but was taken up to heaven.

Apuleius of Madaura | Apuleius, who was born in 125 C.E., is most famous for his "occult" novel *Metamorphoses* or *The Golden Ass*, but he was himself a practicing magician of the Neo-Platonic philosophical school. As the experience of Apollonius of Tyana shows, it was a dangerous time to be known as a practitioner of magic in the Roman Empire. So most magicians merely said they studied the art, and practiced only "science."

The best documented aspect of the life of Apuleius himself is his own trial on the charge of the practice of witchcraft. This came about due to his marriage to a widow some ten years older than himself. The family of the woman charged that Apuleius must have bewitched her into the marriage.

Details of magical practice revealed in his novel show that Apuleius was quite familiar with many technical secrets, and it is likely that the work is at least in part autobiographical. *Metamorphoses* is the story of Lucius, a young student of philosophy, who begins to delve into the practice of magic and witchcraft as he seeks the keys to self-transformation. This leads him to travel to Thessaly, a place traditionally associated with witches. There he becomes attached to a young and beautiful witch named Photis. Her inexperience shows because her magic turns Lucius first into a bird and then into an ass. The mistress of Photis, the more mature witch named Pamphilia, informs him that he must eat of roses in order to be transformed back into human shape. Although this seems simple enough, obstacle after obstacle comes between Lucius and his antidote. Finally, the goddess Isis intervenes and saves the unfortunate Lucius. He then converts to her cult and is initiated into her mysteries.

Plotinus of Rome Plotinus (204–270 C.E.) was Egyptian by birth, but was, like so many of his countrymen of the time, thoroughly educated in the Greek system. He visited Persia and India in the entourage of the Emperor Gordian III. In the latter part of his life he settled in Rome where he gathered many students. In the last years of his life, when almost blind, he wrote down a series of basic treatises on his teachings. These were collected by his student Porphyry and arranged in six groups of nine books each, called the *Enneads* ("the Nines").

Plotinus, like so many other philosophers of his time, practiced ascetic disciplines in order to help himself gain mystical experiences. Plotinus did not write about his practices, however, only the theoretical and philosophical aspects of his teaching. He syncretized the teachings of Plato with those of subsequent Greek philosophers and put this together with what he had learned in his travels. The result is what is usually called "Neo-Platonism." The ideas of Plotinus, and those of his school, had tremendous impact on the intellectual world represented in the old magical papyri; it also had far-reaching effects on the formation of early Christian theology. In fact, most, if not all, of what is called the "western tradition" in magic and mysticism traces its theoretical roots back to Plato through Plotinus.

The Iranian Stream

The Persians are the best known of the Iranian peoples of antiquity. But there are many other Iranian tribal groups that played important parts in the cultural history which led to the ultimate Hermetic synthesis—the Bactrians, Sogdians, Medes, Parthians, Scythians, Sarmatians—and the religious traditions they bore. The Iranians are a branch of the Indo-Europeans, the brothers of the Indian Aryans and the cousins of the Hellenes. As early as 1500 B.C.E. there were advanced Iranian civilizations in the region of modern day Iran, and the plains north of that region were populated with horse-riding warriors whose empires reached to Greece in the North. The Greeks fought a protracted series of wars against the Persians in the fifth century—a long-standing conflict which only ended with Alexander's conquest of Persia in 331 B.C.E.

The importance of Iranian religious and philosophical views is easy to overlook now because of the diminished role of that nation in the world of ideas since its conquest by Islam in the seventh century C.E. But in the ancient world Iranian thinkers and cults developed some of the most powerful ideas which exerted an influence on many traditions. Because of the dramatic impact of the dualistic teachings of Zoroaster (or Zarathustra) it is also easy to forget that not all Iranian thought was dualistic. The older traditions of non-dualistic Iranian religion continued on in the form of many cults including the Magians and Mithrists.

The dualistic and prophetic faith of Zoroastrianism also gave rise to many sub-cults, including Zurvanism and Manicheanism. It was among the Iranian dualistic cults—which saw the cosmos divided into morally good and evil elements at war with each other— that the essence of Judeo-Christian demonology was born. Zoroastrianism also had some effects on Hermetic daimonology. For example, a demonic entity in the Zoroastrian system was *Aêshma-daêva* ("god of wrath")—who eventually developed into Asmodeus in medieval demonology.

The name of Zoroaster is sometimes invoked for magical authority in the old papyri. His role in the history of magic is akin to that of Moses among the Hebrews. As a founder of a religion, much tradition is ascribed to him for the sake of prestige or authority, although we have little evidence that he would have had anything to do with the kind of magical operations recorded in the Hermetic papyri.

Another Persian whose name occurs in the papyri is Ostanes. He came to Greece in the entourage of the Shah Xerxes in 481 B.C.E. He stayed behind after the Persians returned eastward and is reputed to have taught the Greek philosopher Demokritus, one of the founders of the school of Epicureanism. This school holds that all things are material and that all material is made up of atoms (Gk. ατομος, "an indivisible thing"). This seems rather odd because any teaching that Ostanes would have to impart might be expected to have been a part of the dualistic system of Zoroaster. It is perhaps the case that Ostanes was not a dualist at all, but rather a priest of one of the other Iranian mysteries, such as is represented by the Magians and Mithrists.

The Gnostic Stream

The ultimate roots of the ideology commonly known as Gnosticism are in Iranian dualism. But beyond this, Gnosticism was essentially shaped by a mixture of philosophical, theological and mythological streams from Zoroastrianism, Judaism, Platonism, mystery religions, Egyptian magic and philosophy, as well as the recently emergent Christianity.

Gnosticism is unlike the original Iranian model in the belief that the world or physical universe is actually the creation of the evil, dark spirit, not just the zone between the spirits of light and darkness. For the Gnostic, material creation is in and of itself "evil" and must therefore be the result of a creative act on the part of an "evil god."

In the time between the first and second centuries, the period of Gnostic foundations, there were actually dozens of major schools of Gnosticism, including those of Simon (Magus), Basilides, Marcion, Valentinus, and sects, e.g. the Cainites, Barbelites, Sethians, Ophites, and Borborians. One of the major reasons for this tremendous plurality of systems is the fact that Gnostics did not attempt to unify their doctrines into an "orthodox" system, but rather encouraged the creation of diverse schools of thought.

Gnostic sects are especially difficult to study and understand because the creation of differing systems was part of the initiation into these schools at the highest levels. Leaders were encouraged to innovate and generate more sects. But there are certain common characteristics among most of them which make them *Gnostic*.

Most major Gnostic sects adhere to a group of tenets headed by *dualism*, that is, a strict dichotomy between *spirit*, or that which is good and created by God, and *matter*, or that which is evil and created and ruled by the Archôns. Another tenet is that of the *absolute transcendence of God*—God, as the "Father of the Spirit," is in no way contaminated by the matter of this world. A third idea is that of *Gnôsis* itself: "Salvation" is gained by *gnôsis*, "knowledge," of a superrational, experiential kind. This is not intellectual knowledge as commonly thought of, but a direct comprehension of the transcendent absolute: God. A fourth tenet is that of *election*—the individual Gnostic is "called" or "elected" to his status from the transcendent source of light beyond the cosmos (natural order). A fifth cosmological idea is that of the *Aiôns*—cycles of existence that act as gradual barriers between this world and the realm of transcendent light.

Some of these tenets are, in some form, shared by other schools of thought, such as Stoicism and Neo-Platonism, and true Hermeticism incorporates some of them also; but this particular combination of factors sets Gnostic schools apart from all others.

Gnostic sects hold that the material world is ruled by an evil force, and most say that the material world is actually the creation of the evil demiurge. Surprisingly enough when Gnostic thinking is applied to the Judeo-Semitic myth of Genesis, an understanding completely contrary to the conventional interpretation emerges. In the Gnostic mind (*Yahweh) Elohim* of Genesis is identified as the demiurge, creator of this world—that is, the Evil One.

Yahweh, also called Ialdabaoth by many Gnostic sects, created the world and the natural parts of humanity, but tried to keep humankind in slavery and darkness, separate from the transcendent light. The savior of humanity is the Serpent (Heb. *nachash*) who is the bringer of light from beyond the cosmos. Especially those schools that extolled the virtues of the Serpent, e.g. the Ophites (Gk. οφις, serpent) and the Naasenes (from the Greek rendering of Hebrew *nachash*) who could easily be identified on a superficial level as practitioners of the left-hand path. Their spiritual aim is to become godmen in life and to maintain their identities—as spiritual entities—as they pass through the *aiôns* to reach the ultimate source of light. Some see this as a true *imitatio Christi*.

Simon of Samaria | Simon has been called the founder of Gnostic thought. Most of our knowledge of his teachings comes from works written against the Gnostics by early Church Fathers. Their accounts of his philosophy are probably accurate, since they are confirmed by actual Gnostic texts. The stories about his magical duels with the apostles are typical sectarian propaganda—at least in the way they turn out. The figure of Simon Magus is best known from the account given of him in the New Testament book of Acts.

Simon was born around 15 C.E. in Samaria, a region known for its nonconformism from a Jewish point of view. He was the son of an ostensibly Jewish sorcerer, but was educated in Alexandria. Simon became the disciple of an "Arab" named Dositheus, whom some believe had been a follower of "John the Baptist." This Dositheus may or may not have been the author of a text found in the "Nag Hammadi Library" called the *Three Steles of Seth* (or the *Revelation of Dositheus*). Simon is said to have traveled widely, to Persia and Arabia, as well as Egypt and elsewhere, always in search of magical lore. In any event, when Dositheus died (around 29 C.E.), Simon took over his school, called until then the Dositheans, now the Simonians. Dositheus had a female disciple named Helene, and Simon later traveled with his own main disciple, a former slave and prostitute from Tyre, also known by the name Helene. However, they were probably not the same person. But it is certain that Simon did have a companion whore with whom he practiced erotic magic, some of which made use of semen and menstrual blood. Because this and other features of Simon's practices link up with certain eastern ideas, it is likely the accounts were not merely propaganda by his enemies. Simon is said to have died in Rome where he was engaged in a magical contest with the Christian apostles Peter and Paul. One account has it that he died while trying to fly to heaven (while Peter prayed for God to make him fall). Another report has it that he was buried alive, but failed to resurrect himself.

It is possible that Simon was an initiate of a western branch of the "Iranian mysteries," hence the appropriateness of his cognomen "Magus." This priesthood was quite strong in Mesopotamia and Asia Minor at this time. But Simon's true importance lay in his role as a

nexus for certain preexisting ideas, a possible originator of new real-
izations, and a teacher of future Gnostic leaders. He was the teacher
of Menander, who practiced a "bath of immortality" in which a visible fire descended into the water to bestow miraculous power on the
initiate. Menander was in turn the teacher of Saturninus and
Basilides, both important Gnostic teachers.

Simon taught a cosmology that was an inspired combination of
Gnosticism and Neo-Platonism—which will be seen to be a hallmark
of the Hermetic tradition. He held that the One, the undivided and
eternal Divine Mind (Gk. Νους), *reflected* upon and within itself,
thus giving rise to the First Thought (Gk. Επινοια) and thus also
the first Aeon (Gk. Αιων), also called *Ennoia* or *Sophia*, wisdom.
Unity is broken, Duality is begun, and the Fall into manifestation has
been set into motion. Through the first act or deed of self-reflection,
an indeterminate power of the *Nous* is turned into a positive principle given over to the object of its own thinking. This process of ongoing self-reflection is continued through a series of emanations.
Each successive one has a little bit less of the original Unity of divine
Nous than the one before it had.

Simon also taught that the One Mind, the True God of Light,
had nothing to do with the creation of the material universe, and that
in fact the One Mind was not even aware of the existence of matter.
This world, he taught, was the creation of a wicked demiurge, whom
he identified with the Creator God of the orthodox Jewish tradition.
It is because he had determined Yahweh Elohim to be evil that he
concluded that his Laws were also actually wicked and led men to
evil, not to good. This, then, is the root of Simon's libertinism and
antinomianism—the practice of willfully breaking normative codes
to attain higher spiritual truths.

In Simon's system, the First Thought, the Aeon *Epinoia*, fell
through all of the successive Aiôns and was eventually incarnated as a
human woman. She transmigrated from female body to female body
throughout history as each Ruler (Gk. Αρχων) fought to possess her.
She had been Helen of Troy, for example. Simon believed that he had
found the current incarnation of *Epinoia* in the flesh of his consort,
Helene, the Whore of Tyre. He also held himself to be the incarnation of the Divine Mind itself. So in the terrestrial act of saving and

redeeming Helene, Simon saw a reflection of the Ultimate Subject, the *Nous*, redeeming its First Object, *Epinoia*.

The Gnostics used *mageia* extensively. But it was rarely used to cause effects in this world, which would only add to the evil in it; rather they practiced a spiritual form of "higher magic" which was aimed at first perfecting themselves spiritually in this life, and then training their souls to such an extent that they would be able to remember the keys to unlock the barriers to their ascent back to the Light in their after-death state. Each sphere surrounding the world is a time-space structure called an *Aiôn* (or Aeon), each of these is ruled by an *Archôn*. The Gnostic must Know the key magical Words and Names to pass through these barriers back to the Realm of the Father. Chapter 3 on Cosmology shows how these Aeons and Archôns are thought to be arranged around the world of humankind.

Hermeticism is a "gnostic" phenomenon in the technical sense that the Hermetic shares, at one point or another in the initiatory process, all of the characteristic traits of Gnosticism. It differs in that almost all of the historical systems of Gnosticism *per se* rely on Hebrew mythology for their cosmological language, and Hermeticism is more Helleno-Egyptian in this regard.

The Semitic Stream

The Semites are one of the great and manifold mega-nations of antiquity, analogous to the Indo-Europeans in their size and scope. Today the Semitic cultural empire stretches from Morocco in the west to Iraq in the east. The two great living Semitic languages are Arabic and Hebrew. In ancient times the great Semitic nations were Israel, Syria, Babylon (or Akkad/Assyria), and Phoenicia—along with the nomadic peoples of Arabia. Much of the foundation of these Semitic nations was based on the non-Semitic culture of the Sumerians who flourished in Mesopotamia from about 3200 to 2800 B.C.E.

Most of Semitic religion is based on the idea of creator gods who exist in a realm that transcends this world. They are all-powerful, and virtually *own* this world. Their laws must be obeyed, and if they are not, humans can expect to be punished by the gods. The gods are un-knowable except through set rituals in which the gods receive sacrifice. It is easy to see why the magic coming from the Semitic world with such a religious outlook would stress the need to gain power over lower spiritual beings by threatening them with the power of be-ings who are their superiors. In a cosmos in which the divinities were vigilant about punishing those who break their laws, the Semitic ma-gicians were always interested in protecting themselves from negative consequences of interacting with the divine forces. This is repeatedly reflected in the operations of the old papyri.

Mesopotamia | Mesopotamia is merely a geographical designa-tion—Greek for "land between the rivers." The rivers in question are the Tigris and Euphrates. This is present-day Iraq. The oldest civilization to spring up here was that of the Sumerians. Sumerians were non-Semitic, but their culture was subsumed by the Semitic Akkadians around 2350 B.C.E. This began a history of wave after wave of dominant populations coming to power and in turn being driven from power by new invaders—ei-ther from abroad or from subcultural groups within the civilization.

Mesopotamia seems to have been a land perpetually obsessed with control, with rules and regulations. Elaborate hierarchies and strict chains of command were a constant feature of the various cul-tural phases of the region. All of this was perhaps made necessary by the fact that the peoples of the area were heterogeneous, and at the same time the land was constantly vulnerable to aggression from the outside—both situations remain today.

One factor unifying culture in Mesopotamia was its mytholog-ical tradition and religious practice. This tradition was originally Sumerian, but was absorbed by the various peoples who occupied the region over the millennia. Even the Semitic peoples—who controlled the region for most of its history—were largely "Sumerized" in their religious and magical views. This distinguishes them from their more purely Semitic neighbors to the west in Canaan, Syria and Israel, or to the south in Arabia.

Thorkild Jacobsen, writing in *The Treasures of Darkness*, sees the basic Mesopotamian religious values as 1) immanence of the numinous, 2) identity between name and form, 3) intransitiveness of the numinous power, 4) pluralism, and 5) locality.[2] The Mesopotamians responded to their divinities as immanent beings, embodied in the phenomenal world. Each of these beings had a form and a name and was thus isolated as a unique entity—its power was not transferable from it to another being. This aspect ensures continuing plurality and multiplicity, while at the same time localization of the embodied power is made more possible. There has perhaps never been a more *holistic* religious philosophy—with the possible exceptions of those of Taoism and Shinto in the Far East.

This holism led to an obsession with good and evil in magic, however. This is only natural since good and bad things happen to humans and if these "things" (phenomena) are but sensible manifestations of numinous powers—and nothing falls outside that category—the world soon becomes a place inhabited by every sort of powerful entity bent on doing these good and bad things. This aspect contributes little to the spirit of Hermeticism—where a natural sort of dualism reigns. The realm of the spirit shapes and can direct events in the phenomenal world—but the two are not identical.

It is in the technical area of astronomy or astrology where the ultimate Mesopotamian influence on Hermeticism is strongest. The Sumerians may have pioneered the practical applications of the observation of the movements of the stars, but it would be the Semitic Babylonians who would develop the divinatory importance of astrology during the first part of the first millennium B.C.E. However, even this was reformed by the Greeks and it is the Greek or Hellenistic form of astrology which we find in the papyri—not the Egyptian or Babylonian. For example, the constellation we commonly call the Big Dipper (the Great Wain) is called Arktos ("the Bear") in the papyri, whereas it is identified as a bull or the thigh of a bull in Egyptian star lore.

At the time the papyri were written, Mesopotamia was either part of the Parthian (Persian) Empire or was part of the Roman Empire (following its occupation in 165 C.E.).

---

[2]Thorkild Jacobsen, *The Treasures of Darkness* (New Haven, CT: Yale University Press, 1976), pp. 5–7.

Israel | The Hebrew culture must be separated from the rest of the Semitic culture of the period because of its unique religious view. The Hebrews were the first nation to establish a non-philosophical form of monotheism. That is, philosophers had for a long time spoken of an abstract supreme Being, or Unity, which the Greeks might regularly refer to as "God"—Theos. But the Hebrews succeeded in demoting this idea to the status of simply being a god, whose characteristics were much like any one of a hundred other gods of the region, and then promoting the concept to being the *One God.* Their national God, Yahweh, was considered not only their own tribal god, but the one true God of all peoples.

This attitude earned the Hebrews a reputation in antiquity for being a decidedly pre-philosophical people. But the idea of their god being the One God gave their theology a great deal of prestige among magicians because of the natural omnipotence ascribed to him. The Roman historian Tacitus, writing in the second century C.E., referred to the Judaic religion as "superstitious" and their beliefs as "paradoxical and degraded."[3] It seems that the Romans' low regard for the Jews stemmed from the latter's lack of a *rational* philosophy.

Judaic culture had been dominated for the whole first millennium B.C.E. by the idea of monotheism—which led to an ever more centralized state and cultic life. Attempts were made to center this on one city, Jerusalem, and one religious site: the Temple built by Solomon. Solomon was king of Israel between 966 and 926 B.C.E. The Babylonians destroyed his Temple in 587 B.C.E. Between the arrival of the Hebraic tribes in the land of Canaan around 1500 to 1200 B.C.E. and the destruction of the Temple in 587, there was ongoing conflict with the Baal-worshipping Semites of the region as well as with the Dagon-worshipping Philistines in Gaza. It was not until the establishment of the second Temple in 539 B.C.E. that the foundations of the religious form known as Judaism were laid. This took place under the sponsorship of the Persian Empire—hence the great influence of Persian ideas in early Judaic texts.

An important cultural development within Judaism as far as the Hermetic tradition is concerned was the split of the community be-

---

[3]Tacitus, *The Histories, Vol. 1–8*, K. Wellesley, trans. (London: Penguin, 1964).

tween the heavily Hellenized Jews of Alexandria in Egypt and the rest of the orthodox faithful. The Hellenized Jews translated the Pentateuch into Greek and used that language as their preferred linguistic mode. Philosophically the unique aspect of Hebraic and eventually Judaic religion was its fanatical monotheism rooted in irrational acts of faith characterized by blind obedience to a written set of laws (*Torah*) thought to have been directly received from God by Moses (ca. 1250 B.C.E.).

It appears, however, that the bulk of Judaic influence on the Hermetic tradition comes not from the Israelites, but from the Alexandrian Jews who had adopted many features of Hellenistic thought during the time between 200 B.C.E. and 400 C.E.

In the strictest respects, magic is quite antithetical to the spirit of Judaism. If magic is the assertion of the will of the individual magician on the universe, this is bound to be at cross purposes with the will of God on many occasions. Despite this, Judaism was historically relatively open to magical practice. This is especially true when it comes to the implementation of protective magic, amulets (*kamea*), and the phylacteries (*tefillin*). The theurgic aspects of Merkabah mysticism seem to have been borrowed from neighboring peoples in the eastern Mediterranean and from Persia.

The Christian Stream

Christianity is impossible to separate from the personality of Jesus, the supposed founder of the sect. The book *Jesus the Magician* by a renowned scholar of New Testament studies, Morton Smith, is the best single source of information concerning what was probably the true character of Jesus, the man.[4] Among other things, Smith reports what the *non*-Christian contemporaries of Jesus said of him. For us the important elements of this report are that he was said to be the illegitimate son of a Roman soldier (named Panthera) and a prostitute; that he became expert in magic, having been trained in Egypt; that

---

[4]Morton Smith, *Jesus the Magician* (San Francisco: HarperSanFrancisco, 1978).

he became "a son of a god" by these practices; that he taught his followers to disregard Jewish Law (*Torah*) and to practice a sexually lib-
ertine doctrine of love (*agapé*).

Ideological enemies can, and do, simply make up wild and un-
substantiated stories as propaganda. But surprisingly there is plenty
of evidence for this view of things from within the Gospel accounts
themselves—the New Testament books of Matthew, Mark, Luke,
and especially that of John.

Curiously, when Jesus is accused by the Pharisees of casting out
daimôns by the force of Beelzebub—ruler of daimôns—he replies
only with an attempt to baffle them with what are supposed to appear to be sophistic or logical formulas:

> Every kingdom divided against itself is brought to desola-
> tion; and every city or house divided against itself shall not
> stand: and if Satan casts out Satan he is divided against
> himself; how shall then his kingdom stand? And if Beelze-
> bub cast out devils, by whom do your children cast them
> out? (Mt. 12:25–27)[5]

The obvious answer is that the show is rigged . . .

If we assume Jesus to be a historical person who performed acts
corresponding to some of the accounts given in the New Testament
books, what *kind* of man would he have been? Were there others in
that time, and in that region who did similar things? Morton Smith
asks these basic questions and finds that Jesus fits perfectly the profile
of a magician living in the eastern Mediterranean during the first two
centuries C.E. The Greco-Egyptian magical papyri provide many favorable comparisons in his exact time and region for his magical activities. Smith deals with this evidence in detail. What emerges is a
picture of a Hellenized Jewish magician who, among other things,
claimed to be a son of a god, used verbal magical formulas to work
miracles, and who did not send spirits, angels or daimôns to do his
work, but who contained or absorbed a divine spirit and exerted it
directly upon the universe around him.

---

[5]King James Bible, authorized version of 1611.

Several papyri outline magical operations for obtaining a spirit in order to become "a son of a god"—which is another way of saying that ritually the magician has become divine in essence, or more simply that the god has "adopted" the magician. One of these operations (*PGM* I.42–195) says that the magician should purify himself, go onto a lofty roof and, among other things, blindfold himself with a "black Isis band." At one point during the ritual the band is removed and it is said that a "falcon will fly down" and drop a stone as a first sign of the manifestation of the spirit in the magician. This spirit, or *daimôn*, becomes identified with the magician from an outsider's viewpoint so the magician in the words of the papyrus "will be worshipped as a god since [he has] a god as a friend."

There are obvious parallels between such magical rituals and the story of the baptism of Jesus (Mk. 1:9–11) where he receives a "holy spirit" in the shape of a dove which flies down from heaven. After this event he is able to perform magical operations by just "saying the word," that is, uttering some magical formula or "name."

As is made clear in chapter 6, sorcerers who "had" a spirit or daimôn might be called in the Greek of this period a *magos* (pl. *magoi*) and was often considered a "divine man." Such a *magos* was more than a mere *goês*, or sorcerer, who was only able to command spirits outside himself. In Jesus' own time some people seem to have thought he had "obtained" the spirit of the executed John the Baptist—and worked magic with it. But it is the "holy spirit"—that of a god—who Jesus the man seems to have become. It is this holy spirit which is the true agent of his work as a *magos*.

A *magos*—because of his acquired "divine nature"—can cause changes by means of his "word" (directed conscious will) alone. The papyri are full of verbal magical formulas through which the magician can work his will. But there is even one such word recorded in the book of Mark (5:41) when Jesus heals a little girl with the (supposedly Aramaic) phrase: *talitha koumi*.

In fact all the miracles performed by Jesus are paralleled in the Hermetic magical literature of the period. Even the magical power of his own name was enhanced after his death—for magic worked with the spirit (or "name") of an executed criminal was believed to be of special power. This is, of course, further bolstered by the knowledge that Jesus exhorted his followers to do this, saying that he would be "in them always" (Jn. 14:23; 15:4–9; Mt. 18:20; 28:20). For many magicians of the time, deification—and immortalization—was the highest goal of the practice of *mageia*. Jesus' own declarations of his divinity correspond exactly with phrases from magical papyri in which the magician declares his divine qualities:

Jn. 10:36 "I am the Son of God."
PGM IV.535 "I am the Son . . ."
PDM XX.33 "I am the Son of the living God."

Jn. 6:51 "I am . . . the one come from heaven."
PGM IV.108 "I am the one come forth from heaven."

Jn. 14:6 "I am . . . the truth . . ."
PGM V.148 "I am the truth."

Such evidence leads to the conclusion that the man Jesus was a *magos*. He was a dissident, who preached the abrogation of established Jewish Law and was even thought to be "Satanic," or Typhônian by his contemporary rivals and critics. He taught the "salvation of the individual"—while practicing the *deification* of his own individual self.

There are several parallels between Jesus of Nazareth and another contemporary *magos* named Simon of Samaria. Among these parallels is the fact that Jesus (despite later attempts to gloss it over) had as his consort a prostitute, Mary Magdalene. Having such a woman as a consort seems to have been an essential component in the myth of the *magos*.

Principles of the Hermetic Synthesis

The operative Hermetic tradition as a whole is a grand synthesis of all the streams of influence mentioned so far. When we view the tradition as a whole we are tempted to see two different branches. One is philosophical and contemplative, the other practical and operative. The limitations of this view have already been pointed out, but for the sake of understanding at this juncture it provides a useful model. Within the philosophical branch there appear to be two sub-branches: the pantheistic Neo-Platonic school and the dualistic Gnostic school. These differences are probably more apparent than real, however. In *The Egyptian Hermes,* Fowden concludes concerning this "problem":

> Such doctrinal variations . . . in fact reflect an intention that different *successive* levels (or "steps") of spiritual enlightenment should provide different *successive* levels of truth about Man, the World and God, so that for example knowledge of the World, which the Hermeticists regarded as desirable at earlier stages of spiritual instruction is subsequently rejected as "curiosity" (περιεργια, *curiositas*), the pursuit of knowledge for its own sake, and branded as sin.[6]

But the practical and operative form, Hermeticism, which is the focus of this book, is not necessarily subject to such refined philosophical distinctions. The elements of its nature are characteristically more diverse. There are nine principles to the Hermetic synthesis as expressed through the practical tradition of the magical papyri: eclecticism, diversity, pragmatism, worldliness, individualism, natural dualism, immanence of the divine, successive revelation, and emotional fervor. All of these are not necessarily emphasized in the more philosophical branch of the tradition, but when it comes to practical application these are the principles at work to make the tradition come together. In typical Hermetic fashion, all nine of these principles must be applied equally and simultaneously to reach a true Hermetic approach.

The tradition is an eclectic synthesis of differing cosmologies and philosophical perspectives. There appears to be no attempt to make these appear to be reconciled to each other. The key to how this works is concealed in the principle of *successive revelation.* The eclec-

---

[6]Garth Fowden, *The Egyptian Hermes: A Historical Approach to the Late Pagan Mind,* 2nd ed. (Princeton, NJ: Princeton University Press, 1993), p. 103.

tic mixture is allowed to remain dynamic and ever open to change or modification.

In conjunction with the first principle, the tradition is drawn from the widest available variety of cultural sources and mythological traditions. There seems to be a special effort made to catalog the traditions of the world in its meta-mythology. This results in a virtual lack of dogmatism. All operations are subject only to the dictum of whether something *works* or not.

Pragmatism is a key concept in the practical tradition. The aims and purposes of the operations are most often quite down to earth. Even forms of "higher magic" often seem subject to the idea that one evolves one's self to a godlike status in order to be more efficient at operant magic. This sense of pragmatism also lends itself to an openness to innovation. The Hermetic practitioner creates new patterns and combinations unique to a certain time and place based on ancient principles.

When reading the magical papyri one is struck by the worldliness of their aims. The Hermetic magician is not concerned so much with the destiny of his soul after death—the chief preoccupation of the philosophical Hermetic. The operative Hermetic knows he must strengthen himself in this world, become godlike, before his philosophical thought can become more than idle speculation. The practical Hermetic's interest in the materialistic Epicurean philosophy of Demokritus is at least partially explicable in these terms. Also, in later times the development of Alchemy within the Hermetic context is a clear reference to the posited link between the world of nature and its workings and that of the spirit or psychê.

In most ancient societies of the eastern Mediterranean the individual (unless he was a king or pharaoh) had little traditional importance. In the Hermetic tradition, however, the individual comes to the forefront, both as a teacher of students and as a practitioner of magical operations. Hermeticism is not practiced in large group rituals, nor is the individual will and consciousness to be subordinated to that of a group of humans or even to a traditional god-form.

Although the philosophical cosmologies of Hermeticism appear to run the gamut from the dualism of the Gnostics to the pantheism or monism of the Stoics and Neo-Platonists, there is an underlying consistency in the cosmological model implicit in the magical operations. This is already perceptible in the basic operating theory of Hermetic magic which is dependent on a kind of "natural dualism." There is a "higher world" (of the gods, daimôns, etc.) and a "lower world" (of the earth and humanity). There is, however, a "natural" connection between the two as a matter of similarity of kind—this world is a shadow or reflection of that world. This is the reason there are secret correspondences between this world and that. This principle is responsible for the most famous Hermetic dictum of all: "What is below is like that which is above, and what is above is like that which is below." This is part of the second precept of Hermês Trismegistus as recorded on the *Emerald Tablet.*[7] Moreover, this Hermetic principle also became a cornerstone of modern scientific thought.

As a result of synthesizing the ideas of various cultures and philosophical streams of thought, most Hermetics hold two apparently contradictory ideas about the source of true knowledge and power. One of these is the idea that knowledge is revealed from an outside, divine source. This is generally inherited from Judaism and the Egyptian tradition. The other idea is that knowledge is innate in the psychê—awaiting but a catalyst to cause a *remembrance* of eternally real things. This idea is inherited from the Indo-European stream of thought—from the Greek and the Iranian schools.

It seems most likely that the Hermetic synthesis sees that there is an innate, inborn divine essence in (at least some) human beings, but it is hidden from them so that they are generally ignorant of it. Knowledge and use of this faculty leads to salvation. Gaining knowledge and use of this essence depends upon a "revelation" from a divine source or the instruction of a human teacher. Revelation may come through regular contemplation and prayer (or even ascetic practices in some schools), or, as is more usual in the practical school, through regular *practice of magical control.* It is only possible to reveal this Knowledge, or *gnôsis,* in stages (Gk. βαθμοι), and so the non-initiate may see inconsistencies where none exist from another perspective.

---

[7] For information on the *Emerald Tablet,* see Georg Luck, *Arcana Mundi: Magic & the Occult in the Greek & Roman Worlds* (Baltimore, MD: Johns Hopkins, 1985), p. 370.

Common among all Hermetics is a certain emotional fervor, or even fanaticism, which separates them from the more staid philosophical schools around them. Hermetics see an intrinsic hidden value in commitment to an idea or principle as an aid in their magical and philosophical development. This results in an emotionalism present in their works reminiscent of Judaism or Christianity, but always tempered by an underlying Classical pragmatism.

The Hermetic Cult | Another thing we must consider is the question of whether the Hermetics of old were organized into a secret order or cult. The answer to this question is clearly negative. There appears to have been no formal, hierarchized cult or organization of Hermetics in the ancient period, nor was there any in the Renaissance. In fact, later modern attempts to create "Hermetic orders" are violations of some of the very basic principles of early Hermeticism. Within the texts of the magical papyri, nowhere is this aspect more clearly demonstrated than in the fact that many of the texts were written originally as "letters" from an individual teacher to an individual pupil.

The social aspect of the ancient Hermetic tradition was probably based on small closed groups of pupils gathered around a teacher on a comparatively informal basis. There was no distinction among the pupils as to rank or degree of initiation—one was either a "teacher" (or "master"), or one was a "pupil." (Although the papyri sometimes show the pupil teaching the master a few tricks!) Despite this lack of hierarchy, there was a strict sense of an inner group of initiates ("those who have heard the Word") set apart from the profane world around them.

The schools or groups gathered around individual masters would appear to have been based on the systematic reading and interpretation of certain "sacred texts," such as those represented in the *Corpus Hermeticum* and the "Nag Hammadi Library."[8] In the course of the guided reading of these texts, revelations would take place in

---

[8]For information on *Corpus Hermeticum*, see Walter Scott, *Hermetics* (Boston: Shambhala, 1985), and James M. Robinson, ed., *The Nag Hammadi Library* (Leiden: Brill, 1977).

the minds of pupils. These revelations constituted the true spiritual initiation. Interestingly the fact that many of the old papyri seem to have come in the form of correspondence between masters and pupils would indicate that the ancient Hermetics were the first to practice a sort of "mail order occultism." This has again become popular in this dawn of the postmodern age.

Mircea Eliade points out that the enormous importance of written works in the Hermetic tradition follows from two factors in the history of the first half of the first millennium C.E. First, there is the triumph within the establishment of a "religion of the book"—Christianity. Written texts gained in prestige, even if they were not Christian. Second, the formerly established Mystery Cults and initiatory schools had been destroyed and the living initiators had largely disappeared, or were increasingly difficult to find. Eliade goes on to say that in this new system a new type of entirely spiritual initiation was based not on contact with living teachers but upon contact with written sources—"the sacred text can be forgotten for centuries, but if it is rediscovered by a competent reader its message becomes intelligible and contemporary."[9] This too is after all a major premise in the postmodern thesis itself.

It is clear that the philosophical Hermetics did practice certain ritual forms, although they were for the most part not as elaborate as those found in the magical papyri—the need for which had been superseded by the more interiorized practices of the philosophical Hermetics. The philosophical rituals may have been as simple as a regularized focusing of attention on a symbol of divine unity—such as the Sun (Hêlios-Rê) or the ritualized offering of "spiritual sacrifices" in the form of hymns of praise and thanksgiving to the deity. (An example of this is the Formula of Thanksgiving [*PGM* III. 591–610] on page 252.)

At the dawn of this postmodern age we have witnessed a revival of the idea that spiritual development can be fostered through exposure to books or sacred texts. The question remains an open one as to whether genuine development is possible without recourse to a living

---

[9] Mircea Eliade, *History of Religious Ideas*, W. Trask, A. Hiltebeitel, and D. Apastolos-Cappadona, trans. (Chicago: University of Chicago Press, 1978).

teacher who can at least act as a guide through the maze of written material. Clearly the Hermetics of old believed that in large measure the texts alone could play a vital role in the "initiation" of only certain elect individuals, predisposed to be able to "hear the Word"—to understand the essence of the texts unaided by human contact. *But* for the vast majority of students it remained necessary to have teachers to open their ears. But even in these cases the Hermetic teacher is not a master of *indoctrination* into a set dogma, but rather an "opener of the way."

The living teacher remains the single most vital component in the Hermetic tradition. The fact is that no tradition would have been possible without the cells of teachers and students who were personally attached to each other.

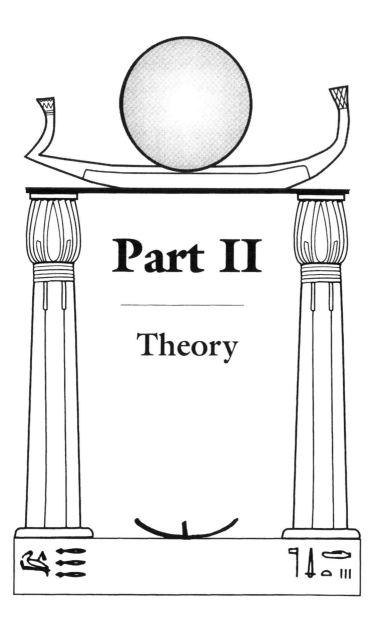

Part II

Theory

Cosmology

A cosmology is the conceptual framework of an individual, school of thought, or whole culture by means of which the world is understood. This is necessary for serious magical work because if you want to change the world around you, you need to have some idea of how it is made up.

Hermetic cosmology, you will learn, can be a fluid concept. It is not necessary, or perhaps advantageous, to have a "scientifically accurate" map of the world for magic to work. This is why a geocentric physical model of the cosmos is still effective. We are each the center of our *own* universe, after all. All such cosmologies are in fact creations of the inner self, the subjective universe, of some individual teacher whose doctrine had a significant impact on a whole historical tradition.

The original Hermetic cosmology was derived from four major sources: the Neo-Platonic and Stoic schools of Hellenistic philosophy, the Gnostic school, and the Egyptian religious tradition(s). Any individual Hermetic cosmology can be seen to be a representation of one, or a synthesis of two or more of these schools of thought regarding the universal order. The collection of philosophical texts known as the *Corpus Hermeticum* contains some books which seem totally Neo-Platonic or Stoic, while others are heavily tinged with Gnosticism. You can read:

> . . . God ordained the births of men and told mankind to increase and multiply abundantly. And he implanted each soul in flesh by means of the gods who circle in the heavens. And to this end he made men, that they might contemplate heaven, and have dominion over all things under heaven, and that they might come to know God's power, and witness nature's workings and that they might mark what things are good and discern the diverse natures of things good and bad, and invent all manner of cunning arts.

Or you can read words such as these:

> The Good then is in God alone . . . . [T]here is not room
> for the Good in a material body, hemmed in and gripped as
> such a body by evil—by pains and griefs, desires and angry
> passions, delusions and foolish thoughts . . . . I thank God
> for this very thought he has put into my mind, even the
> thought that the Good is absent, and that it is impossible
> for it to be present in the world (*kosmos*). For the world is
> one mass of evil (*kakias*) even as God is one mass of Good.[1]

Here you see two radically different attitudes toward the *Kosmos* and
its role in the spiritual life of humankind. In the first text you hear of
how goodness is in the nature and that higher truths can be intelligi-
bly derived from observations of the workings of the world. This is
the attitude of the Stoic and Neo-Platonic schools. But in the second
text you see the Gnostic position that the material world is devoid of
goodness and that nothing is to be gained by observing it and certainly not by interacting with it—as it is "one mass of evil." Yet *both*
of these radically different views are—or can be—equally Hermetic.

The reason for this is, as we have learned, may be because various books of the *Corpus Hermeticum* are the products of different
schools and teachers within the vast Hermetic tradition. But it is
more likely that these represent differing *levels* of understanding, and
are in fact not contradictory. A persuasive case is made for this point
of view by Garth Fowden in his book *The Egyptian Hermes*.[2] In any
event it can be said that in the Hermetic tradition individuals are
challenged to arrive at unique philosophical syntheses based on experience—not to follow the teachings of petrified dogmas slavishly.
And so it continues today.

The development of such philosophical theories is also important to practical magical work as the staging points for advanced per-

---

[1] For information on *Corpus Hermeticum*, see Walter Scott, *Hermetics*, Vol. I (Boston:
Shambhala, 1985), p. 169. Text here and on p. 47 from Libellus III and VI.
[2] Garth Fowden, *The Egyptian Hermes: A Historical Approach to the Late Pagan Mind*
(Princeton, NJ: Princeton University Press, 1993).

sonal development and initiation. These theories are additionally essential as expressions of your understanding of the elements (*stoicheia*) of the universe and how they fit together in the cosmic order.

Neo-Platonic Cosmology

The most dominant single aspect of Hermetic cosmology is that provided by the Platonic school. By the time of the writing of the Greek magical papyri and the *Corpus Hermeticum,* this system had developed into a Neo-Platonic branch and a Stoic school. The basic difference between the two latter schools is that the Stoics hold that the entire cosmos is rational and limited, whereas the Neo-Platonists hold that there remains an irrational, completely unknowable and mysterious aspect beyond the ability of rationality to comprehend. The basic idea behind the Neo-Platonic view of the world is the emanation of the Good (Gk. αγαθον) or the One. In this cosmology there is a progressive admixture of darkness and density the further something is from the source of all emanation—the "fullness of being."

Neo-Platonism as it would have been known to the writers of the magical papyri also contained admixtures of Stoic and Gnostic elements, and has its roots in the even more ancient school of Pythagoras. The major features of Neo-Platonic cosmology are already presented in Plato's dialogues—especially in the *Timaeus.*[3] But they are given their distinctive form by Plotinus in his *Enneads.*[4] These concepts also find extensive expression and elaboration in medieval Judaic Kabbalism—for example in the *Sefer Yetzirah* (third to sixth centuries) and the *Zohar* (13th century).[5] Some of the earliest roots

[3]For translation of *Timaeus,* see Edith Hamilton, *Plato: The Collected Dialogues* (Princeton, NJ: Princeton University Press, 1963), pp. 1151–1211.
[4]Plotinus, *The Enneads,* Stephen MacKenna, trans. (London: Penguin, 1991).
[5]Aryeh Kaplan, *Sefer Yetzirah: The Book of Creation* (York Beach, ME: Samuel Weiser, 1990). Gershom Scholem, ed., *Zohar: The Book of Splendor* (New York: Schocken, 1949).

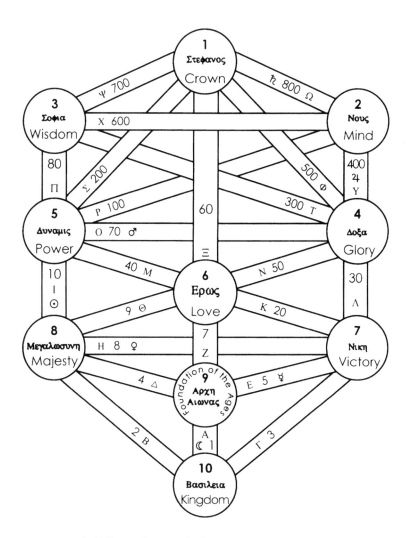

Figure 1.   The Hellenistic Cosmographic Tree.

of what was to become Kabbalism can be discerned in the Hermetic-Platonic cosmology. In figure 1 on p. 50 you will see the form of the Kabbalistic "Tree of Life" as it might have been framed by the Hellenistic cosmologists.

To oversimplify, the Neo-Platonic cosmogony and cosmology shows a threefold emanation. (See figure 2.) The One is the origin of all things, equated with God. God created as an intermediary the "Maker"—the *demiourgos* (demiurge) also called the Word (*logos*). The creation of the Word is called the All- or World-Soul. The Word is the active agent of divine creation, while the All-Soul is the very plan or blueprint of manifestation.

Now, to be more exact, all three members of the triad are but three parts of the Divine. The first part is the *One*, the First Existent, also called the Good (*agathon*) or sometimes "the Father." The second part is the First Thinker and the First Thought—the vision of the Divine. This is the Maker, often called the "Son of God." Part three is the expression of the outgoing activity or *energy* of the Divine. It becomes the basis for material manifestation.

Fundamental to an in-depth understanding of Neo-Platonic thought is the notion that an essence or Being is the equivalent of its characteristic action. Love is the equivalent of Loving—for the relative Being of Love can have no other action than *to Love*. Also, each

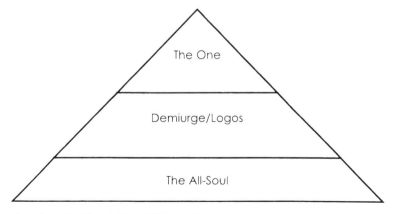

Figure 2. Neo-Platonic Threefold Emanation.

entity in the chain of Being is a reflection, or "shadow," of that which is above it—from which it emanated. It then both contemplates and aspires toward that which generated it, *and* in turn also generates an image of itself below itself. And so the chain of Being goes until its energy ebbs and it finally ceases. Being is seen to be analogous to a light shining into the darkness—the light is strongest where it is closest to its source, the further it is from its source, the more diffuse it is.

Matter arises at that point where the creative power of the All-Soul comes to an end. Matter is almost non-Being, it is a mixture of Being and non-Being. Absolute non-Being cannot, strictly speaking, *exist* in a cosmos that ultimately emanates from the fullness of Being.

The supernal triad of the One-Divine Mind-All-Soul reflects itself continually in levels below, or "after" it. Here the origin of the principles by which the Neo-Platonic cosmology was used to construct the Hebrew "Tree of Life" became clear. There are three times three spheres, with the world of matter separate from and below the three triads above.

It has long been suspected that the cosmology of the Hebrew Kabbalah—as outlined in the *Sefer Yetzirah* and the *Zohar*—was based on a now lost Greek original. The "loss" of the Greek original was probably due to the persecution of Neo-Platonic and Gnostic schools and sects by officials of the orthodox churches. But now, the lost Greek original can be restored. The restored version is based on simple principles using the classic cosmological pattern inherited by the Hebrew Kabbalah together with what we know of the Hellenistic philosophical tradition.

The role of the Greek "letters"—or *stoicheia* (elementa)—is essential. These are 24 in number, of course, so the number of pathways between the 10 spheres would be 24, not 22 as in the Hebrew tradition. It is known that the 7 vowels of the Greek *alphabeta* were connected to the 7 then known planets and that the many vocalic incantations found in the Hermetic magical tradition were considered keys for invoking the subtle forces of the planets—or more particularly of the *gods* which the planets manifested. With this knowledge, I applied the simple principle that the ordering of the *stoicheia* should proceed in such a way that the first *stoichion* would be between the two spheres yielding the highest sum when the numerical values assigned to those spheres were added together. When this mathematical principle was followed, the configuration represented in figure 1 (p. 50) was obtained. I determined this must indeed be the correct ordering and configuration of the elementa concerned because with no other is there the possibility of ascending from the Kingdom to the Crown by means of the 7 vowel sounds—AEHIOYΩ—in an unbroken and continuous line. This is the original Hellenistic-Hermetic cosmography as represented in two dimensions. Further aspects of this figure will be discussed in detail and made practical in the section on *Stoicheia* on page 115.

It is not the aim of this book to explain in its entirety the depth and breadth of the Hellenistic magical cosmography—if such a thing were possible. It is introduced here for *practical* reasons and in order to give the right framework for the working exploration of the *stoicheia*—the signs, sounds, and meanings of the Greek letters. However, the door now stands open for those who would discover more about the foundation of this understanding of the world. It should be noted that the *names* of the spheres reflect those translated into Aramaic and Hebrew in ancient times, but that the Greek was not as strict as the Hebrew when it came to the names of the spheres. Other names of the spheres, conveying other dimensions or aspects of their being, were also known. For example *Sophia* might also be called *Epinoia* or *Ennoia* with approximately equal meaning.

Although the pattern shown in figure 1 (p. 50) is fundamental to esoteric and magical understanding of the triads and their functions—as well as that of the elementa (*stoicheia*)—the more usual form of diagraming the Neo-Platonic (and Gnostic) cosmos is found in figure 3 on p. 54. In this second diagram, a number of other things become clearer. Whereas figure 1 emphasizes the Neo-Platonic concept of triads and emanation from a distant source *downward* toward earth/matter, figure 3 emphasizes the inner/outer dichotomy or opposition also important to Neo-Platonic, Gnostic, and Egyptian cosmology. Like all such models or diagrams, these are only partial images of realities which cannot be reflected in two or even three dimensional models. To be truly seen, the models must be grasped entirely by understanding itself—by the Intellectual Soul.

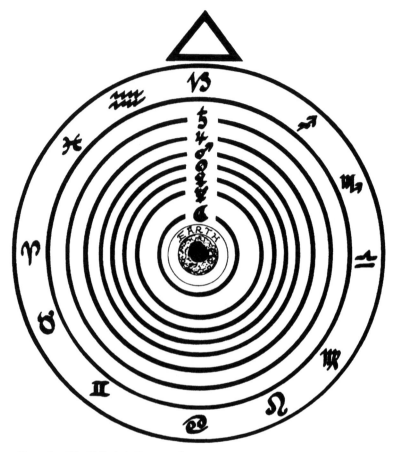

Figure 3. The Hellenistic Cosmograph.

The cosmograph shown in figure 3 is closely related to the scientific model of pre-Copernican antiquity. Its basic shape, although not its basic meaning, was shared by many Gnostic teachers as well. The cosmos can be seen to be divided into three great zones—the trans-Saturnian realm, the planetary realm, and the terrestrial sphere. The firmament, defined by the heavenly sphere of the fixed stars of the Zodiac, divides the planetary realm of change and flux from the supernal realm beyond wherein dwells the Divine Triad. Seven concentric circles or spheres define the realm of the planets, which are

seen as expressions or equivalences of the gods and goddesses of
mythology. In the center is the realm of the elements—aether, fire, air,
water, and earth. The terrestrial sphere is in the innermost midst of
this whole system. There are also chthonic realms below the earth,
known to Greek tradition as Tartaros, Hadês, and Erebos. This basic
map of the universe was elaborated in specific ways by the Gnostics
and both were synthesized in the Hermetic view.

Gnostic Cosmology

Neo-Platonic and Stoic cosmology strove to be scientific in that it
was an attempt to describe the physical universe in objective detail.
This is not so of Gnostic cosmology. Gnostics strove only toward
spiritual knowledge—toward *gnôsis.* Subjective, inner truths have pri-
macy over all else. For this reason it is common for Gnostic teachers
to develop widely differing cosmologies. The details vary from school
to school but the principles remain fairly consistent. Often our only
sources for the various schools are Christian writers who are writing
against the Gnostics. But we have many authentically Gnostic texts
also, such as the *Pistis-Sophia* or the whole body of texts found at Nag
Hammadi.[6]
     The main differences between the Gnostic and Neo-Platonic
views of the universe often lie in the origin and value of the physical
cosmos—not in its shape or form. For the Gnostic the physical universe is in itself evil—and the creation of an evil god. In this attitude
the Gnostics were opposed by the Neo-Platonists, such as Plotinus
who devoted one tractate of the *Enneads* (II:9) to this opposition:
"Against the Gnostics; or Against Those that Affirm the Creator of
the Cosmos and the Cosmos itself to be Evil."[7]
     Ultimately, the source of Gnostic cosmology lies in Iranian du-
alism. However, this Iranian form was significantly influenced and

---

[6]C. Schmidt, ed., *Pistis-Sophia*, V. MacDermot, trans. (Leiden: Brill, 1978).
[7]Plotinus, *The Enneads*, Stephen MacKenna, trans. (London: Penguin, 1991), pp.
108–132.

reshaped by Hellenistic philosophy, Judaic mythology and mystical theology, and perhaps even Egyptian tradition until it developed a distinctive character beginning in the first century C.E. Essential to *most* Gnostic schools is the idea that the material universe was created by a god they characterize as being *evil.* When considering the Judaic cosmogony, then, the clear Gnostic conclusion is that Yahweh is the creator of the physical universe and is therefore to be identified as the evil demiurge.

According to the *Apochryphon of John* in the Nag Hammadi texts, the material universe originated when Sophia desired to create a being without the cooperation of her consort, the Invisible Spirit. She created Ialdabaoth, also called Yahweh, who then created the material universe through a vast series of Aiôns, each ruled over by an Archôn (ruler).

> And the archôns created seven powers for themselves, and the powers created for themselves six angels for each one until they became 365 angels. And these are the bodies belonging with the names: the first is Athoth, he has a sheep's face; the second is Eloaiou, he has a donkey's face; the third is Astaphaios, he has a hyena's face; the fourth is Yao, he has a serpent's face with seven heads; the fifth is Sabaoth, he has a dragon's face; and the sixth is Adonin, he has a monkey's face; the seventh in Sabbede, he has a shining fire-face.[8]

Here we see the cosmic importance of the number 365 and recognize many of the names also found in the Hermetic magical literature.

Humanity was also created by the Demiurge Ialdabaoth/Yahweh and his host of Archôns. When the Demiurge breathed life into the human form, the struggle between the light of spirit and the darkness of matter in human existence began. Christ is a pure spiritual creation of the Invisible Spirit and comes to humanity to remind

---

[8]For information on *Apochryphon of John*, see James M. Robinson, *The Nag Hammadi Library* (Leiden: Brill, 1977), p. 105.

them of their kinship with the light, and to help provide the knowledge (*gnôsis*) necessary for that return.

The figure of Christ is usually important in Gnostic schools. This is not so in Neo-Platonic or Hermetic schools. But among the Gnostics Christ is seen not as the son of Yahweh, but of his Father in Heaven, the Invisible Spirit. Christ is often identified with the serpent in the Garden of Eden, who encouraged humankind to seek Knowledge. Certain Gnostic sects saw the role of the serpent (Heb. *nachesh*) as central. Two of these groups were known as the Naassarenes (from the Grecicized form of the Heb. *nachesh*, which was *naas*), or the Ophites (from the Greek *ophis*, serpent). It has been theorized, since no town named "Nazareth" existed in the first century C.E., that the epithet "Nazarene" referring to Jesus really means Naassarene—"the Serpentine."

The Ophite sect provides us with an example of Gnostic cosmology. A diagram of the cosmos as they understood it appears in figure 4 on p. 58. Clearly this cosmology has much in common with that posited by the Neo-Platonists. Again we have a threefold division—but the borders are defined differently. The "Kingdom of God" is made of pure spirit—the Pleroma. It consists of the outer two circles—of the Father (the Invisible Spirit) and the Son (the primeval spiritual man). The Son forms the link between the World of the Spirit and that of Life below. The Father and the Son are bound together by Love—*agapê*. The second realm is that of Life. It also consists of two circles, one of Light (signified with the color yellow) and one of Darkness (seen as blue). This realm is ruled by spirit and soul mixed together.

Within its midst is the Circle of Life—the active realm of Sophia. This is the seed of the Divine Soul in Man. Its complex structure appears in figure 5 on p. 58. Within the Circle of Life is the Providence of Sophia, and in the midst of that are two intersecting circles—*gnôsis* (Knowledge) and *synesis* (Insight). Where these intersect is the definition of the Nature of Sophia (Wisdom).

Below the Realm of Life is the Cosmos itself. It is usually seen as the creation of the first Archôn—and is material (and hence evil in the Gnostic understanding). It is a mixture of matter (body), soul, and spirit. At the outermost boundary of this realm is the Garden of Eden. In it are the trees of Knowledge and Life—and at its innermost gate is

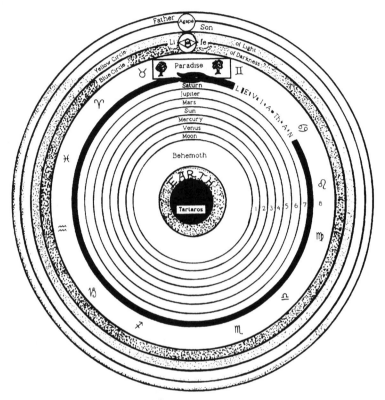

Figure 4.   A Gnostic Cosmograph.

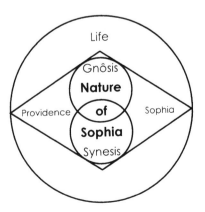

Figure 5.   Circle of Life.

a revolving flaming sword. Just below this realm are the fixed stars and most importantly those of the Zodiac. This region is the gateway to the higher reaches through Eden. Entry to this realm is blocked by the cosmic serpent encircling the Cosmos. In Gnostic tradition this is identified with the Hebraic sea-monster Leviathan, while more Hellenistic tradition simply calls it the Ouroboros—the serpent biting its own tail. Below the serpent are arranged the familiar seven planetary realms— each one ruled by a hierarchy of Archôns meant to block and prevent the individual's soul from returning to its home in the Pleroma.

At the center of the world order is the Earth. Just above the Earth, and below the sphere of the Moon, is the atmospheric realm filled with aerial entities—daimôns, angels, and so on. Also, the Earth is not quite the nethermost region of the world—below it are the infernal regions such as Tartaros and Erebos. It is from these aerial and infernal realms that the early Hermetic magicians most often acquired the aid of entities in their practice of *goêteia*.

To the Gnostic all this cosmological speculation was intended to explore the machinations of the evil cosmos so that the individual Gnostic could come to understand them and eventually escape them in a perilous journey out of the almost infinite material traps of the world. Magic as such was only important to the Gnostic as a tool for escape and safe passage through the Aiôns back to the realm of pure spirit. A Gnostic would never engage in the magic of the sort found in the magical papyri. Magical technologies were used purely for purposes of bringing an individual to *gnôsis* and for aiding the spirit in its struggle to pass through the Aionic hierarchies. Some Gnostic texts, for example the Coptic *Book of Jeu*, give the necessary "spells" of incantations needed at each level to force the Archôn to allow the spirit to pass through.[9] These incantations and the names of the various entities inhabiting the Aiôns are often identical in type to those found in the magical papyri. The purpose of the spells is also very similar to that of the formulas found in the much older Egyptian *Book of Coming Forth by Day*.[10]

---

[9]C. Schmidt, ed., *The Books of Jeu and the Untitled Text in the Bruce Codex*, V. Mac-Dermot, trans. (Leiden: Brill, 1978).

[10]This text is better known as *The Book of the Dead*. There are several translations. The best is by T. C. Allen, trans., *The Book of the Dead* or *Going Forth by Day* (Chicago: University of Chicago Press, 1974).

Egyptian Cosmology

Because the Hermetic tradition has its geographical roots in Egyptian soil and surely contains Egyptian concepts just below the surface, a discussion of the basic ideas of the ancient cosmology of Khemet is needed to understand the elements present in the Hermetic worldview. All aspects of the study of ancient Egypt pose enormous difficulties. The history of that culture spreads out over 5,000 years and seems deceptively constant in its external shape. In fact, Egyptian culture and religion underwent many changes through its millennia-long history—and the country was always more a mosaic of local cultures (each with its own particular values and myths) than a unified culture.

The one thing that held these cultures together was the Nile river. Geographical considerations must have suggested some aspects of cosmology to the Egyptians. Egypt is called the Black Land (Khemet) because the annual overflowing of the waters of the Nile brings fertilizing soil and posture to the land just a few miles either side of the banks of the river. This makes the land rich and fertile due to the deposits of dark silt—all without rainfall. The land beyond the fertile dark strip is entirely desert and is called the Red Land. This regular, yet mysterious, process of annual inundation, and the strict division between the *inner* fertile land and the desolate *outer* land also proved important to Egyptian cosmological conceptions.

Actually there are several major cosmogonic myths in Egyptian tradition. Different cities or regions had their own local myths concerning the origin of the world. Two of the most important and the two most interesting to the would-be Hermeticist, are those of Heliopolis (City of the Sun) and Hermopolis (City of Hermês = Thoth). Before the birth of the cosmos could take place, three qualities or powers had to be present: Hu (divine utterance), Heka (magical power), and Sia (divine knowledge). Atum (Rê), the first entity, wielded these powers to shape the cosmos. In the cosmology of Heliopolis this first entity, Atum (the All), gave birth to the first cosmic pair: Shu (Space or Air) and Tefnut (Moisture or Water) through a masturbatory act of creativity. This pair then gave birth to Osiris, Isis, Set, Nephthys, and Horus the Elder. The whole Heliopolitan cosmogony is shown in figure 6 on p. 61.

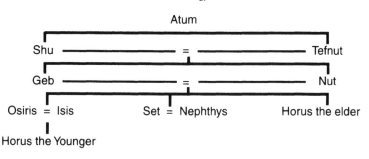

Figure 6. The Heliopolitan Cosmogony.

Another, perhaps more abstract and sophisticated myth comes from Hermopolis where we read of four pairs of entities representing Nothingness or Hiddenness, Endlessness or Formlessness, Darkness and Inertness who all coalesce to form a great cosmic egg—from which Intelligence (Thoth) is born. The whole Hermopolitan cosmogony appears in figure 7 on p. 62.

The actual shape of the world as understood by the Egyptians is only slightly more singular. In the earliest times the Egyptians faced the south for ritual purposes—the south is the direction from which the rising waters of the Nile come. This must have been the source of life—of the earthly kind in any event. We know they originally faced south because the Egyptian word for north meant "back of the head," while those for east and west are "left" and "right" respectively. In later times this "australization" became a true *orientation* when, with the increase of the importance of the sun in Egyptian cultic life, the ritual direction was changed to the east. The solar cult was apparently developed in the Nile delta, and spread throughout the country when the north conquered the south around 2950 B.C.E.

The Egyptian cosmology is impressive by its apparently primitive nature. Abstract principles upon which the cosmology is based are often obscured by the multiplicity of external images and the mutability of those images. The basic cosmological principles of the Egyptians hinged on their desire for *symmetry* and their sense that space was *limited*. In its simplest form the Egyptian cosmos appeared as shown in figure 8 on p. 63.

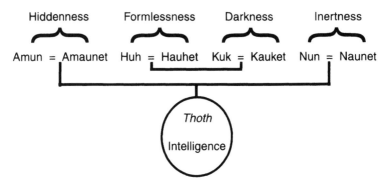

Figure 7.   The Hermopolitan Cosmogony.

Nut is the Sky or vault of heaven. She is held up by four columns or pillars in the four cardinal directions. These are sometimes equated with *tcham*-scepters. (See the discussion of the god Set on page 89.) Shu is the Space between the Sky and the Earth (Geb). Geb is a flat plain—which is Egypt with the Nile running through its middle. Around the edges of this plate the land is hilly or mountainous. These are the foreign lands outside Egypt. This whole plate of land floats on a primeval water-mass—Nun. Below this is a realm called the Dat or Duat: the "Underworld." It is into the Duat that the Sun descends nightly, and it is into this place that the souls of the dead also descend.

The question of the "location" of the "Underworld" is a problematic one. In the most ancient times this realm was identified with the northern part of the night sky—where the stars "know no destruction." This refers to the circumpolar stars which are always in the sky and never dip below the horizon. The Duat contains the "Field of Reeds" and the "Field of Offerings" where the dead may live eternally as an *akh*, "effective spirit." In later times the location of the entryway to the Duat shifted from the north to the west.

An alternate special arrangement suggested by some texts is shown in figure 8 on p. 63. Here the Sun rises in the east after renewing itself in the waters of Nun. It then travels below the vault of heaven in the undersky (*nenet*)—thought of as polished metal—until it again dips into the watery realm only to rise along the outside of the inner plate. It is the Sun's light coming through the holes in

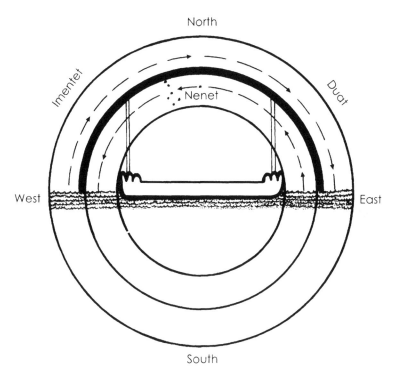

Figure 8.   The Egyptian Cosmograph.

the plate that accounts for the light of the fixed stars. The Field of
Reeds lies in the east in the Duat where the Sun is reborn each day,
and the Field of Offerings (*Hetep*) lies in the west in *Imentet*.

Hermetic Cosmology

Hermetic cosmology is an original and multifaceted mosaic of cosmologies drawn from Hellenic philosophies (such as those of Plato
and Aristotle), Hellenistic Stoicism and Neo-Platonism, as well as Judaic and Egyptian mythologies and religious traditions. There is no

one single Hermetic cosmology, just as there is no one single Gnostic cosmology. There are only individual cosmologies revealed by individual Hermetic teachers through texts they wrote. In order to understand fully the Hermetic cosmology—and ultimately the anthropology and theology as well—you must do several things. First you must read and study a wide number of individual Hermetic teachings. The systems contained in the *Corpus Hermeticum*[11] should be studied, as well as the doctrines of the Neo-Platonists, Stoics, and especially those of the Gnostics. Next these doctrines must be *activated* through the highest forms of operative work of which you are capable. After this has been done for some time—usually a period of several years—you must begin to create your own personalized doctrine based upon your operative and experiential work. Then, and only then, can you begin to teach your doctrine—and thereby truly understand it yourself.

The principal elements of a Hermetic cosmology can be derived from the material already provided in this chapter. However, wider study is necessary for further progress. Other cosmologies can be accepted or adopted by the postmodern Hermetic. The ultimate aim is the creation of your own cosmology based on a particular synthesis of component elements. From all objective evidence this eclectic cosmological creativity is one common denominator among all "schools" of Hermeticism in ancient times. The lesson to be drawn from this fact will be left for you to ponder.

---

[11]For information on *Corpus Hermeticum*, see Walter Scott, *Hermetics*, vol. 1.

First Part of an Epistle
from Abaris to Ammonius
(Translated from an Unknown Tongue)

I. INTRODUCTION:

1. In the name of the first born son of Chaos, who is Intelligence, I greet thee from the land of eternal day!

2. Thou hast asked of me to set down in words my Knowledge of the origins of the orderings of the world. Herein are my thoughts perfectly concealed. It is for thee to reveal and open them.

3. What thou readest here is but a continuation of what thou hast learned while thou didst dwell with me long ago.

II. COSMOGONY:

1. Before time began and before Nature moved upon the face of the void, God—the Mind—dwelt in darkness and solitude; as an egg in space was the Mind.

2. Even the Mind knew nothing, for there was nothing Intelligible. But at once the Mind thought the first Thought—and then there were two. Between these two—the Mind, who is the bridegroom, and his bride, who is his Thought, and whose lips drip with honey because she is wise—did all intelligent things come to be.

3. In their bliss the Mind and his Thought, who dwelt with him, brought forth myriad offspring—though they knew them not. From the honey sweet lips of Sophia, as the Thought of Mind is called today, sprang forth an eternity of circles, each one smaller and less like her than the preceding one.

4. Though she Knew not what she did, her creations gave her great pleasure.

5. Thus were born the Archôns, and their Aiôns, which they govern and watch over and guard with ferocity.

6. But when her creative pleasure had passed, there was born in her a burning desire to Know what lay beyond.

7. This desire was bequeathed to her by her bridegroom on their wedding night. This was his first gift, but his last will be the revelation she receives when they are reunited.

8. Gifted with her burning desire to Know, she set off into the created realms. As she entered each of the succeeding Aiôns which had issued from her own lips, she expected to find the bliss she had known with her bridegroom—but found only pain and sorrow as she was violated and caused to suffer at the hands of each of the Archôns. With each of her violations, the Aiôn wherein she dwelt was filled with creatures and given shape and form. When her violation was complete in one Aiôn, she was passed on to the next below.

9. As she fell below the realm of the Aiôns she reached the center of all wherein there shimmered a heavenly water. In this water was reflected the image of the realm above, whence it came. In this vastness dwell twelve creatures who gird it from without and twelve who anchor it from within. And the second twelve are seven and five in number.

10. While on the earth Sophia took upon herself a body, that she might come to Know the ways of the earth. But on earth it was little different from the way it was among the Aiôns. And in the earth, creatures were brought forth from her violations.

11. Memory of her bridegroom had all but faded from her memory. But what she had of it, she imparted to her children that they might be instilled with some measure of his gift of desire.

12. And thus was the cosmos and the earth in its midst made complete through the sufferings of the First Thought.

13. Now, I could tell thee of the search of Mind for his Thought, and how he quested after her through the eternities of the ages, but that must wait for another day.

III. COSMOLOGY:

1. Today what thou must learn, however, is the shape of the cosmos as it is today.

2. The realm of Earth, where thou dwellest now, consists of four base elements. These are Earth, Water, Air, and Fire. A fifth, Aether, connects these to the realms above and to the heavenly forms of the base elements.

3. Below the Earth lie the infernal, or nether, regions wherein Chaos still reigns and Typhôn is king. There are three chthonic realms: Hades, Erebos, and Tartaros.

4. But above the Earth stretches a great expanse of Air. In this Air dwell all manner of daimôns. At the outermost reaches of the Aerial realm, the Earth is wreathed by a halo of Aether and in this dwells a host of 365 daimôns.

5. Beyond the Aetherial realm surrounding the Earth are seven circles, each one outside the last.

6. The first of these is inhabited by the Moon, who is called the Goddess Selênê, whom the Romans call Luna.

7. Then there is the realm of Hermês, or Thoth, whom the Romans call Mercury.

8. Then there is the realm of Aphroditê, whom the Romans call Venus.

9. Then there is the realm of the Sun, who is also known as Hêlios or Rê, and whom the Romans call Sol.

10. Then there is the realm of Ares, whom the Romans call Mars.

11. Then there is the realm of Zeus, or Ammon, whom the Romans call Jupiter.

12. Then there is the realm of Kronos, whom the Romans call Saturn.

13. Beyond the reaches of Saturn lie the gateways to the supernal regions beyond. These are the twelve living creatures of Zodiacus who rule over the realms below.

14. But of the stars there are none more powerful than those we call the Immortals, who never know death or decay. These are the eternal ones of the Northern heaven, wherein dwells the Ageless Intelligence.

15. There are many gateways to the supernal regions wherein dwells the infinity of Aiôns.

16. Each Aiôn is ruled by an Archôn and each is an expression of a Word which issued from the first Word uttered by God, the Mind, which was an embodiment of his First Thought, and who remains hidden from him until he is able to find her in the nether region.

IV. CONCLUSION:

1. This is all I have to say at this time concerning the shape and nature of the world.

2. Seek the Mysteries!

The theories of cosmology are essential to true progress in the art and science of mageia or theurgy. Such theories act as a framework for magical operations which in turn refine the "mere theories" into true teachings—*doxa*—based on experience and real Knowledge (*gnôsis*).

Many ancient Hermetics rarely indulged in operative magic—but they all practiced an abstracted form of *mageia* nevertheless. Still others evolved to a point after which they no longer needed to in-

dulge in operative workings. In both cases what was eventually practiced was a pure form of mageia in which the individual subjective
universe—the *nous*—directly entered into, and worked its will
(*thelêma*) upon, the greater subjective universe: the *Nous.*

The original magical papyri are full of references to cosmological models which indicate the magicians recording the operations
were intimately familiar with complex images of the world. A complete analysis of the cosmological references in the ancient papyri
would reveal interesting results. Such mysteries should be left to the
individual to discover. From an operative viewpoint it is most important to understand that the earth and earthly life is the focal point
of Hermetic mageia. Influences are chiefly drawn from gods,
daimôns, or angels dwelling in the elements—Earth, Water, Air, Fire,
and Aether—as well as in the heavens or below the earth in the
chthonic realms. There are further powers (Gk. δυναμης) that are
informed in these spheres from which magicians can draw both
knowledge and personal power if they understand how to gain access
to these spheres.

HERMETIC ANTHROPOLOGY

Mageia is the art of effectively expressing the will of the individual in the world. But what is the true nature of the individual, of the self, of Man—the *Anthrôpos*? The answers to these questions are essential in the practice of Hermetic mageia. This is because the development or transformation of the self must occur in tandem with the increase in personal technical power. The magician must have an understanding of what makes up the human being (*Anthrôpos*), as well as what makes up the world (*Kosmos*) in order to know how to practice mageia.

What I speak of here is an actual *anthropology*—an understanding of the nature of the whole human being. What, in today's terms, might be considered a combination of physiology (body) and psychology (mind, soul, and spirit). Although the most ancient Greeks seem to have had an instinctual understanding of the distinction between *psychê* (soul) and *physis* (nature), this dichotomy was less well understood by the Egyptians and other systems of the east. Different cultures have had different ideas about what it is to be a human being.

But whether Hellenistic, Egyptian, or traditional Judaic anthropology is being considered, the system indicates a much more detailed and precise set of terms for the make-up of the total human being than is commonly available in modern terms. This is due to the fact that the ancients were more familiar and intimate with these parts of themselves. It is this understanding that we seek to recover in the study of ancient anthropologies.

As elsewhere in the Hermetic tradition, Hermetic anthropology is eclectic and drawn from sources we have learned to expect by now: Hellenistic philosophies and religions, Gnosticism, Judaic teachings, and Egyptian religious traditions. And again the would-be follower of the postmodern Hermetic path must drink deeply from these sources and eventually create a personal synthesis from those elements.

Hellenistic Anthropology

Although other anthropologies may also be important to the total understanding of Hermetic teachings, it is clearly that of the Greeks which gives us the greatest insight into the magical system of the papyri, as well as being the one with the most profound links to our own ways of thinking today. The link is provided by two things. First, the ancient Greek system is linked to our own by reason of their primeval identity. The language of the Greeks and that which we speak today were once *one*. This proto-language is called Indo-European by the academics, though it has been called "Aryan" by the more romantic. (Actually "Aryan" only refers to the eastern branch of the Indo-European family and technically has nothing to do with the European tradition except through later influences.) Also a link is provided by the widespread, but secondary, Hellenization of our own technical jargon. Most of our "scientific" terminology for things to do with *physiology* or *psychology* are derived ultimately from Greek (usually through a learned Latin intermediary).

The ancient Greek term for the whole human being was *anthrôpos*. This included the complex psychic structures together with the natural physical parts. These physical components were called either *demas*, which meant the framework of anatomical structure of the body, or *sôma*, which is more narrowly confined to the material substance. *Sôma* is also the word used for the lifeless corpse.

The widely used term for the soul, *psychê*, originally had a very specific, if broad, meaning. The *psychê* could be called the active form of the person. It is the life-force capable of being separated from the body by death (or through magical techniques). It can exist in Hades or Tartaros and be reborn. The *psychê* is the "shade" or disembodied "spirit" which can survive death. It is, however, particular to each individual—although it can also be raised to the level of a god (*theos*) or daimôn (*daimôn*).

Most characteristic of the Indo-European psychology is a structural distinction between a cognitive or intellective and a reflective or emotive aspect of the mind. (This is no doubt an intuitive, "pre-scientific" realization of the dichotomy of functions

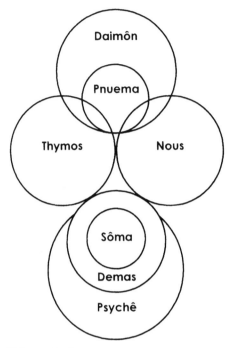

Figure 9.   The Hellenistic Soul.

usually explained today in terms of the left and right hemispheres
of the brain.) The ancient Greeks usually called the emotive or vi-
talistic aspect the *thymos*. This word comes from a root-word meaning "to storm, rage or rush." It is originally the seat of vitality,
desire, anger, courage and so on. The ancient writers would never
think of the *thymos* as being in Hades. It is vitally connected to life
in this world. The other aspect of the mind is called the *nous*. Its
mental and intellectual character made it more prominent in the
language of philosophical writers of all traditions. The *nous* contains the intellectual forms and structures of thought and the power
of memory (*mneme*). Later philosophers used the terms *phrenes*
(senses), originally practically a synonym for *nous* meaning *reason*.
Both the *thymos* and the *nous* have traditionally been located in the
"heart" (*kardia*) of the individual. Some have taken this to mean

the physical heart, while it may also simply mean the innermost essence or *core* of the person.

The use of the term *pneuma*, breath, to mean anything but the physiological process of respiration came only with Judeo-Christian influence in the latest Hellenistic period. Ultimately it is a translation of the idea of the Hebrew *ruah*. Otherwise its meaning is contained in the Greek *psychê* and *thymos*.

Of tremendous interest to magicians is the idea of the *daimôn*. A *daimôn* is essentially a demigod or quasi-divinity of good or evil propensities, which can, through the application of magical techniques, become attached to an individual. The individual can, by an act of will, assimilate himself or herself to the essence of a *daimôn* and assume its powers as his or her own. The *psychê* of an individual can be raised to the level of a *daimôn* after physical death—or conversely the *psychê* and the pre-existing *daimôn* can become fused during the life of an individual. The *daimôn* and its relationship to the related concepts of the *angelos* and *theos* will be discussed in the next chapter.

A conceptual structure of the Hellenistic soul is shown in figure 9 on p. 72.

Egyptian Anthropology

Concepts of the ancient Egyptian psychosomatic complex have been included in a wide variety of occult-type literature for well over 100 years now. Much of it has suffered from two tendencies often found in such literature—it has been out-of-date and out-of-touch with the most recent Egyptology, and it has often tended to project onto Egyptian evidence concepts already familiar to whatever occult school the author happened to belong. To the theosophist, the Egyptian concepts looked "remarkably theosophical," and so on. In fact, the Egyptians looked at themselves and the world around them in a unique way. The postmodern Hermetic should try to understand this viewpoint as much as possible *from within itself.*

There are many aspects of Egyptian anthropology that might seem strange to the modern European mind. The degree to which the individual person only had meaning in the context of the social is just one of these. It was not until the 18th dynasty (around 1500 B.C.E.) that the word for human being, *remetch* (rm<u>t</u>), was used in a singular sense—it previously appeared only in the collective *remetchu* (rm<u>t</u>u). (Forms in parentheses refer to phonetic values of hieroglyphic characters. See Table 1, page 108.) Also the degree to which the Egyptians did not recognize a dichotomy between the body and the soul(s) is remarkable. This is why they thought it so important for the future of the soul to keep the physical body preserved in the process of mummification.

Egyptian anthropology consists of three great categories—the corporeal self, the social self and the psychic self. These are three parts of a whole—which is most identified with the physical or corporeal self, the *ha* (h'). This word could also mean "body," as could the words *djet* (<u>d</u>t), *hemef* (hm.f), or *het* (<u>h</u>t). The *djet* also means the "inner self," while *hemef* is used only of gods and kings. *Het* is the most "physical" of all the terms as it is also used of animals and even of plants. It really means the "belly." The region of the abdomen was thought of as the seat of the affects or instincts by the ancient Egyptians—and the place where magical power (*heka*) was stored. All of these terms indicate an entirely physical state of being, all of which would also be thought to be "psychological" by the modern European mind.

The utter lack of the body/mind or image/reality dichotomy gives rise to the idea that the image or shape of a person has a determinative effect on the soul—especially in the after-life. The most important aspect of the image is the face. This is why the sarcophagal images portray the shape of the body indistinctly, while concentrating with great detail on the features of the face. This is also why the Egyptians put so much emphasis on *cosmetics*. The very word "cosmetic" really means "to arrange or order (properly)," that is, "to make in the image of the world (*kosmos*)." This, like so many other Egyptian terms, was translated into the Greek language. When the Egyptians applied cosmetics to their faces, they were actually creating immortal images within their beings. Individual characteristics were minimized in favor of a stylization of the self as an archetypal human image that was immortal.

Another external aspect is the "shadow," called in Egyptian the *khaibet* or *shut* (h3jbt or shwt). This is the appearance or image of the person as a whole, but is sometimes equated with the physical body or lifeless corpse itself.

Two principles governed the social self—favor (*hezut*) and right-order (*ma-at*). All efforts made by individual selves were thought to be instigated by the king whose "favor" initiated such efforts. All actions of individuals were seen in the cooperative context of *ma-at*—and by the power of *ma-at*, collective action was rewarded. This social aspect of the body-soul was in a decayed state by the time of the Hellenistic period in Egyptian history. The magical papyri and the *Corpus Hermeticum* are testimonies to the ascendancy of the individual will over the collective will of ancient Egyptian statism.[12] It should be noted that from the earliest times the cause of the individual will was championed by the god Set (Typhôn). Although the official cult of Set declined in the latest periods of Egyptian history as that of Osiris ascended, the Typhônian spirit gained power as foreign philosophical and religious schools from Greece and the East gained strength.

The chief organ of true "psychic" activity—that is, thinking, feeling, and so on—is the *ab* ("heart"). This is the innermost self, the seat of knowledge and reason as well as emotion. It is here that the intrinsic conflict between the assertion of the individual will and the right sense of cooperation with social complexes is played out. The balance and harmonizing of these was the task of the Egyptian *ab*. The outermost self is embodied in the tongue and is symbolized by the name *ren*.

Terms most frequently discussed as "soul concepts" among the Egyptians are the *ba* (b3) and the *ka* (k3). In fact these are not normally used by the living person at all—although they are present in life. They only become active after death. The *ba* is the *post mortem* body or soul—the "life in death," while the *ka* is the "body double" of the person. The *ka* may, however, be activated in life through certain magical technologies.

---

[12]For information on *Corpus Hermeticum*, see Walter Scott, *Hermetics*, vol. 1 (Boston: Shambhala, 1985).

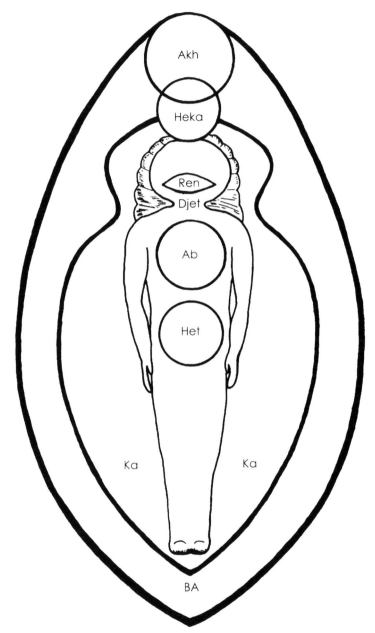

Figure 10.   The Egyptian Anthropology.

Of perhaps greater importance to the magician than these two functions are the *akh* (j3h) and the *heka* (hk3) or *akhu* (3hw). The *akh* is the "effective spirit" which can become immortal in the imperishable regions of the northern night sky. This is the true *post mortem* individual entity. It must possess *heka* ("magical power") in order to survive. This is stored in the "belly" (*het*) in life and must be carefully guarded and protected after death. (See figure 10, The Egyptian Anthropology, page 76.)

The *heka* is important to the magician both in life and death. This force is that by which the creator god Atum-Rê created the cosmos. It is personified as the god Heka—without whom the other gods themselves could not exist. It is the "First Work"—also called Khunum in the Egyptian pantheon. In life magicians use the *heka*, also synonymous with the "magical word," to make their wills potent. This is also done through a kind of charisma used to exercise influence over the hearts of others. Words for this emphasize either the idea of fear—*neru* (nrw)—or the idea of life—*merut* (mrwt).

It is perhaps impossible to understand totally the way in which the Egyptians thought of themselves and the world around them. But because of the importance of people of Egyptian heritage in the Hermetic tradition, we must try to bridge the gap with rationally intuitive tools as an exercise in using these tools. Many Hermetic Egyptians perhaps first exposed as adults to Hellenistic philosophical and magical thought may have had to exercise similar faculties to grasp the truth by which the Hellenized systems challenged them. In struggling with the problems in reverse, we reverse the flow of time and recreate their experiences in reality.

Mystical Judaic Anthropology

Although Judaic or Hebraic mythology and theology played a major role in the development of Hermetic magical and cosmological conceptions, the anthropology or psychology of the ancient Hebrews was relatively less important. However, because of the vitalism promoted by these worshippers of the Demiurge (as the Hermetics saw it), the concept of the physical breath as a dominant psychic conception became widespread. The more complex psychology presented in medieval Kabbalistic literature is actually directly related to Neo-Platonic psychology as well as to the ancient Semitic beliefs on the topic of the soul.

The *Zohar*, compiled by Moses de Leon in the 13th century, contains a succinct discussion of the tripartite soul.[13] The three souls are: the *nefesh* (vital soul), the *ruah* (spirit), and the *neshamah* (inner soul). When a person's body dies the *nefesh* remains with it, perhaps continuing for a period as a disembodied soul and even interacting with the living. The *ruah* goes to "the earthly Garden of Eden" and vests itself with a new form resembling the one it had in earthly life. But before the *ruah* can enjoy the delights of the lower Garden, the *neshamah* must ascend and be reunited with "the One who embraces all sides." When the reunion of the *neshamah* with the One is complete, the *ruah* is crowned in the lower Garden and the *nefesh* rests easy in the grave. So then the task is for the *neshamah*, which has its origins in the One, to be reunited with its source—the Holy One. This may involve some difficulties.

The text of the *Zohar* also indicates a basis of necromantic magic in the Kabbalistic context when it says that when the living are troubled they go to the graves of the dead and awaken the *nefesh* which goes out to activate the *ruah*, which in turn rouses the patriarches and the *neshamah* which is united with the Holy One who then "has pity" on the living and their woes.

Ruah is the soul-breath breathed by the Demiurge, Yahweh, into the inanimate form of Adam. This idea of the breath bearing the divine component in humans is heavily emphasized in Hebraic lore. Before contact with the Semitic teachings, the terms for "breath" in Greek (*pneuma*) or Latin (*spiritus*) had little or no "psychic" connotations. It is equally clear, however, how much of the systematic Kabbalistic teachings of the *Zohar* are based on the Neo-Platonic triad of the One, the Demiurge, and the All-Soul. Each of the three soul-components is the creation of the corresponding aspect of Divinity, and each ultimately returns to its creator. All are conceived of as being one on a certain level.

---

[13]Gershom Scholem, ed., *Zohar: The Book of Splendor* (New York: Schocken, 1949).

Second Part of an Epistle
from Abaris to Ammonius
A Hermetic Anthropology

I. INTRODUCTION:

1. I now continue on the topic of the character of the Anthrô-pos, as thou hast also asked me to set down in words my Knowledge of the origins and character of the Anthrôpos. Again, my thoughts are herein perfectly concealed. It is for thee to reveal and open them.

2. Know thou that the Anthrôpos is a creature of intermediate nature, and can become like unto a creeping vine or like unto an angel or god. The key is found in the will of the Anthrôpos himself.

II. ANTHROPOGONY:

1. Man, or the Anthrôpos, it is said by some, was created in the image of God. This is indeed so, but his origin is not singular, but manifold.

2. In the Anthrôpos is contained the seed of all possibilities, both physical and spiritual. In the Earth are contained all physical possibilities, and so it is in the Body of Man. But only the Soul of Man contains the seeds of all spiritual possibilities.

3. This is so because the Anthrôpos is indeed a reflection of the totality of the Most High, the One, the very God, who could do naught else but create, and create he did by means of his Thought and his Word, which is embodied in his Thought.

4. In the Anthrôpos were coalesced the potential quintessence of the Most High, but this quintessence can not be realized unless it receives impetus from within the creature—whereupon he hears the Word.

III. ANTHROPOLOGY:

1. The Body of Man is the focus of the perfect reflection of the essence of the Cosmos, of the universal ordering of the World.

2. Man need not study the Cosmos to learn its secrets, but by studying the Body to which his Soul is for a time wedded, he shall be able to Know the Mysteries of nature.

3. The Soul is wedded to the Body now and again for a purpose. That purpose is revelation.

4. In the Body there is a system of hidden affinities or correspondences, and between certain Bodies there are other hidden affinities and correspondences. So it is in the larger Cosmos. By Knowing thine own Body, thou canst Know the Cosmos.

5. For as it has been said: "That which is above is like unto that which is below."

6. In the same way, the Anthrôpos, being endowed with a Soul, which originates in those realms beyond the physical universe, and from beyond the stars, can come to Know the realm of the Spirit and the Aetherial realms beyond the Earth by coming to Know his own Soul.

7. But before it can be Known, it must be discovered.

8. Having been discovered, it can now become the object of the inquiry of the Will of the Anthrôpos.

IV. DESTINY OF THE SOUL:

1. What the Soul comes to Know depends entirely on the innate character of that Soul and then what the Will of that Soul undertakes to cultivate the seeds which are found in that character.

2. If they follow their appetites, and are nothing but Creatures of Nature, and do naught else with their Lives than consume and excrete, be that food, money, or effort, they will be little else than plants, or at best earthworms.

3. If they follow their senses, and are nothing but Creatures of Nature, and do naught else with their Lives than gratify their five physical senses, following pleasure and avoiding pain, they will be little else than beasts of the field. Perhaps therein they shall become as noble as a hound or eagle—but they shall not be Human.

4. If, however, they apply the rationality of their Souls and by means of their own efforts rise above the appetites and beyond the senses—to them a great Mystery shall be revealed. For they will have become truly Human, and will come to understand their connections with the realm above.

5. But yet greater Mystery will be revealed to those who learn how to cultivate the seeds of divinity which are innate in the Soul of the Elect of the Earth. Such seeds are cultivated by exercising the faculty of magic, the ability to use Knowledge to alter the nature of the Soul, or to alter the order of nature surrounding the Soul.

6. Upon the death of the Body, it returns whence it came and becomes one with Nature once more.

7. This will also be true of those Souls which have been consumed by their own appetites, or which have been imprisoned by their own illusionary existence in the realm of images presented to their senses in life.

8. But for those who have applied their rational faculties, some part of their Souls may indeed survive, though they will by force of Necessity forget all which they have learned in

Life, only to return to Life and in time go beyond the gifts of the rational Soul to ascend to the realm of the daimôns and angels.

9. Only those who have in Life exercised the faculty of the divine, and themselves become as one with an angel or daimôn will be able to drink of the waters of Memory and thereby retain that which they have learned and developed of the divine in the time of Life, when the Soul was wedded to the Body.

(Here the epistle ends.)

Theology and Daimonology

In the Hermetic magic of the papyri we find two kinds of external entities the magician constantly deals with: divinities and daimôns. A god or goddess (Gk. θεος or θεα) is an entity of a transcendent nature. They are usually drawn from one of the major national religious mythologies of the eastern Mediterranean—Greek, Egyptian, Hebrew, or Mesopotamian.

The daimôn (Gk. δαιμων, pl. δαιμονης) also later called *daimônion* (pl. *daimônia*) is a being between the gods and humanity. To the ancient Greeks, daimôns could be either helpful and good (the *agathodaimôn*) or maleficent and evil (the *kakodaimôn*). The former might of late be referred to as an "angel." In Greek this would be αγγελος, which is simply Greek for "messenger." The *angelos* was the messenger of a god or the gods, a thing which is essentially the active agent of the will of God or a god.

Hermetic theology poses a number of questions or problems for the student to solve. What is a god? Is there only One, or are there many? By what names are the gods to be called? The most philosophical branches of the tradition may provide one set of answers, while the more magical branch seems to give quite different ones. This is not unusual in complex traditions with long histories. The gods are characterized by Mind. Consistency and regularity can only be expected in Nature. Therefore it is not even necessary for your Mind to hold internally consistent views on such questions—although you may strive for such if you wish.

Philosophical Hermeticism holds that the gods are creations of the universal Mind or Intelligence (*Nous*) and are in fact abstract functions or archetypes of relative Being. This is the root cause of the happy sense of eclecticism in the Hermetic tradition. In reality the various gods and goddesses of national (natural) traditions are mere *images* of real archetypes which in fact exist beyond their sensible images. This is why, to the highly initiated Hermetic, there is no *real* difference between Thoth and Hermês, Rê and Hêlios, or Set and Typhôn.

But to practical-minded magicians, the images can not be dispensed with just because they are quasi-illusions. Magicians must inspire and motivate their own psychês to effective action. In the early stages of initiation such motivation is virtually impossible to accomplish with abstract philosophical jargon. The soul is stirred to action by myth and poetry. This is why the magical formulas are usually based on mythic understandings. This practical stage may not be dispensed with—and this is a great secret of postmodern Hermetic magic.

Egyptian Gods and Goddesses

The two most important theological systems for understanding Hermetic magic are those of the Egyptians and the Greeks. As noted elsewhere, in the Hermetic philosophy, focused on the *principles* of which the various gods and goddesses are expressions, the differences between various mythological pantheons is secondary. It is most essential to see beyond the images to the reality which lies above and within.

The Hermetic theology is a synthesis of the Egyptian and Greek systems with a strong, but secondary, admixture of Hebraic or Judaic theurgy. But the actual original devisers of the Hermetic synthesis were first Egyptians, who were educated and trained in the Hellenistic tradition. They would have felt very much "at home" with the Egyptian gods and goddesses; the Greek divinities would probably have seemed more *universal* and abstract to them, while the Hebraic god would no doubt have seemed quite materialistic and concrete.

The Egyptian idea of a "god" was itself rather abstract in some respects. The Egyptian word for "god" is *neter* (ntr), the plural form is *neteru* (ntrw). These *neteru* seem to have been something akin to "principle substances." This is why they could be so easily mixed and combined in the Egyptian mind. Whereas the Greek might have distinguished clearly between the god (*theos*) and the principle (*archê*) of which the god might be a manifestation or image, the Egyptian recognized no division.

Most of the major divinities of the Egyptian pantheon make regular appearances in the ancient magical papyri: Thoth, Osiris, Isis, Horus, Set (Typhôn), and others. Some basic understanding of who or what these gods and goddesses are and how they might function in the Hermetic magical philosophy is essential.

Thoth (= Hermês) | The Greek form of this god's name is the label under which the whole eclectic philosophical and magical tradition of the eastern Mediterranean is found. But it is likely that it is with the Egyptian *neter* that the root of the tradition is to be discovered.

In the magical papyri the name of Thoth appears in various forms and spellings: *Thôth, Thooth, Thôouth, Thouth,* or *Theouth.* Each has its own philosophical power in the Hellenistic system of operant phonology. The actual Egyptian form of his name is *djhuti* (d͟hwty). He is closely associated with the Moon.

In the Hermopolitan cosmology Thoth is clearly shown to be a god of Intelligence and Wisdom. He is the god of writing and of the magic of writing and of the spoken word. It is for this reason that the particular form of magic represented in the papyri is ascribed to him.

Thoth can act as the Great God in the literature of the magical papyri. His name is found in workings designed to provide release or liberation as well as to reveal hidden things. He is often invoked in conjunction with Moon workings and for victory or to restrain the anger of others. In operation 42 he is equated with Abrasax and called the "soul of darkness" (from a Coptic title *Bainchôôôch*).

Rê (= Hêlios) | Rê is the god of the Sun. The formula PHRE occurs quite often in the ancient magical papyri. This is a Hellenized form of the name of the Egyptian sun-god, Rê, with a definite article attached, meaning therefore "the Sun." This is the name of the god in the later periods of Egyptian history.

In ancient Egyptian theology Rê is the creator god, the first of the gods. He is called Atum as the setting Sun and Rê at midday. The disk, or better said, the orb, of the Sun is called Aten. (This became the focus of the "heretical" monotheistic aberration under Akhnaten between 1377 and 1358 B.C.E.) Rê is clearly the god of creativity and the originator of motion and change in the cosmos. Rê is commonly combined with a wide variety of other god-forms and often equated with others. Two of the more notable of these combinations occur in the papyri literature with Aresonophre (the Sun of Arsinoe—the City of Crocodiles) and with Helioros (Hêlios-Horus).

Mnevis, which appears in operations 10 and 45 in Part IV of this book, is the sacred bull of the Sun, worshipped at Heliopolis. Mnevis is the Greek form of the entity, which the Egyptians themselves called *Ur-mer*, which is described as the "life of Rê."

Rê, or Phre, as he usually appears in the magical papyri, is a sovereign figure of centralizing and general magical force. Obviously the image of Rê was rehabilitated through later contact with the astro-philosophical views of the Greeks, who viewed Hêlios as the sovereign of heaven. If Thoth-Hermês is the synthesizer of the Hermetic tradition, Rê-Hêlios is the symbol of the focus of that synthesis.

Osiris | In the common religion of the Egyptians at the time of the writing of the magical papyri no god was more important than Osiris. This dominance is not reflected in the ancient papyri, however, since not only foreign gods but also diverse intra-Egyptian religious factions—such as those of Thoth and Set-Typhôn—were even more strongly represented.

The name of Osiris generally appears in the Greek form in the old papyri as *Osiris*. The actual Egyptian form of the name is *Usyr* 𓊨 (wsyr). Various magical forms of the name, obviously derived from originally Egyptian words or phrases, are incorporated as magical formulas or *voces magicae* in the papyri. These include OUSERRAN-NOUPHTHI ("Osiris of the good name"), OUCHICOCH, OUSENARATH, OSORNOUPHE ("Osiris the Beautiful"), and OUSERSETEMENTH.

In the ancient Egyptian pantheon, Osiris eventually became a sort of "supreme god." But this development was slow and never quite complete. Oddly enough, Osiris was originally a foreign god imported from the Semitic world at an early date. His chief function involved the agricultural cycles of birth, life, death, and renewal. In this capacity he also became a god of the Underworld and of the dead—himself a sort of deified mummy.

Magically Osiris is usually connected with the underworld or the world of the dead. The clearest example of how Osiris functions in the magical texts is found in *PGM* VII.429–58 (operation number 45 in this book). This is an operation to restrain or banish things. There the magician is told to engrave his desire on a "lead plate from a cold water channel" and to do this "late in the evening or in the middle of the night." The plate is to be tied to a cord and thrown into deep water. The text written on the plate commends the matter at hand over to Osiris to deal with.

Serapis (Gk. Σαραπις) is an interesting development of Osiris. His name comes from the Egyptian Usar-Hapi, a combination of Osiris and Apis—who is the Lunar Bull of the West or of the Under-world. Tradition has it that Ptolemy Sotêr (305–286 B.C.E.) estab-lished the worship of Serapis as a god of the Underworld which both Egyptians and Greeks could worship in common.

Isis | Isis is another highly popular deity in the late Egyptian pe-riod who is relatively rarely mentioned in the magical pa-pyri. Her name appears in the papyri in the form *Isis*. One magical papyrus mentions several of her secret names as being: LOU, LOULOU, BATHARTHAR, THARESIBATH ATHERNEK-LESICH, ATHERNEBOUNI, EICHOMO and CHOMOTHI. For most of the ancient Egyptians Isis was their greatest goddess. She personified the force of life and the feminine power to give life and to renew it.

Perhaps the most frequent mention of Isis comes in her con-nection with the black swath of cloth used to blindfold the magician for certain workings. This is called the "black Isis band," and was originally supposed to be taken from a cloth used as drapery on stat-ues of the goddess.

In operations in this book she is sometimes mentioned in con-nection with Osiris. In operation number 12—a general invocation

(*PGM* VII.490–504)—she is connected to the star called Sothis (the rising of which signals the annual rising of the Nile), the Full Moon, and it is mentioned that the "Agathos Daimôn permitted her to rule the entire Black Land."

Horus   There were, of course, two distinct gods in the Egyptian pantheon called Horus. One was among the most ancient of the Egyptian deities: Horus the Elder (*Hr-wr*). The other was the son of Osiris and Isis: Horus the Younger. In the latest period the two were identified—at least by the Osirians. The symbol of both was a falcon.

In the papyri the name of Horus commonly appears as 'Ωρος. Horus the Elder, or Greater, appears in magical formulas as AROUER, a Hermetic rendition of *Hr-wr*.

In the ancient Egyptian pantheon the two Horus figures originally had very different functions. The older one, true to the actual meaning of his name, was a deity of the horizon and the chief god of the inhabitants of Lower Egypt. Horus the Younger, son of Isis, seems to have been engendered simply to avenge the death of his father Osiris who was killed by the Eternal Set.

References to Horus are surprisingly rare in the old papyri. Most of the time when he is mentioned it is simply to evoke a mythic situation in which he plays a part—such as his fight with Set.

Amon (= Zeus)   The name of Ammon (Egyptian 𓇋 , *amn*) or Amon, or Amen, appears frequently in the papyri. There the name is usually spelled Αμουν. His name originally indicates "he who keeps his name hidden." He was thought to be beyond the ability of men or gods to conceive of him.

Although Amon was an ancient god, he was only of local importance until later in Egyptian history. He gained his greatest popularity in combination with the Sun-god, Rê, in the form of Amon-Rê. But his importance in the later Hellenistic age stems from the identification of Zeus with Ammôn. In the form of Ammôn the Egyptians and Greeks worshipped the god in common.

Sekhmet | The lion-goddess Sekhmet makes only rare appearances in the old papyri. For example, in operation number 23 of this collection one of her esoteric names, SACHMOUNE PAELIOGOTEREENCH, appears. Her main function in the ancient Egyptian pantheon was that of a goddess of war, plague, and aggression. Her name is derived from the Egyptian word *sekhem*, power. As such her essence was certainly understood by the writers of the papyri.

Khnum | Khnum, or Khnemu, was one of the oldest gods worshipped by the Egyptians. His chief seat of worship was in Elephantine in far Upper Egypt. Compared to his diminished popularity in the latest phase of Egyptian history his name occurs quite frequently in the magical papyri. There his name appears most often as *Chnum* and, in Part IV of this book, it appears in operation number 44 in a *vox magica* as CHNEOM.

His continued importance in the magical tradition reflects the primeval power of Khnum as a total god—the primal shaper of life and of the gods themselves. He is also the creator of humanity. He is often depicted creating a man as a potter turning the human form on a wheel. It is his function as a *maker*, as a *creator*, which is most important to the Hermetic magician.

Set (= Typhôn) | The name of Set appears quite frequently in the papyri. Despite the fact that in the more common cultic life of the Egyptians Set had become largely diabolized by the late Hellenistic and Roman periods of Egyptian history, Set is unabashedly used in the magical papyri. The form of his name is usually rendered as Σηθ or in Coptic as *CHΘ*. (It must be remembered that the Greek letter *theta* was pronounced as an aspirated t+h, not as in our Germanic "thorn." This is why the more phonetically accurate spelling "Set" is generally preferred.

Other magical names or formulas in which the name of the god Set appears include BOLCHOSÊTH and ATHEREBERSÊTH. Also the formulas ERBÊTH and PAKERBÊTH occur so frequently

in operations which also use Set, that they too must be considered secret names of certain aspects of Set-Typhôn.

In the history of ancient Egyptian religion no god is older than
Set. No other god underwent such radical changes in attitude toward him by the people. In the beginning, Set was a regional god of
Upper Egypt. He was a warlike and aggressive force with tremendous creative powers born of chaos and darkness. When foreign invaders came to dominate Egypt on occasion, it was Set with whom
they most often identified their own god. Due to a combination of
Set's original ambiguities and his subsequent "alliance" with hated
foreigners, many of the other Egyptian cults vilified Set as a god of
evil. This found its ultimate expression in the late and decadent
Osirian cult.

The Setian force was never fully rejected by the Egyptians. His
symbols—and his power—were thought to be indispensable by all
Egyptians. For example, the *tcham* or *uas* scepter carried by many
Egyptian gods bears the distinguishing marks of Set—the head of the
Set-animal and the characteristic forked tail.

Other symbols of Set include his red color (hence the general
tabu on the use of lamps colored red in the historical papyri). The animals closely associated with him are the donkey (ass), pig, and fish.
It is for this reason that the papyri often speak of the use of the blood
of an ass (especially a black one) or the prohibition on the eating of
pork or fish to maintain ritual purity.

In the old magical papyri Set-Typhôn may be invoked for any
number of purposes. This is certainly because, among the old Egyptian gods, no other god would more exemplify the role of the Hermetic magicians in the social order than Set. By the twilight of
Egyptian culture, typical magicians were figures "out of step" with
their native Egyptian society. They had enthusiastically embraced
foreign thoughts and practices and had rejected the domination of
the Osirian cult of the establishment. Thus it is easy to see why Set
would have become one of their models. Nevertheless, warnings are
often made in the old papyri not to use certain Setian symbols (such
as the color red) or to eat fish, pork, and so on. In another spell,
however, the god may be invoked freely and his name exalted. This
shows as much as anything the degree to which the magicians were

free of normal moral constraints, and just how much they considered their craft a pure technology.

Hellenic Divinities

The gods and goddesses of Greece (Hellas) are of almost equal importance to those of Egypt for the magical technology of the magicians who wrote the ancient papyri. It is sometimes clear that in fact Egyptian divinities are hiding behind Greek names. This is especially true of Hêlios (= Rê), and to a lesser extent of Hermês (= Thoth), and Typhôn (= Set). Clearly the writers of the papyri were deeply schooled in Greek culture, philosophy, and religion. An understanding of the Greek divinities is repeatedly demonstrated—for example when Hermês is invoked to help in finding a thief (*PGM* V.172–212). The papyri often use Homeric verses for magical purposes, which is only something somebody familiar with the Hellenic national epics would do.

But the Egyptians' understanding of the Greek gods was also thoroughly *Hermetic*. They understood that the gods and goddesses were real forces—yet ones whose names and shapes were only keys to the inner, transcultural and truly objective core principles which such gods and goddesses embodied.

Hermês (= Thoth) | Hermês appears with extreme frequency in the papyri as Ἑρμες. Beyond all other names it was this one that the magicians writing the old papyri seemed to identify with the most. This was also true of the more philosophically minded Hellenized Egyptians of the period who also called themselves Hermetics.

The Greeks honored and worshipped Hermês for a variety of purposes. Some of his functions had been taken over by Apollo, but he remained a god of communication, commerce, eloquence, healing (the *caduceus* is his scepter), and athleticism. This latter trait was his because of the speed with which he was thought to be able to go from place to place. One of his most important areas of activity was as a *psychopom-*

pos—a conductor of the souls of the dead. Because of all these traits, he was the chief messenger of Zeus, and could with all speed carry communications to and from Olympos. His connection with the power of speech earned him the divine title of *Logios*—God of the Word. His most important function in the magical tradition of the papyri is *philosophical.* The Greek Hermês embodies the spirit and soul of the intellect, of the power of the Word and quick-wittedness—of communication. The other level of importance is how he actually works in the operations. Through the power of Hermês, the will of the magician could communicate most directly with the Olympian realm of the gods and goddesses. In later astrological symbolism, of course, Hermês is equated with the planet Mercury (his Roman name).

The Roman philosopher and orator Cicero, writing in the first century B.C.E. in his *Nature of the Gods,* identifies five forms of Mercury worshipped in his day. The fifth of these he says killed Argus, and for this reason fled to Egypt where he gave "laws and writing to the Egyptians."[14] He is further identified as being the same as their Thoth.

Hêlios
(= Rê or PHRE)

The name of Hêlios (Gk. 'Hελιος) is constantly mentioned in the papyri. In the Greek pantheon Hêlios is the personification of the Sun itself. His cult was very ancient and universal among the Greeks. The island of Rhodes is sacred to him, and it is there that the colossal statue of him stood.

The chief functions of Hêlios in the Greek pantheon were both natural—as the orb of the light-giving Sun—and psychological—as a symbol of omniscience. As a god of light he can see everything and knows everything. Also because of his focus of light he is a symbol of the unified focus of the soul necessary to continued success in magical operations. This is why it is often said to be so important to have a link with Hêlios before great magical operations can be carried out.

As the cult of the stars and planets became more important in ancient Greece, the symbolism of Hêlios was expanded to include all of the powers and attributes belonging to the Sun.

---

[14]Cicero, *The Nature of the Gods* (London: Penguin, 1972).

Zeus (= Ammôn) | Zeus is the chief of the Olympian gods of Greece. His name occurs repeatedly in the magical papyri in the Greek form Ζευς [zdews]. Zeus is again and again referred to as the king or master of the gods and is equated with other chief gods of other pantheons, such as Mithras or Iaô/Adônai.

In the tradition of Hermetic magic Zeus is a figure who is usually invoked for quasi-religious purposes, or for the establishment of complex mythic analogies, although Zeus himself seems to have little to do with magical operations. *PGM* V.459–489 is a general invocation to the universal powers of Zeus. In terms of planetary mythology, Zeus is the equivalent of the planet Jupiter (which bears his Roman name).

Selênê | Selênê is the personification of the Moon. Her name appears both as a designation of a goddess and as the magical name of the Moon herself—for they are one in the Hermetic system. For this reason she is also known by her more ordinary name: Mênê.

As with Hêlios, to Selênê may be attributed all of the magical powers attendant to the astrological meaning of the Moon. She is called the "ruler of Tartaros" in *PGM* IV.2241–2358 and in *PGM* VII.429–458, it is said of her that "when she goes through the underworld, she breaks whatever spell she finds."

Apollo | The Greek god of the light of the Sun, Apollo, was a foreign god who was syncretized into the Greek pantheon at an early time—either from the Luvians (Trojans) in the East or some northern tribe. The Greeks themselves most often associated him with Hyperborea: the Far-North. His name appears in the papyri as *Apollon*. In the ancient Greek pantheon, Apollos had myriad functions. He was the god of light and a destroyer, the god of healing and prophecy, the god of music and wolves.

Apollo is a divinity who may have whole hymns dedicated to him in the old papyri (e.g. *PGM* I.262–347). Because of his close relationship with the power of Hêlios and because of the various kinds of power he has to bestow, this becomes understandable. The main power the magicians who wrote the papyri seem to be interested in is that of *vision*—the gift of prophecy—for example as in *PGM* VI.1–47.

Typhôn (= Set)	For the most part, when the name of Typhôn is invoked it is a Hellenic substitute for the old Egyptian god named Set.

The name of Typhôn appears regularly in the papyri in the form of *Typhôn*, although other spellings are known in Greek (*Typhaon, Typhoeus*, and *Typhos*). Also the *vox magica* forms of ERBÊTH and PAKERBÊTH occur regularly in connection with Typhôn, as they do with Set.

For the Hermetic magician there is little difference between Set and Typhôn, but it is certain that the writers of the old papyri would also have known the myths of Typhôn in his purely Greek context, as these were widespread and are found in Hesiod's *Theogony* and many other old sources. In the ancient Greek sources Typhôn is referred to as a *drakôn* (dragon), although he is more than a large reptile. His shape is described as being rather amorphous—with reptilian parts of shining red and green colors, along with wings and parts of various other beasts. Some give him the head of an ass. He is usually said to be the offspring of Gea (Earth) and Tartaros (the chaotic Underworld), and to have fought Zeus in the last battle between the deposed Titans and the Olympians led by Zeus. It was the stated will of Typhôn to overcome Zeus and win back heaven for the chthonic forces. At one point it is said that Typhôn forced all the Olympians to flee in terror to Egypt—where they all took on animal shapes to disguise themselves.

To the Greeks Typhôn was a figure of cosmic rebellion, though his link with the chthonic (subterranean) realm also connected him with the prophetic power of the Pythôn. In the magical papyri, Typhôn appears in roles as varied as those of Set—his burning passions and fiery nature seem to be the energy from which the magical power to effect the will of the magician is drawn.

Aphroditê | In the magical papyri her name appears as Αφροδιτη. Her name is likely of Phoenician origin. There were few goddesses more widely worshipped in Hellas than Aphroditê. She was a goddess of fertility and vegetative abundance, to be sure, but her functions went well beyond this to include all aspects of erotic love. Aphroditê Ourania is the celestial goddess of ideal love, Aphroditê Genetrix promotes and protects marriage, Aphroditê Nymphia is the matron of unmarried young girls, while Aphroditê Pornê is that of prostitutes and the arts of erotic love. The courtesans of Corinth were also the priestesses of Aphroditê there.

As the winning of lovers is an extremely common aim of magical operations, and as there is no more unequivocally erotic goddess than Aphroditê, her function in the Hermetic tradition of magic is clear. Astrologically Aphroditê is the equivalent of Venus.

Semitic Divinities

The Hebrew God(s) | The creator god of the Hebrews, Yahweh Elohim, is found in the often repeated formula IAÔ. Indeed the IAÔ formula is the most repeated single name of power in the old magical papyri. Also references to Judaic or Hebraic religious figures (such as Moses, Solomon, Abraham, Isaac, and Jacob) are extremely frequent in the papyri. But few of the ancient papyri are based on Hebraic theological constructs and none is based on any orthodox, truly Judaic understanding of theology.

Yahweh = IAÔ | The name of Yahweh, in its peculiar Greek vocalic representation *IAÔ* (Gk. Ιαω = 811), is a magical power of great popularity among Hermetic magicians. But IAÔ is not prayed to as a personal god, but more often *wielded* as a quasi-natural force—through the pronunciation of the name itself.

Of course, in orthodox Judaic theology Yahweh is the one and only true god. In practice he has so many special names and func-

tional titles (El, Adonai, Shaddai, Yahweh Tzabaoth, etc., etc.) that
for all intents and purposes the old polytheism of the ancient Hebrews is to some extent still preserved at least in the early forms of
Judaism. In that religion Yahweh is the creator god, of course, but
also the giver of the Law—the *Torah*. It is his function as creator of
the natural cosmos that most interests the Hermetic magician.

IAÔ is a vocalic rendering of the pronunciation of the name
of the Hebrew god usually spelled Jehovah, or Yahweh (Heb.
YHVH). This is the most often invoked single god-name in the
papyri. This does not mean the Hermetic magicians were Jewish or
Christian in their beliefs. Quite to the contrary. They invoked *Iaô*
simply because he was supposed to be the "god of this world"—the
creative Demiurge (also according to the Gnostics!)—who was
therefore highly potent in workings designed to cause changes to
occur in *this world*—the Kingdom. The meaning of IAÔ and the
orthodox theological interpretation of Yahweh are therefore in-
compatible.

It is widely thought also that the Semitic high god was identified by many Egyptians as their own god Set, who is also a god of
storm and war. This was further enforced by the fact that Set was
considered the "god of foreigners" and many Semitic and other foreign invaders of Egypt identified their high god (Ba'al or Yahweh)
with Set.

By invoking the power of IAÔ the Hermetic magician helps ensure that the things being willed shall become manifest in the objective universe inevitably and as a matter of "natural course"—because
it is being channelled through the universal creative framework represented by IAΩ.

Moses	Although the ancient and semi-mythical Hebrew prophet Moses was supposedly a historical man, he functions in Hermetic magic as a god or as a deified ma-

gician—that is, as a *daimôn*. As with the god of Moses, *Iaô*, the Hermetic magician sees nothing of the religious in him—only the
magical. Moses is not a prophet, but a mighty worker of wonders
who defeated the sorcerers of the pharaoh. As an inventor of writing,
Moses is sometimes made the equivalent of Thoth.

Gnostic and Iranian Divinities

Besides references to the gods and goddesses of the peoples of the eastern Mediterranean region, the old papyri contain many references to more exotic and mysterious deities. One who makes an occasional and dramatic appearance is Mithras. Mithras is a god of ultimately Iranian origin. But his cult was not Gnostic or dualistic. Because his cult was in many respects identical to that of the Iranian Magians (or *magûs*), from whom the term *mageia* was derived, the figure of Mithras became important in the purely pragmatic and functional pantheon of the Hermetic magicians of the first few centuries after the time of Jesus.

Certain other entities treated as gods have their origins in abstract magical constructions with their roots in Gnostic thought. One of the most often seen is ABRASAX (also spelled ABRAXAS). The spelling is irrelevant because this is nothing other than a numerical formula of the expanse of the heavenly orb—the *Hôros* ('Ωρος)—the sum of the numerical values of the letters in the name is 365—the number of degrees in the astronomical circle, and the perfect number of days in a year. Another abstract cosmological god is Aiôn (Αιων). The word means "Age"—an enormous expanse of time—but also refers to the encirclements of the cosmos by successive aiôns, as we saw in chapter 3 on cosmology.

Other abstract ideas unknown in the Greek pantheon such as Anankê (Αναγκη), which simply means necessity or compulsion, or Tychê (Τυχη), meaning good fortune, are divinized and addressed as goddesses. This process of divinization of abstract principles represents a magical approach to some of the same questions wrestled with by philosophers. Whereas for the religious practitioner, gods and goddesses are intermediaries between the world of humanity and the realm of the perfect and permanent archetypes or ideas such as Love, Truth, Beauty, and Justice, philosophers attempt to *understand* these things directly with their own intellects, while magicians try to *exercise* these principles by means of their own wills.

Jesus, the King | The best documented example of such a magician is Jesus the Naassarene (that is, the Serpentine). Although those who wrote and used the magical papyri were not Christian in any orthodox or generally accepted sense, occasionally they might call on the name of Jesus for purely pragmatic ends—just as they called on Yahweh (*Iaô*). By the time the papyri were recorded, the name of Jesus was being widely used as a magical *word* by Christians and non-Christians alike. He was a famous holy man or magician known to have been *executed* as a criminal. Using the *name* or *power* (Gk. δυναμις) of any executed criminal was magically powerful—how much more so if that of an executed *magos*!

The donkey or ass is an animal closely associated with Jesus. In what might *seem* to be an ironic twist, in the cultural context of the Hermetic magical literature, the donkey or ass is identified with the god-form Set-Typhôn—by this time a god of evil in Helleno-Egyptian mythology. So for some Hermetic magicians Jesus had already been identified with Set-Typhôn. It is possible he was considered a "son" of this god. We know that the Hebrew god *Yah(weh)* is represented in Hellenic manuscripts as *Iaô*, who was identified with Set-Typhôn by the Egyptians themselves. This seems right enough since Set was the "god of foreigners" among the highly xenophobic Egyptians and the Jews were perhaps the largest foreign population in Egypt. Besides, the Egyptian (Coptic) word for donkey happens to be *io* or *eio*—which sounded much like the Hellenic representation of the *Yah—Iaô*. Gospel evidence pointing to this constellation of symbols includes the story that Jesus rode into Jerusalem on a donkey which he instructed his disciples to steal from the city (Mt. 21:1–7).

This unexpected complex of symbols can also be found in the early Christian use of the sign of the fish, ⊂✕. This is also clearly the sign of the first letter of the Greek *alphabeta*, but the fish is also a sign of the god Set-Typhôn. The magical papyri often emphasize the common Egyptian tabu against eating fish, because fish are thought to be Typhônian. But for a Typhônian initiate, the eating of fish would be sacred and empowering. This is an idea Jesus would have acquired during his magical training in Egypt.

Daimonology

For the most part, the magicians would try to convince the power of a god to work for them, while the daimôn would be something they would eventually try to absorb and make their own to work with at will. By this process a magician could become "a son of a god"—which is what Jesus the *magos* seems to have done. He and his daimôn became one. The magicians are united with their own personal daimôns. What they will the daimôns will—and the will of daimôns can make things happen in the Kingdom.

Likewise, a daimôn can also be seen as a demigod—an independent, relatively immortal and powerful entity, but not as powerful as the great gods of the official national cults. In Roman terminology an entity similar to the daimôn was the *genius*—a familiar spirit inherited along genetic lines in the family or *gens*.

Daimôns are in and of themselves neither good nor evil. They are rather like humans that way. Their characteristics are, however, much more fixed and permanent than those of humans, who tend to manifest a number of differing character traits at any given moment. The magical papyri mention two major classes of daimôns—the *agathodaimônês* (good-daimôns) and the *kakodaimônês* (evil-daimôns). The good ones are used for beneficent purposes, while the evil ones are employed to effect maleficent ends. But more often daimôns are mentioned in a neutral sense—as demigods worthy of respect and worship.

Angels on the other hand are quite different from daimôns. The chief difference between them lies in the fact that the angel is not independent. It is the mere *messenger*, or "active principle," of a greater god. It is only fully useful to the magician if the magician has some measure of control over the god or goddess from whom it is sent. Of course, one god-form famous for the number of angels he has around him is Yahweh—the creator-god of this, the natural world. For example, the names of the three archangels of the god, Michaêl, Gabriêl, and Raphiêl are all found in the texts of the old papyri.

A single entity might be called a god, an angel, or a daimôn because often from an operative, practical perspective these terms might be seen to be equivalent. Also one entity might in fact be all three—

having attained godhood after first having been a daimôn who attached itself to the will of another god for a time, having begun its existence as a human soul (*psychê*).

From this elementary presentation of the theology and daimonology of the magical papyri certain principles of the eclectic use of the relevant pantheons should be apparent. The ability to be eclectic in any effective way must be based on a deep level of understanding of the core principles that the gods and goddesses of various pantheons represent. It is not based on arbitrary choices predicated on questions of style or fashion. Eclecticism based on superficial images and misunderstanding is doomed to be simply impotent.

GOÊTEIA, MAGEIA
AND THEOURGIA

The term "magic" has been associated with techniques of sleight of hand trickery as well as notions of "evil"—when it is put side by side with "religion." As we will also see in chapter 12, this distinction between magic and religion, while sometimes useful, is often invoked hypocritically by those who think their spiritual technology is "good," and therefore "religious," while those of other people is "evil," and therefore "magic."

The ancients were closer to true magic than we are today. This becomes very clear when we look at how many terms they had for magical operations—each seemingly with its own technical difference. In order to practice Hermetic Magic, you must understand it. To understand it you must study and learn by experience what it really means.

The Hermetic magician is not obsessed with ideas of "good" and "evil" the way, for example, a Zoroastrian, Jewish, Islamic, or Christian one might be—the Hermetic magician is focused on initiation, self-development, if you will, and on obtaining results. The Hermetic magician is a pragmatic magician.

In other words, none of the types of magic discussed here is "off limits" to true Hermetic magicians. They may use one kind of operation for one kind of effect, and another type of operation for another. Also, magicians must gauge their own abilities and powers at any given moment and use the best kind of technique within their powers at that moment.

The three kinds of magic most often seen in the ancient sources are: γοητεια (goêteia), μαγεια (mageia) and θεουργια (theurgy).

Goêteia

Goêteia is the "lowest" of the three forms—not in any "moral" sense—but simply because it is the easiest to perform successfully. *Goêteia* is often referred to as "mere trickery," or the art of jugglers. Well, such things are even used in the most noble and philosophical schools. The Buddhist tantric, for example, might use such illusionary tricks as a major teaching tool to demonstrate to those who can understand that all of sensory existence can be seen as illusory. Teachers who present half or partial truths when conveying complex data to a student are engaging in such *goêteia*—and such teaching techniques are absolutely necessary for success.

But in essence *goêteia* is in fact what most people practice as "magic" today. With *goêteia* the sorcerer, or *goês*, uses elements in the objective universe to affect the will generated in his own subjective universe. Gods, goddesses, angels, or daimôns, or even material magical substances (such as herbs, sacrifices, and so on) are called upon or used to do the will of the sorcerer. Each time the *goês* wishes to have a magical effect on the objective or subjective universe, he or she must engage the formula and do the magical operation particular to that effect. Most of the workings in this book are therefore, technically speaking, *goêteia*. Most Western occultism has practiced what is essentially *goêteia*.

Mageia

Although to the non-initiate, to the outsider, works of *goêteia* and works of *mageia* may sometimes appear the same, they are in fact quite different. The magician, or *magos*, is one who has attained a certain level of personal initiation which causes him or her to act on a divine level. The *magos* does not ask gods to do things for him or her, or use substances to create wondrous effects—he or she acts directly (usually through signs or words of power) from his or her subjective universe upon the objective universe. This is usually not put in terms of the magician "commanding" a god, but rather as "having" such a god as an indistinguishable part of himself or herself. He is said at that point to have become the "son of (a) god"—he or she has been adopted by the god and elevated to a divine stature while still in life.

Another term used in ancient times that conveyed some of the same meaning as *mageia* was thaumaturgy (Gk. θαυματουργια), which generally means "wonder-working." Wonders are worked by means of the will of the magician without the necessity of intervening gods, angels, or daimônions.

The term *mageia* is, of course, derived from the name of the priest-class, and/or particular sect of Iranian origin. By the early years of the present era, this sect was widespread beyond the borders of Persia or Iran proper and into the lands that are present-day Turkey, Iraq, and Syria. It was members of this sect, the *Magoi*, or Magi, that the Gospels say visited the infant Jesus. Perhaps this was but the first sign of his future development as a *magos*.

The practice of *mageia* extended well beyond the confines of the Magian sect and, especially in those schools free of the particular theology of the Magians, it developed into the forms we see in the Hermetic papyri. In the Hermetic school the magician is free to do his own will, constrained only by the contents of his own psychê.

With time the term *mageia* began to fall into disrepute, so that it eventually became synonymous with *goêteia*. As this was happening, the philosophical schools of the early centuries of the era were growing, and within them there was some interest in *mageia*.

Theourgia

Theurgy is a term coined by the philosophical writer Julianus, a Hellenized Chaldean, living in the time of the Emperor Marcus Aurelius (161–180 C.E.). But theurgy was not, and is not, merely another word for "magic." Literally the term means "divine-work." In his *Enneads* (IV.4.26) the Neo-Platonist Plotinus says of theurgy that it depends on "the sympathy of enchained forces."[15] Theurgy must work

---

[15]Plotinus, *The Enneads*, Stephen MacKenna, trans. (London: Penguin, 1991, and Burdette, NY: Larson, 1992), p. 310.

in harmony with the gods, in harmony with the laws of the objective universe, or at least with the characteristics of the powerful subjective universes that surround the theurgist, and that are called gods, angels, daimôns, and so on. In a way, theurgy has more in common with *goêteia* than with *mageia*. The theurgist must take much that is in the macrocosm outside himself into account when designing and executing his operations; the *goês* too must discover the minute details of the entities and substances he is going to work with before his magic will work. What makes theurgy unique is its concern with being "philosophically correct"—and harmonious with nature—rather than just being effective and powerful. *Mageia* is also concerned with the discovery of philosophical truth—but truth of a far more subjective kind, rooted not in nature but in consciousness, not in *physis* but in *psychê*. The Hermetic magic recorded in the Greek papyri preserves the purest strain of the highly individualistic tradition of Western *mageia*.

MAGICAL WRITING SYSTEMS

Historically, systems of writing have been important to many schools of magical practice. The magical papyri, especially those written in Greek, sometimes contain references to the numbers of letters in a given formula or give precise information about the pronunciation of these formulas. The act of writing and the written (as well as spoken) word are essential to the Hermetic tradition. Three writing systems are important to the ancient Hermetic tradition of magical communication—the Egyptian (which is preserved in three forms: hieroglyphic, hieratic, and demotic), the Greek, and the Coptic. All three systems are used in the Hermetic magical papyri. The Semitic writing system, which was to become so important later in the western magical tradition, was relatively unimportant in the early Hermetic system. But because of its indirect influence it is presented and discussed in a basic way in Appendix G.

Scripts or writing systems have been involved with magical practice from the beginning. Some systems of writing appear to have been created from a magical or religious impetus from the beginning. Examples of this would be the Egyptian hieroglyphics and the Hebrew *alef-bet* as well as the Germanic runes and the Celtic ogham. We can tell this was the case because all of these systems have huge amounts of lore attached to the written characters—both individually and collectively. In such systems the names of the characters typically have some definite meaning in the language the characters are designed to represent. In Hebrew, for example, *alef* means "an ox," *bet* means "a house," *gimel* means "a camel" (or "a rope"), and so on. *Writing* itself was fully incorporated into tradition from the very dawn of literacy in such cultures.

There is another approach to sacred writing systems, however. Originally some seem to have been created on a purely practical or pragmatic basis, and only later acquiring religious or magical connotations. This is the case with the Greek *alphabeta* as well as the Latin ABC. This is clear because the lore built up around the letters only comes at a later date, and the names of the characters have no special esoteric meanings: they are just mnemonic formulas such as *alpha, beta, gamma*—none of which have any intrinsic meaning in the Greek language. (They are sound-imitations of the Phoenician letter-names.)

But this latter group of systems has one advantage over the former: the early practical phase opened the system up to abstract and divergent elements that the tradition-bound systems resisted. The greatest examples of this are found with the Greek *alphabeta*. The Greeks, for purely practical reasons, began to write the vowels that their Semitic models had left unwritten. A system with no vowels would be relatively more difficult to read and learn to write. Thus the craft of writing was better preserved among professional scribes and priests. Reading such a system—wld b n mr dffclt thn rdng ths wrds fr spkrs 'f 'nglsh. But the Greeks simply and practically used characters to spell out words just as they sounded. New vowel characters were added to the system and so merchants and shopkeepers could learn to read and write and use the new skill in their day-to-day affairs.

This practical Greek innovation took place sometime during the eighth century B.C.E. Merchants and shopkeepers deal quite a bit with numbers, so the Greeks also came up with the idea of using the same characters they used to write words for arithmetic as well. This aspect of the esoteric lore is covered in the section starting on page 115. Here I just want to point out that the invention of a practical, easy-to-learn system of mathematical figures, making use of the same characters as used for writing words, was the gateway to the possibility of interpreting written texts according to numerological symbology.

The Hebrews borrowed the idea of using letters for numbers as early as the second century B.C.E. Many of the oldest manuscripts of the Old Testament have the chapters and verses enumerated with *Greek* letters, not Hebrew ones!

Something should also be said about the distinction between a language and a writing system. A writing system or script can be used to represent an infinite number of human languages—as the Roman alphabet is now used to write languages from English to Japanese (Romanji), and from Italian to Xuasa. Theoretically, you could write

Chinese in Egyptian hieroglyphics, as awkward as that might be. The Egyptian *language* is to be distinguished from the hieroglyphic writing system. In fact Coptic is really a dialect of Egyptian written in a modified Greek *alphabeta*. Languages exist apart from the graphic systems used to represent them. But when they do come to be written, languages are seen in a new, more objective sense. The way in which language works is mysterious. Writing systems help to objectify this mystery and make it more operational.

The Egyptian Systems

The Egyptian language itself is best described as Hamito-Semitic—from its earliest stages it shows itself to be a mixture of the type of language spoken in northeastern Africa (Hamitic) and that of the Semites (e.g. later Hebrew, Akkadian, Arabic). The language was written in hieroglyphics from the beginning of Egyptian history. The term "hieroglyphic" is a Greek one meaning "priestly writing." This system usually required that it be carved carefully into stone, wood or other hard surfaces or just as meticulously painted on flat surfaces. By about 2600 B.C.E. an abbreviated version of hieroglyphics had been developed for writing with pen and ink on papyrus. This type of writing is called hieratic—or "priestly." Much later, sometime between 900 and 650 B.C.E., an even more abbreviated system was devised called demotic—or "popular."

All of these systems were merely versions of each other. Their internal structures were the same. None of them was a form of "picture writing" as is sometimes assumed. There is a phonetic system of 24 sounds. (See Table 1 on p. 108.) Vowels were not written, only consonants. So-called determinatives were often appended to words to indicate to which part of speech or category of meaning the word belonged. Such determinatives have no sound-value. For example, the image of a papyrus roll ⊏⊐ determines that the word it is appended to is an "abstract idea." So ⌂⌐ is phonetically *ht* (see Table 1 on p. 108 for sound values), and the ⊏⊐ indicates abstraction. Therefore *ht* means "an abstract thing." Note that there is no vowel

Table 1.   The System of Egyptian Phonemes.

Number	Hieroglyphic	Hieratic	Demotic	Phonetic Value	Meaning
1				a (=3) father	eagle/vulture
2				y ruby	reed
3				a car	arm and hand
4				w too	chick
5				b boot	leg
6				p pool	box
7				f feel	horned viper
8				m moon	owl
9				n noon	water
10				r right	mouth
11				h hat	courtyard
12				h ha!	wick (flax)
13				h loch	disk/placenta
14				h huge	club
15				s saw	folded cloth
16				"	door-bolt
17				s show	pool
18				k queen	hill
19				k basket	basket
20				g go	jar stand
21				t tap	loaf
22				t church	tether rope
23				d dog	hand
24				d adjust	snake

sound indicated in the example just given. The vowels must be reconstructed from information provided by Coptic. We can never be sure of just how ancient Egyptian was actually pronounced.

Hieroglyphics also contain ideograms. These are single signs representing whole words. For example, 𐎒 can stand for *ḫpr* ("to become; be"). This could also be written 𓆣𓏏𓏤. Notice that in this second form we can discern the phonetic signs 𐎒 + 𐎒 + 𐎒 (*ḫpr*) as well as the ideogram and abstract determinative—and all the elements are combined not in a linear or "logical" way but in a way guided by balance and symmetry of form.

There are several things about hieroglyphics that should be obvious. First they were (and are) difficult to learn—special hieratic training was necessary. This ensured that the art of writing—and its powers—would remain property of the priesthood. Another obvious factor is the importance of writing to religion and magic. Language—the *word*—has special power in Egyptian magic and religion.

This last point indicates a tremendous shortcoming of the Egyptian writing systems (hieroglyphic, hieratic, or demotic) for those who would attempt to revive old Egyptian forms of magic. From the written forms we can simply never know exactly how the words were pronounced, because the *vowels* are missing. It is these very vowels which are later shown in the Hermetic tradition to be the backbone of verbal magic, that we call phonosophy or operative phonology. We can guess that the science of the vowels was both known to and practiced by the ancient Egyptian hieratic magicians—and it is precisely because of the power these sounds had that they were kept *secret* and unwritten. When the last member of the Egyptian priesthood died, the secrets of their vocal magic would seem to have died with him.

Another aspect of ancient Egyptian religious and magical lore lost to us is the esoteric significance of the 24 phonetic signs. No ancient work survives that indicates their hidden meanings, but the connections between them and the Creto-Semitic system are obvious. (See Appendix G.) Several of the 24 Egyptian phonemes correspond to some extent with the meanings of the Creto-Semitic, and hence to the Hebraic system of letters as shown in Table 2 on page 110. Other, deeper correspondences can be found by those who look.

Table 2.   Correspondences between Egyptian Phonemes and Hebrew.

Egyptian Form	Egyptian Meaning	Hebrew Form	Hebrew Name	Meaning of Hebrew Name
⌐	a (arm and hand)	י	*yod*	hand
~~	n (water)	מ	*mem*	water
◯	r (mouth)	פ	*pe*	mouth
⊓	h (courtyard)	ח	*heth*	fence
●—	ḥ (club)	ו	*zain*	sword
—•—	s (door-bolt)	ד	*daleth*	door[-leaf]
▭	t (tether rope)	ג	*gimel*	rope
◠	d (hand)	כ	*kaf*	palm of hand
⌐	ḏ (snake)	נ	*nachash*	serpent

The Greek System

The Greeks did not begin to write until around the 14th century B.C.E. It is from this time that the Mycenean inscriptions can be dated. But this system died out in subsequent centuries. The writing system used in the Greek magical papyri, that of the familiar 24 letter *alphabeta*, was not developed until around 750 B.C.E. This was ultimately based on the Phoenician writing system. But its development was one more in a succession of bold cultural innovations instituted by the Greeks during the first millennium B.C.E. Their *alphabeta* system is innovative because it is totally *phonetic*. It is spelled as it sounds. All sounds, the vowels included, could be represented by Greek letters. This is of tremendous importance to us as the sacred *voces magicae* could now be written down so that we can know exactly how to pronounce them today. In the original papyri from which the magical operations in this book are taken, not only are the Greek words written in Greek letters, but so too are Egyptian or Coptic and Hebrew words and phrases. As opposed to the purely Egyptian tradition preserved in hieratic or demotic material, the

Table 3. The System of Greek ΣΤΟΙΧΕΙΑ.

alpha 1	beta 2	gamma 3	delta 4	epsilon 5	zeta 7	eta 8	theta 9
iota 10	kappa 20	lambda 30	mu 40	nu 50	xi 60	omicron 70	pi 80
rho 100	sigma 200	tau 300	ypsilon 400	phi 500	chi 600	psi 700	omega 800

Greek tradition has been recorded in written form—to be revivified by magicians today.

For inscriptions the Greeks used capital letters, but for writing on papyrus cursive versions were developed. Most esoteric speculation and lore is based on the shapes of the capitals, although magically the cursive signs carry just as much force as the capitals. This is understandable since the Greek esoteric tradition surrounding the letters came along as a part of the development of philosophy and through contact with the more anciently literate peoples of Babylon and Egypt. To the Greeks their letters were more purely *abstract signs* for abstract principles than anything rooted in an ideogrammic or ideographic tradition. But by the time the Greco-Egyptian magical papyri were written down, there was a complete system of Greek esoterica embodied in their letters or *stoicheia* (elements) as they called them. Appendix E demonstrates how to write the Greek letters properly, in an aesthetic and powerful way.

The Greeks adapted the Semitic letter-names as virtually arbitrary names. As opposed to the Semitic letters or Celtic oghams or Germanic runes, the Greek letter-names have no natural meanings. They do however, contain mysteries. In the section on *Stoicheia,* these mysteries are explored in depth. Now it is only important to understand the external body of the tradition.

The purely numerical Ϝ (*digamma*) has the value of 6 but is not part of the codified system of the 24 *stoicheia*. Similarly the sign Ϙ is used for 90 and 🝞 for 900 in numerical computations. Most of the names of the Greek letters have no intrinsic meaning. The ones that do have such down to earth meanings as: *o-mikron*, "little O," or *o-mega*, "big O." More detailed instruction on how to pronounce the letters in Greek are provided in Appendix F.

On this exoteric base, the Greeks built up an elaborate and extremely complex set of teachings from various philosophical schools. It is as though practical innovation had unlocked a deeper esoteric potential based on abstract thought and mathematical models.

The Coptic System

The Coptic language is actually a dialect of the language spoken by the ancient Egyptians. It died out as a living language by the 17th century but continued in use for ritual purposes in the Coptic Church. It was able to isolate itself and survive as long as it did because it was the language of Christian sects in Egypt—some of them Gnostic—which remained apart from the Roman and subsequent Arabizing Islamic influences. As discussed in the earlier chapters of this book, there was, however, an obviously close relationship between the Hellenistic and Coptic societies in Egypt at the time the magical papyri were written. Coptic uses a modified Greek *alphabeta* (and so represents the vowel sounds). Coptic words and words written in the Coptic *alphabeta* are regularly found in the magical papyri, and there is a parallel tradition of Coptic magical papyri. The writers of the papyri knew how to read and write Egyptian in both demotic and Coptic scripts, although their preferred language seems to have been Greek. There were close cultural ties between the Coptic speakers and the Egyptian Hellenics. This is shown by the famous "Nag Hammadi Library"—a group of Gnostic texts discovered in 1945 in Egypt some sixty miles from Luxor. These are written in Coptic but experts agree that they were translated from originally Greek texts. They were probably buried around 400 C.E. to save them from orthodox Christian persecutors.

Table 4.   The Coptic System.

Number	Coptic	Nubian	Name	Phonetic Value	Numerical Value
1	ⲁ	ⲁ	alpha	a	1
2	ⲃ	ⲃ	beta	b	2
3	ⲅ	ⲅ	gamma	g	3
4	ⲇ	ⲇ	dalda	d	4
5	ⲉ	ⲉ	ei	e	5
6	ⲍ	ⲍ	zeta	z	7
7	ⲏ	ⲏ	heta	e	8
8	ⲑ	ⲑ	theta	t + h	9
9	ⲓ	ⲓ	iota	i	10
10	ⲕ	ⲕ	kappa	k	20
11	ⲗ	ⲗ	lauda	l	30
12	ⲙ	ⲙ	mi	m	40
13	ⲛ	ⲛ	ni	n	50
14	ⲝ		xi	x	60
15	ⲟ	ⲟ	ou	o	70
16	ⲡ	ⲡ	pi	p	80
17	ⲣ	ⲣ	ro	r	100
18	ⲥ	ⲥ	simma	s	200
19	ⲧ	ⲧ	tau	t	300
20	ⲩ	ⲩ	he	u	400
21	ⲫ	ⲫ	phi	p + h	500
22	ⲭ	ⲭ	khi	kh	600
23	ⲯ	ⲯ	psi	ps	700
24	ⲱ	ⲱ	o	o	800
25	ϣ	ϣ	shai	sh	
26	ϥ		fai	f	90
27	ϩ	ϩ	hori	h	
28	ϫ		djandja	j	
29	ϭ		chima	ch	
30	†		ti	t + i	

Magically the Coptic *alphabeta* is especially important because although it is used to represent Egyptian sounds the vowels are also written—which allows us to hear the vowel sounds in the operative *voces magicae*. Surely also the Coptic, that is *Egyptian*, pronunciation of the letters must have had a tremendous influence on the performance of the *voces magicae* as reflected in the magical papyri. Coptic is written either in the Coptic style or in a variant, more cursive, Nubian style, as shown in Table 4 on p. 113.

Learning how to read and write the characters of strange alphabets has always been an arcane fascination. Mysteriously such activity has its practical benefits. It strengthens the memory and makes the mind more agile and facile at processing data in new ways. There is also a great deal of lore and magical wisdom encoded in many systems of writing. This type of teaching is explored for the Greek system on page 110. The decoding of this wisdom is the equivalent of magical initiation. This comes not by believing what you are taught about a system but by discovering for yourself some of the intrinsic meaning concealed and encoded within the structures and substructures of the system. This process can be undertaken with Hebrew letters—about which the surviving literature is most vast—or the Greek *stoicheia*, or even Celtic *ogham* or Germanic runes.

Understanding the *sounds* the letters represent is an important part of your exploration. This is essential to practical work in operant phonology. In order to pronounce the phonic magical formulas correctly you must know how each letter and letter combination is spoken. (This is covered in more detail in Appendix F.) But beyond this the Hermetic magician should be familiar with the way the writing of each letter *feels* and *looks* after it has been correctly executed on paper, papyrus, or in carvings.

THE SCIENCE
OF THE *STOICHEIA*

The Greeks call the letters of their alphabet *stoicheia*, elements, which is suggestive of the way in which they were thought to describe the building blocks of the *kosmos* as well as act as a blueprint for the modification or alteration of the order of the world through *mageia*. The world is said to consist of 24 essential elements, or *stoicheia*, each of which finds manifestation in the 24 letters of the alphabet as bequeathed to humankind by Hermês. The science of these elements can be classified according to four levels of knowledge the magician might have concerning them: they are expressed as shapes, sounds, meanings and numbers.

Hermetic magicians will first seek to discover the meanings hidden within each of the elements, and then experimentally implement those elements to modify or influence the subjective and objective universes in a meaningful way. Magic is communication. We communicate along natural channels using natural (physical) manifestations of the *stoicheia*. By the same token we may communicate in a non-natural or *psychic* way with the non-natural aspects of those same *stoicheia*. There are both natural and non-natural aspects to all four levels of meaning the *stoicheia* possess.

The Esoteric Study of Letters

Many readers of this book will already be familiar with the mystical and magical speculations surrounding the Hebrew letters in the system of Hebrew mysticism popularly called the Kabbalah. These traditions and those of the Hermetics are closely related, both in type and in historic terms. In fact, it was surely through Hellenistic mysticism that the Hebrews further imbued their already magical writing system with numerically mysto-magical significance. This is witnessed by the fact that the technique of adding up the total numeri-

cal value of a word is called "*gematria*," which Gershom Scholem
cites as being derived from the Greek *geometria* ("measurement of the
world"), or alternatively from the Greek formula "*gamma* = *tria*" ("Γ"
= "3").[16] Another major method of Kabbalistic work with letters is
called *notarikon*, which is derived from the Latin word *notaricum*,
"acrostics." However, it must also be said that innovations and em-
bellishments of the system made by Hebrew Kabbalists over the centuries were later borrowed by the latter-day medieval and Renaissance
Hermeticists.

Theory | The basic premise of the esoteric study of "letters" is
           | that there is a hidden affinity between and among the
           | various aspects—shapes, sounds, meanings, and num-
bers—and that this affinity extends from the realm of Being or reality (the realm of the God) from which it emanates to the terrestrial
realm of Nature. Each "letter" is a true symbol of a higher principle.
That is, it is not a mere arbitrary *sign* of a principle, but is in fact an
essential *part*, or manifestation, of it.

   If the *kosmos* was created by means of the Word (an idea common to Egyptian, Judaic, and Indo-European traditions) then the
"letters of the word(s)" are indeed the *elements* of the cosmic ordering.
By consciously absorbing the patterns inherent in the system of letters (elements) the magician will have the divine meta-grammar to be
able to create effects in the objective and subjective universes just as
the gods do.

   Knowledge of the esoteric lore of the *alphabeta* allows the magician to understand the workings of other magicians, as well as provides a blueprint for effective magical operations. A total map of the
four aspects of a *stoichion*, in this case the *alpha*, might appear as
shown in figure 11.

   Number is over all and the highest of the aspects because it is
nearest to deity in its abstract quality. Number comes the closest to
describing the element in its purest form. Knowledge of the numerical science, or arithmosophy, is primary because the ancient Hermetics, with the Pythagoreans, thought of number as the root

---

[16]Gershom Scholem, *Kabbalah* (New York: Meridian, 1974), pp. 337–343.

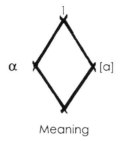

Meaning

Figure 11. *The Four Aspects of a* Stoichion.

(*archê*) of all things. In this they have been proven correct when it comes to the manifestation stage of existence. Every manifest thing can be *quantified* on many levels, from its dimensional measurements to the atomic number of the physical elements that make it up. If we "have the numbers" on something we can create or recreate it in the physical world—we ourselves can cause that thing to manifest, remanifest, or even "dismanifest." If this is true in the world of five senses and three dimensions, how much more true is it in the more subtle realms?

The shape and sound of a *stoichion* exist on the same level and give physical manifestation to the element. These are what the senses can both "see" and "hear" of the manifestation of the element in question. For practical reasons these are the most potent magical tools for the implementation of the powers of the *stoicheia*. Most of what we see in the historical record of Hermetic magic as recorded in the magical papyri involves the use of the elements on this level—by writing out formulas and/or uttering them. It would be a misunderstanding to think that the shape and sound are *merely* physical manifestations, however. The physical phenomena are in fact reflections of corresponding higher, more subtle principles which are numinous and supernal. Beyond the physical *stoicheia* are the *stoicheia spermatikon*—the "seed-elements." Realization of the seed-elements comes through *experience* of the totality of the *stoichion*.

The meaning of a *stoichion* is by far the most complex aspect—because it is so manifold and multileveled. But ultimately it is the meaning that is the most important aspect for working Hermetic magicians. It is the meaning they seek most of all, and it is through the meaning that the keys to operating with *stoicheia* are to be discovered.

The Hebrew   In no other cultural group has the esoteric study
Tradition   of letters been better cultivated and preserved
                 than among the Jews. Surely they must have inherited religious and magical lore concerning the letters, or *'otiyyot* (signs), from their neighboring Semitic sources, but that only accounts for a portion of the surviving lore in the Hebrew tradition. A great deal of it has obviously been borrowed from Hellenistic sources. This is noted by Gershom Scholem in his book *Kabbalah* where he writes concerning the composition of the *Sefer Yetzirah*: "Some of the terms used in the book were apparently translated from Greek, in which the term *stoicheia* indicates both elements and letters: this usually finds expression in the Hebrew term *'otiyyot yesod* (elemental letters), i.e. letters which are also elements."[17]

The Jewish philosopher and historian, Philo of Alexandria (30 B.C.E.–50 C.E.), wrote this concerning the Word in Hebrew theology: "(Moses) would say that the Intelligible World is nothing else than the Divine Logos engaged in the act of building the cosmos. . . ."[18] Of course, this is a prime example of the entry of Neo-Platonic, Neo-Pythagorean, and Stoic philosophical ideas into Jewish theology through the Alexandrian, Hellenized, branch of the culture. A second-century Jewish writer, Artapanus, even equated Moses and Hermês, as both were characterized as the inventor of writing.[19]

In Hebrew the word for letter is *'ot*, which also means "sign." This could be a sign given by God or one addressed to God in ritual. It is the word used for signs and omens through which God made his will known to people. (By the way another word used in Hebrew for letter is *siman*, borrowed from the Greek *semeion*, sign.)

---

[17]Gershom Scholem, *Kabbalah*, p. 27.
[18]See Philo's *On the Creation of the World*, in *The Works of Philo Judaeus*, C.D. Yonye, trans. (London: George Bell, 1855), pp. 6–7.
[19]For information on *Artapanus*, see Garth Fowden, *The Egyptian Hermit* (Princeton, NJ: University of Princeton Press, 1993), p. 23.

In the Jewish ideology of the letters, they are seen as the "twenty-two workers" used by God to construct the universe. Therefore, command over them gives the magician (or *ba'al shem*—"master of the word") an analogous power to alter the shape of events. Knowledge of them will allow the master to unlock the mysteries of the kingdom of God.

As mentioned, there are three principal ways to manipulate the *'otiyyot* for magical purposes: *gematria* (numerology), *notarikon* (acrostics), and *temurah* (permutations). In its simplest form gematria is the addition of the numerical values of the letters in a given word or phrase to arrive at a sum. This sum is the numerical signature of the word—its essence in principle, its *archê*. Also, whatever words add up to the same value are obviously identical in essence, despite whatever differences may appear on the surface in the sensible world. *Notarikon* is the practice of taking phrases and creating words out of them. *Temurah* is a method of encoding one word (or interpreting it) through a system of letter substitutions.

All of these methods only became extremely popular in Hebrew mysticism in the Middle Ages, although they were known at least from the time of the composition of the *Sefer Yetzirah* (perhaps as early as the second century C.E.), and it is likely long before that.

As methods for interpretation of texts or the objectively philosophical elucidation of linguistic symbols these techniques may often appear ridiculous to some. This is because in the modern period, once they were dislodged from certain *traditions* and approached in an arbitrary fashion, all kinds of manipulations of the data became possible. It is likely that in the ancient traditions there were specific uses of these techniques, not the least of which would have been *operative* in character.

The Greek Tradition | Although we are relatively less informed about the mystical and magical uses of the Greek *alphabeta*, all evidence points to many of the well-preserved and cultivated Hebrew traditions involved in the use of the *'otyyot* being borrowed from Greek practice. Therefore most of what is missing can be restored with some effort.

As noted earlier, the Greek tradition of magical and mystical speculations regarding the letters was not original to the system. In the very beginning of literacy among the Greeks the letters were used for purely practical and mundane ends. The early development of the numerical values was more for bills of sale or invoices than mystical speculation. But soon after its establishment the system became the object of magical and mystical insight.

By calling the letters *stoicheia* (elements) the ancient Greeks revealed their magical—and even "scientific"—attitude toward them. An attitude that is somewhat different from the Hebrews who called their letters *signs*. An element is a building block of a larger whole, whereas a sign is mainly a medium for communication between two entities (e.g. God and Human). The Hermetic combines these approaches for maximal operative and philosophical use.

The Greeks used a form of gematria, also called *isopsêphia* in Greek, very similar to the one developed in the Hebrew tradition. The Greeks speculated deeply on the *stoicheia*—on the numbers they represented (or manifested), their sounds, their shapes, and ultimately their meanings. Even in modern times scientists have continued to use Greek letters as designations for abstract principles of mathematics, physics, and other sciences. This is a tradition begun by the ancient Greeks themselves.

Earlier I presented a reconstruction of the original cosmological schemata which later became known as the "Tree of Life" in the Kabbalistic tradition. At that point I noted that there are 24 connecting paths between the 10 spheres of being that emanate from the One. The 10 qualities, which are the 10 numbers, studied and expounded by Pythagoras and others, are connected in a network of elements on a secondary (cosmic) level as represented by the 24 letters of the Greek *alphabeta*. The abstract numbers are purely of the intelligible world whereas the letters (paths) are extensions of the intelligible world into the sensible realm. They are the blueprint of the World Soul and the means of communication between the realm of the senses and the realm of the spirit.

What I present in the following sections is based on this blueprint as expressed through the Greek *stoicheia*. The early Hermetic tradition as we know it was almost exclusively expressed through the medium of the Greek language and alphabet. Therefore, it is by understanding this system that we can come closest to grasping the basic principles of Hermetic practices in this area.

The Mithraic Use of the Greek Stoicheia

Of the several schools that contributed to the Hermetic understanding of the *stoicheia*, Mithraism is one of the most interesting and useful for us today. Mithraism swept into the west from Iran at the same time that the development of Hermeticism was ebbing. Although its roots are Iranian, it soon syncretized with the Greek modalities of thought and in turn with the Roman system. An examination of Mithraic doctrines concerning the alphabet reveals many *arcana*—including those connected with the symbols used in the system of images known as the Tarot—which would otherwise remain unknown until the late Middle Ages.

In fact the Greek magical papyri contain many references to Mithras (Gk. Μιθρας or Μειθρας). Mithraism is a later development of Iranian religion being practiced at the time of the expansion of the Roman Empire to the borders of Persia (from the first century B.C.E.). This religion found a receptive public in the Roman army, where it developed into an all male warrior religion. These soldiers then disseminated the faith, along with all its magical features throughout the Empire (where it was syncretized with the Greco-Roman mystery religions). It was these Roman soldiers who built the numerous Mithraic temples to be found throughout the territories of the Roman Empire.

Mithraism brought with it a whole body of lore and magical technology. It inherited this from Iranian religio-magical systems from which it sprang. This was tremendously influential in the formation of the Hermetic synthesis. As is well-known, the terms *mageia* and *magos* are borrowings from the Iranian terminology. The terms probably were passed on from the Mithraic cult or one closely related to it. A priest in the cult was known as a *magû* in Iranian. It is presumably three such *magûs* (pl.) who are said to have come to visit the Christ-Child guided by a "star."

At some point in the early centuries C.E., a connection was forged between the letters of the Greek *alphabeta* and the lore of Mithraism. Curiously enough this Mithraic lore in turn seems to be an unmistakable link with the symbolism of the Tarot. Connections between various alphabetic systems and the Tarot have been the subject of speculation throughout the modern occult revival. Most, if not all, of this has centered on the Jewish Kabbalah and hence the Hebrew *alef-bet*.

A Swedish scholar, Sigurd Agrell, who worked in the early part of this century, points out the well-known fact that the attribution of Hebrew letters to the Major Arcana of the Tarot is of relatively late date. This was first done in the late 18th or early 19th century. According to Agrell, however, the connection between the Tarot and an alphabet occurs first in the Greek cultural sphere, not the Hebrew.[20]

Interestingly, the reduction from 24 to 22 letters for esoteric practice came not through Hebrew influence, as might be expected, but through *Roman* practice. At that time, the Latin alphabet consisted of 23 letters, but since "y" could not be used in initial position, it was not employed in Roman divinatory practice which depended on the use of the initial letters of words to form formulaic readings. This Latin 22-letter system then became the underlying one for later magical practice (to which the Hebrew was also added). We can not rule out the possibility that the Tarot symbolism was shaped by either the older Greek or by a kindred, perhaps even Iranian, system.

Agrell uses the Greek *alphabeta* and its magico-mystical correspondences to explain the Tarot. Table 5 on p. 123 is a somewhat modified version of the one printed in *Die pergamenische Zauberscheibe und das Tarockspiel*.[21] This reconstruction rearranges the Tarot order to agree with the esoteric meanings of the Greek letters in the Mithraic tradition. Agrell is of the opinion that the original Tarot order followed the system of Greek letters, but that it became altered

---

[20]Sigurd Agrell, *Die pergamenische Zauberscheibe und das Tarockspiel* (Lund: Gleerup, 1936), pp. 60–61.
[21]Sigurd Agrell, *Die pergamenische Zauberscheibe und das Tarockspiel*, pp. 97–98.

Table 5.   The Greek Alphabeta and Mithraic Correspondences.

Greek Name	Number	Arcanum (Esoteric Roman Name)	Mithraic Meaning
alpha	1	The Fool (Apis)	the Bull
beta	2	The Magician (Bacatus-Typhôn)	the Daimonic
gamma	3	The Priestess (Caeles-Isis)	the Divine
delta	4	The Empress (Diana)	4 Elements
epsilon	5	The Emperor (Eon-Aeon)	Aiôn
zêta	7	The Hierophant (Flamen)	Sacrifice
êta	8	The Lovers (Gaudium)	Joy, Love
thêta	9	The Chariot (Hamaxa)	Crystal-Heaven
iota	10	Justice (Iustitia)	Anankê
kappa	20	The Hermit (Kronos)	Kronos, Death
lambda	30	Wheel of Fortune (Libera)	Plants
mu	40	Strength (Magnitudo)	Trees
nu	50	The Hanged Man (Noxa)	Hekatê
xi	60	The Star (Stellae)	Stars
omicron	70	The Sun (Victor-Unus)	Sun
pi	80	The Devil (Quirinus)	Serapis-Mithras
rho	100	The Moon (Trina)	the Feminine
sigma	200	Death (Orcus)	Bearer of Dead
tau	300	The World (Zodiacus)	Human
ypsilon	400	Temperance (Pluvia)	Water
phi	500	Judgment (Xiphias)	Phallus
chi	600	— ? —	Possessions
psi	700	The Tower (Ruina)	Zeus
ômega	800	— ? —	Riches

when fused with the *Roman* tradition of 22 divinatory letters, as outlined above. Notice in Table 5 on p. 123 that each of the esoteric
names begins with a different letter in the Latin alphabet, and that if
these are arranged in their traditional ABCDEFGHIXLMNO-
PORSTUXZ order, the traditional order of the Major Arcana of the
Tarot is likewise revealed! These few pages of lore are, I believe, sufficient to set a whole new course in the investigation of Tarot symbolism, as well as being a door to new understandings of Greco-Roman
esoterica.

From this material, we can suppose that the symbolism of the
Tarot is ultimately based on a syncretized Irano-Hellenic model, not
an originally Semito-Hebraic one. Furthermore it points to the possibility of there being an original 24 Major Arcana, not 22. This
would cause the whole body of Tarot *arcana*, counting the Major and
Minor Arcana together, to equal 80, not 78.

As far as any connection between the Greek alphabet and the
Tarot made through this Mithraic theory, it seems possible that
(proto-)Tarot was indeed shaped by this, or some related tradition. It
is also worthy of note that the "Gypsies," so often connected with the
Tarot, are actually of *Central Asian* origin (not Egyptian!). The language they speak, Romany, is closely related to the Iranian that must
have been spoken by those original *magûs*. These facts strengthen the
connection of the Romany people with the Tarot, while placing them
in their true Indo-Iranian cultural sphere.

Among academics in the 1970s and 1980s there developed a
new theory of how magic works in traditional societies. This is best
described as a semiotic theory, which, briefly stated, means that magical acts are seen as symbolic actions meant to *communicate* between
realities. Symbolic acts performed in the mundane world will be received (and it is hoped acted upon in return) by a transmundane
world. Any act of communication is perhaps best understood as a *linguistic* act, and an elemental part of such an act hinges on the letters
(sounds) used to make up the words, and ultimately the "sentences"
of that communication. I will return to the theoretical basis of magic
in the section called "Magical Theories."

Operative Phonology: Names of Power

The *stoicheia* are sounds. Sounds are vibrations in the air which may be heard by others—they are modulations in the atmosphere which can trigger changes in the objective universe or in subjective universes that might be sensitive to them. The One created the *cosmos* by means of the Word: the *Logos*. To the ancient Greek the idea of the λογος was more than a mere "word." It indicated a whole discourse of (often abstract) meaning, which *could* be encapsulated in a single, magically charged *word of power*.

The science of sound, phonosophy, was well cultivated by the ancient Hermetic magicians. By means of the right pronunciation of the right sounds, in the right order, at the right time, by the right person, changes can be wrought in the universe. When we look at the verbal portions of the ancient operations in the magical papyri, we see two types of formulas. One is in "natural speech," that is letters represent words which are easily understood on a mundane level and represent more or less the speech that would be understood readily by other contemporary humans. The other type of formula is something else. It is not readily understood by the non-initiated, or even by most human beings at all. It is a kind of speech known to the gods, the angels, and the daimôns. It is ordinary practice in the old operations recorded in the papyri to shift back and forth between these two modes of communication. Common examples of shorter formulas or "names" of this kind are ABLANATHANALBA, ABRASAX, PAKERBÊTH, or the most famous IAÔ. Sometimes words or names of this kind are extended into whole sentence-like formulas, or even into entire passages. As they are written they are meant to be performed vocally (as well as often written in some special way).

Each sound is a certain type of vibratory modulation of the air in the environment. These vibratory rates can have, according to the ancient Pythagoreans, specific effects on the atmosphere. For example, the Pythagoreans thought that to each of the planetary spheres surrounding the Earth a specific musical note was ascribed. This is the origin of our western scale of music with seven notes and an octave.

When magicians, with full attention and concentration, can perform the στοιχεια—can make or visualize the visible sign while perfectly performing the sound, and at the same moment fully realize the numerical quality and the semantic meaning(s) of the "elements" in their souls—then the doors to perfection will open.

The Greeks had a system for revealing the correspondences between the *stoicheia* and their cosmic qualities, which is nowhere openly stated and has remained a quasi-secret. This system is broadly alluded to in a number of classical sources, is briefly mentioned by Agrippa at the end of Book I of his *De occulta philosophia*,[22] and is discussed at some length by Franz Dornseiff in his landmark work on our subject, *Das Alphabet in Mystik und Magie*.[23]

It is well-known that the Greeks ascribed the seven vowels to the seven planetary spheres. The question of whether *alpha* was the highest or the lowest sphere was open until the discovery of the original form of the Alexandrian "Tree of Life" depicted in figure 1 on p. 50, where it is made clear that *alpha* must be ascribed to the Moon, and *ômega* to the sphere of Saturn. The 17 remaining letters are to be ascribed to the elements and to the 12 signs of the Zodiac—as perhaps also suggested by the "literal cosmology" outlined in the Jewish *Sefer Yetzirah*.[24] In the Greek system there are fully five "elements"— Aether, Fire, Air, Water, and Earth. Five plus twelve is seventeen, and we have our perfect correspondence. The question of which letter is to be ascribed to which sign is again answered by the key provided by the Alexandrian "Tree of Life."

One school of thought has it that the key to which sounds are to be attributed to which element is contained in the Greek names of the elements: αιθηρ, πυρ, αηρ, 'υδωρ, and γη. It just so happens that there are only five consonants used in all five of these words: ρ =

---

[22]For information on Agrippa's *De occulta philosophia*, see Heinrich Cornelius Agrippa van Nettesheim, *Three Books of Occult Philosophy* [1651] (London: Chthonios, 1986).

[23]Franz Dornseiff, *Das Alphabet in Mystik und Magie* (Leipzig: Teubner, 1922), pp. 83–91.

[24]Aryeh Kaplan, *Sefer Yetzirah: The Book of Creation* (York Beach, ME: Samuel Weiser, 1990).

Air, δ = Water, π = Fire, θ = Aether, and γ = Earth. Another school has it that the elemental letters are near the ends of the three rows of symbols as represented in Table 3 on page 111. In this system *theta*, at the end of the first row, is ascribed to Earth (it is seen as an iconic representation of matter in space). Near the end of the second row, *xi* is ascribed to Water. The last three consonants of the system, *phi, chi,* and *psi,* are ascribed to Air, Fire, and Aether respectively. In the examples that follow, the second system is used.

When considering the astronomical factors in the definitions of the vowel/consonant combinations, you should not think of them in the usual way we are perhaps taught to think about astrology as a predictive science. Rather it is astronomy as a descriptive, cosmological map of the archetypal possibilities present in the world at all times and in all places. To understand the syntheses formed by the vowel/consonant combinations, you should consult a good book of basic astrological interpretations.

Astrological lore is essential to a full understanding of Hermetic principles. Being true to the philosophy of this book, and being true to the Quest for the Mystery, one should ideally explore the most root-level, or radical, sources available. In this regard we are fortunate to have the work of "Project Hindsight," which sets about to make available the basic source books of astrological lore. Among the volumes is the invaluable *Liber Hermetis* (Book of Hermes).[25]

The combined vowel/consonant unit can be thought of as a compound of elements forming a substance which is combined with other substances to create the entire formula. These are the second level of building blocks above those formed by the elements themselves. Each formula is designed, much like a "chemical" or alchemical formula for a specific operative purpose. These combinations are the entities referred to by the ancient Greeks as the λογοι σπερ–ματικοι (seed-words). (See Table 6 on p. 128.) A transliteration of this table is shown in Table 7 on p. 128.

Note that the metathesized forms of these combinations (i.e. *ba* for *ab*) do not effect their meaning on this level of interpretation.

---

[25]Robert Zoller, trans., *Liber Hermetis: Part I* (Berkeley Springs, WV: Golden Hind, 1993).

Table 6. Seed-Words.

Planets	Vowels	♈ β	♉ γ	♊ δ	♋ ζ	🜃 θ	♌ κ	♍ λ	♎ μ	♏ ν	🜄 ξ	♐ π	♑ ρ	♒ ς	♓ τ	🜁 φ	🜂 χ	⊛ ψ
☾	α	αβ	αγ	αδ	αζ	αθ	ακ	αλ	αμ	αν	αξ	απ	αρ	ας	ατ	αφ	αχ	αψ
☿	ε	εβ	εγ	εδ	εζ	εθ	εκ	ελ	εμ	εν	εξ	επ	ερ	ες	ετ	εφ	εχ	εψ
♀	η	ηβ	ηγ	ηδ	ηζ	ηθ	ηκ	ηλ	ημ	ην	ηξ	ηπ	ηρ	ης	ητ	ηφ	ηχ	ηψ
☉	ι	ιβ	ιγ	ιδ	ιζ	ιθ	ικ	ιλ	ιμ	ιν	ιξ	ιπ	ιρ	ις	ιτ	ιφ	ιχ	ιψ
♂	ο	οβ	ογ	οδ	οζ	οθ	οκ	ολ	ομ	ον	οξ	οπ	ορ	ος	οτ	οφ	οχ	οψ
♃	υ	υβ	υγ	υδ	υζ	υθ	υκ	υλ	υμ	υν	υξ	υπ	υρ	υς	υτ	υφ	υχ	υψ
♄	ω	ωβ	ωγ	ωδ	ωζ	ωθ	ωκ	ωλ	ωμ	ων	ωξ	ωπ	ωρ	ως	ωτ	ωφ	ωχ	ωψ

Table 7. Transliteration of Seed-Words.

Planets	Vowels	♈ b	♉ g	♊ d	♋ z	🜃 th	♌ k	♍ l	♎ m	♏ n	🜄 x	♐ p	♑ r	♒ s	♓ t	🜁 ph	🜂 ch	⊛ ps
☾	a	ab	ag	ad	az	ath	ak	al	am	an	ax	ap	ar	as	at	aph	ach	aps
☿	e	eb	eg	ed	ez	eth	ek	el	em	en	ex	ep	er	es	et	eph	ech	eps
♀	ê	êb	êg	êd	êz	êth	êk	êl	êm	ên	êx	êp	êr	ês	êt	êph	êch	êps
☉	i	ib	ig	id	iz	ith	ik	il	im	in	ix	ip	ir	is	it	iph	ich	ips
♂	o	ob	og	od	oz	oth	ok	ol	om	on	ox	op	or	os	ot	oph	och	ops
♃	y	yb	yg	yd	yz	yth	yk	yl	ym	yn	yx	yp	yr	ys	yt	yph	ych	yps
♄	ô	ôb	ôg	ôd	ôz	ôth	ôk	ôl	ôm	ôn	ôx	ôp	ôr	ôs	ôt	ôph	ôch	ôps

The methods of analyzing magical formulas, or *voces magicae*, are demonstrated in the examples given below.

Let us interpret a few of the best known magical name formulas from the ancient papyri using this key. True Hermetic magicians will set about proving the validity of this key to themselves both theoretically and practically, so there is no need to interpret an exhaustive number of formulas in this way. In fact, such an exhaustive cataloging would be counter productive to the real aims of Hermetics.

ABLANATHANALBA (= **AB-LA-NA-TH-AN-AL-BA**): The fact that only the A-vowel occurs in the formula demonstrates its Lunar nature. *Theta* (9) is at its center, and it is a palindrome (the same forward and backward). It consists of only three vowel/consonant combinations (AB, LA, AN) and their metathesized forms. AB/BA is the sound of the Moon in Aries; LA/AL is the sound of the Moon in Virgo; AN/NA is the sound of the Moon in Scorpio. *Thêta*, the *stoichion* of Earth, is the axis about which this array turns. So it is fairly clear that the formula is one that expresses and gives command over the material realm of Earth among the elements in the sub-Lunar sphere.

ABRASAX (AB-RA-SA-AX) is also seen as ABRAXAS (AB-RA-AX-AS): Again only the A-vowel occurs, once more indicating a sub-Lunar or Lunar sphere of activity and potency. This is the preferred sphere of practical magical activity for the Hermetic magician. AB is the sound of the Moon in Aries; RA is the sound of the Moon in Capricorn; SA is the sound of the Moon in Aquarius; AX is the sound of Lunar Water. The fact that the gematria value of the formula is 365 cannot be ignored here. ABRASAX expresses, and gives command over, the entire spectrum of 365 degrees of activity within the sub-Lunar sphere.

PAKERBÊTH (PA-KE-ER-BÊ-ÊTH): PA is the sound of the Moon in Sagittarius; KE is the sound of Mercury in Leo; ER is the sound of Mercury in Capricorn; BÊ is the sound of Venus in Aries; ÊTH is the sound of Terrestrial Venus. PAKERBÊTH is a magical epithet of Set-Typhôn—to whom is ascribed the planet Mercury in Egyptian astrology. It is obvious that there is a strong, aggressively erotic component to the composition of this formula. PAKERBÊTH is strong in love and in hate in workings meant to effect the material universe.

IAÔ (I-A-Ô): These are three vowels, so they are all ascribed to the planetary spheres: I is the sound of the Sun; A is the sound of the Moon; Ô is the all encompassing sound of Saturn—the outermost planetary sphere and gatekeeper to the outer reaches. IAÔ is the *alpha* (the innermost) and the *ômega* (the outermost), ruled from the primary head of the Sun (Hêlios). IAÔ is the creator of the Earthly sphere from these primary stations of creativity in the system. The IAÔ formula can also be seen as a magical abbreviation of the entire vocalic spectrum: AEHIOYΩ.

All the magical formulaic elements in the tradition of the ancient papyri can be interpreted in this way, and made to unlock their secrets for the working magician today. It is important to realize that when the old magical papyri instruct the magician to recite a formula such as ABLANATHANALBA, it is not understood as purely irrational mumbo-jumbo. Each letter and each sound of the formula is to be concentrated upon with the entire Being of the magician—otherwise it is ineffective.

Arithmosophy: Hermetic Numerology

In the ancient papyri it is always made clear that the idea of *number* is an important part of the constitution of magical formulas. Within the texts themselves, quite often the writer will tell us that a given name is to be made up of a certain number of letters. Other formulas, such as the famous ABRASAX are obviously first and foremost numerical formulas in the shape of words.

As we have already mentioned, some Greek schools of thought held that "number is the root of all things." We have also observed how true this is on what we like to call a "scientific" basis today. But for the ancient Pythagoreans and Platonists, this logical use of the qualities of numbers was only a beginning to what could be done with them. Their secrets, if unlocked with wisdom and insight, can yield understanding of the very qualities of Being dwelling with the eternal One.

The numerical system of the Greek *stoicheia* has already been presented in Table 3 on p. 111. Each letter has a numerical value. In Greek practice when a letter was meant to be understood as a number a mark would be inscribed next to it, for example, $\rho' = 100$.

In the Greek system of number-letters, *theta* is unique and stands alone in the ninth column (the signs for 90 and 900 being purely numerical symbols). Also, the simple representation of the number 6 is impossible without recourse to the obsolete *digamma*.

Numbers have been imbued with symbolic qualities by most cultures. The ancient magical papyri are full of references to such culturally specific numerical symbols. For example, when the number 7 is mentioned, it is most often a reference to the god Set-Typhôn, whose seat is behind the constellation of the Thigh (*Kephesh*)—which consists of seven stars. We most commonly call this constellation the "Big Dipper." However, the usual use of numerical symbolism at the deepest level of understanding is one we know about from the writings of the Pythagoreans and Neo-Platonists. For them each of the numbers one through ten had a special, if manifold, *qualitative* meaning. Note that for them the idea of number was not confined to a matter of quantity. Here are a few of the qualities ascribed to each of the numbers in the *Theology of Arithmetic*,[26] thought to be based on the works of the Neo-Platonist and theurgist, Iamblichus:

ONE—the Monad: It is called the First (*prôteus*) and the Maker (*demiourgos*), it is Life and God, it is Darkness and Matter. The One excludes nothing, and is in so Being, Nothingness itself. In many ways, the One shared many qualities with what we know as zero today. (The concept "zero" came to the West from India via the Arabs, and is a borrowing from Sanskrit *sunya*.) The One is both Order (*taxia*) and "Infinite Space" (*chaos*).

TWO—the Dyad: It is Nature in motion, dynamic growth. It is the Ratio (*logos*) in Proportion (*analogia*).

THREE—the Triad: Here is Harmony in Knowledge (*gnôsis*). The triad is the Mean between extremes.

FOUR—the Tetrad: This is called "the Nature of Change," and that which holds the key to Nature.

FIVE—the Pentad: It is called the "Immortal" and equated with Light and the manifestation of Justice.

SIX—the Hexad: This is called the Form of Forms and the Reconciler. The hexad possesses wholeness. Here is the marriage between male and female.

SEVEN—the Heptad: It is known as the Citadel (*akropolis*), and the one which Preserves. The heptad is the "Reverend Seven."

---

[26]Robin Waterfield, trans., *Theology of Arithmetic* (Grand Rapids, MI: Phanes, 1988).

EIGHT—the Octad: This is the Steadfast and the Seat which is called All-Harmonious.

NINE—the Ennead: This is called Perfection because it is the Oneness of Mind. Here there is not the Oneness of the One beyond the ability to be conscious, but Oneness in a conscious state. It is equated with Prometheus (who sees ahead) and who brings to perfection. The Ennead is the *hôros*, the horizon—the border between the outer realms and the return to the One in ten.

TEN—the Decad: Here there is a return to the quality of One, but on a different level. It is equated with Eternity, or Aiôn, with Memory and Necessity. Ten is the number of *Kosmos*.

These qualitative discussions are highly relevant to understanding the essences of the ten spheres of Being as depicted in the Alexandrian "Tree of Life." They are in fact something separate from the qualities represented by the *stoicheia* bearing the same number designations. The *stoicheia* are manifestations and quasi-sensible signs of that which is only fully intelligible in the pure abstract numbers of the spheres.

Gematria | The practice of adding together the numerical values of each of the letters of a word or phrase and deriving the hidden meaning of the word or phrase from the resulting sum is called gematria or *isopsêphia*. Gematria is the more common term because it is also used in Hebrew mysticism. The term *isopsêphia* literally means "equal-stone," which means "of equal value." *Psêphos* is the word for stone used in calculating with a device similar to an abacus, it is also the word for a stone used in voting or for divinatory purposes. When the sum of two words is the same, they reveal a hidden affinity or identity otherwise unknown. This is in accordance with the Hermetic laws of sympathy.

Here we will only concern ourselves with the practice of Greek gematria, because that is all that would appear in the Hermetic tradition (whether undertaken by Jews or pagans). There are certain rules of Greek gematria. For example, when a *sigma* and a *tau* come together, they may be written ς and their combined numerical value is to be read as 6. In the Book of Revelations the number of the Beast is recorded in the original text as χξς. (But in some of the oldest manuscripts of the text the number appears χας, which would be read 616.) Also, if two numbers are within one unit of each other, they can be read as equals. A key for the transliteration of *voces magicae* back into their original Greek forms can be found in Appendix F.

In the section on operative phonology we discussed four common names of power in the old papyri: ABLANATHANALBA, ABRASAX, PAKERBÊTH, and IAÔ. Now let us look at them in terms of their numerical values.

ABLANATHANALBA = 1+2+30+1+50+9+1+50+1+30+2+1 = **179**: The numerical sum is a poetic interpretation of the meaning of the name in this case. It is unity (1) throughout all of the 7 heavens (planetary spheres), ruled from a higher plane of unity which is the recurrent 9 in the "center."

ABRASAX = 1+2+100+1+200+1+60 = **365**: Here we have a formula that was primarily created as a numerical entity. The deity it is meant to conceal is certainly revealed when we discover that the Greek spelling of Mithras (Μειθρας) = 40+5+10+9+100+1+200 = 365! ABRASAX (and Mithras) are the gods of the 365 degrees of the orb of heaven.

PAKERBÊTH = 80+1+20+5+100+2+8+9 = **225**: This is known to be a Typhonian name from the contexts in which it appears throughout the magical papyri. Its key number is 9 (the number of the digits of the sum when added together), and it is the higher octave of another Typhonian name ERBÊTH = 124 (key number 7). Another name used in the papyri, IARBATHA, also has a gematria value of 124 and can also be identified as a Typhonian name.

IAÔ = 10+1+800 = **811**: This is the Greek version of the famous Hebraic divine name YHVH (the gematria for which is 27). The key number of the Greek form is 10 (= 8+1+1), which is the highest form of perfection, the decad.

The last thing the true Hermetic will wish to do is make all of the foregoing into idle speculation and pseudo-intellectual game playing. These ideas are meant to be used as tools—first for the exercise of magical aims, then for the contemplation of the universe with the understanding that comes with experience.

In this regard you should be forewarned that *accurate* use of the principles of gematria will depend on access to the original Greek texts, some knowledge of the language (the more the better), knowledge of the rules of the process, as well as an understanding of the qualities involved. It is very easy to be led astray or down blind alleys, or worse, by using this precise science in an imprecise way.

Obviously, I can only begin to scratch the surface here. There are a thousand secrets waiting to be uncovered. All true Hermetic magicians will set out to uncover these for themselves. I have been told that a hundred volumes could be written from the basic material offered in this one chapter alone.

MAGICAL THEORIES

In ancient times magic was often very much a part of the everyday life of people, both common and noble. But even in ancient times not all humans acknowledged the power of magic—there were probably just as many sceptics then as now, proportionately speaking. Also, many people today are fully engaged in a magical universe and do not realize it—or consistently deny that such is the case. It must be said at the outset that there is nothing intrinsically advantageous to using magical operations. They are not a universal panacea that can be applied in a uniform way by all individuals with uniform results. That is the hope of science. Magic was always thought to be the domain of special, elect individuals and groups.

Ancient Theory

Generally the ancients believed that the magical arts were things that must be revealed to humans by means of some divine communication in the first instance, and then something that had to be carried on along secret lineages from that point forward in time. It was the art and science of the gods and goddesses themselves, and it was supernatural in origin. Magic made use of the principles of the cosmos, and was the means by which the gods and goddesses were able to create and to some extent guide the development of the world. To some elect members of the human species the gods imparted at least a portion of the keys necessary to begin to make use of the principles known to the gods. Those with this knowledge formed priesthoods and brotherhoods for the cultivation and extension of this special kind of knowledge.

For the ancients, be they Egyptians, Greeks, or Jews, the art of magic was a matter of applying mysterious *principles* revealed to the magician either by a teacher or directly by a god or other occult source. Its practice was limited to the gods themselves and to the elect of this terrestrial sphere. This was because those who were not elect simply could not make magic *work*. It was not only a matter of what you did, it was also a matter of who or what you were—what you had become through initiation and/or election.

For the ancient Hermetic magicians the ultimate aim of their pursuits was certainly not simply catching thieves, obtaining lovers, or protecting themselves from malevolent daimôns. Operations of this kind are to *mageia* what basic laboratory experiments are to chemical engineering. The discovery and realization of the highest of principles may be the aim, but practical experimentation can be the foundation and proving ground.

The theoretical underpinning of ancient Hermetics was provided by the idea that all that existed was derived from the *Plêroma* (the Fullness of Being) and was thus of one essence, and that all of this was therefore linked—from the cosmological orderings, through the theological/daimonological realms down to the psychic or anthropological—Humans, Gods, and Cosmos were linked. Discovering ways to work with the hidden linkages was the essence of initiation and magic.

An Alexandrian magician of the third or fourth century would tell us that magic works because it is formulated according to eternal principles hidden within the supernal realms (in the Mind of God). These principles are hidden from the mundane mind by reason of the lack of the mundane mind's ability to perceive them. He would also insist that although logic and reason is able to bring one close to an understanding of this higher reality, it alone can never cause one to realize and have true knowledge (*gnôsis*) of it. This is because although the higher and lower worlds may be similar in structure (as above so below) and be linked by hidden correspondences or sympathies, they are still different in kind.

The science of the *stoicheia* holds the greatest single key to the theoretical understanding of the magic of the ancient Hermetics—at least as far as the evidence of the Greek magical papyri allows us to discover. Magic works chiefly on the basis of a theory of complex correspondences between elements in the supernal realm and the mundane world. This was the basis of all the occult sciences, astrology, alchemy, and so on, and the basis of the famous Hermetic dictum "as above, so below." The *stoicheia* represent a multidimensional system of symbolic correspondences with a ready made communicative context. As humans can communicate by means of the *stoicheia* (sounds and visible signs in writing), so too can humans communicate with gods (as gods must be able to communicate with one another) by means of the more mysterious aspects of these *elements*.

Modern Theory

Modernism, the school of thought prevalent in western civilization since the 17th century, is marked by a firm belief in the dogma that humanity can save itself through the application of reason and scientific methods when and if these methods are applied in a cooperative and rational way. This new faith might be called "Scientism." In the wake of modernism two schools of thought arose concerning magic. One, the more orthodox "Scientistic" approach, held that magic was merely erroneous science. This school rejected the reality of magic altogether, claiming that it was merely superseded pseudo-knowledge.

The other approach taken by those who did not want to give up the ways of magic, but wanted to try to make them "respectable" in the eyes of a populous ever more under the spell of modernism and its Scientism, held out the possibility that magic was just "undiscovered science." By the same token, those who wanted to correlate rational science with magic always seemed anxious to grasp any new scientific discovery that seemed to corroborate the past or present claims of magicians. Additionally, magic was theoretically couched more and more in terms of material science. Magic was no longer the domain of spirits and gods, but of energies and forces, analogous to newly discovered forces such as electricity. Perhaps the most famous modern magical theorist on the friendly side of things was Aleister Crowley whose avowed theoretical position was, "The Method of Science—the Aim of Religion."[27]

---

[27] This is the motto of Crowley's journal, *The Equinox*.

Modern understandings of magic, either friendly or hostile, served a great purpose in keeping interest alive in the reality of magic throughout the modern period. But as the ancients could have told modern would-be magicians, logic and rational science is precisely what magic is *not*—the fact that it is not is what makes it *magic*. Rational thought is, indeed *must be*, the springboard to the magical realm of operative power and intellectual enlightenment, but its rules are insufficient to allow the soul to make the transition from the sensible realm (where methods of natural science are valid) to the intelligible realm where those same methods can be applied only by analogy at best.

Postmodern Theory

Postmodernism is a general school of cultural thought which has been growing in western European societies since the end of the Second World War. No premise of postmodernism is more important than the abandonment of the "myth of progress" based on the cooperative, monolithic application of scientific rationalism. The events of the 20th century showed that despite a quantum leap in science and technology, the human species, if it had changed at all, had only become worse. Quantum leaps in rationality, education, and practical applications of science had not equaled even a moderate amount of *true* human progress. Modernism had proven itself, at least to some, to be a failed experiment.

Only a very small group of magicians working in the world today could be characterized as practitioners of postmodern magic. Just because a label has been attached to a school of magic in the past twenty or thirty years does not make that school *postmodern*. Attempts by current magical schools to accord their theories with "modern physics" is just more of the same modernism.

An essential component of a postmodern theory of magic is the realization that *magic is real*, and it works. Modernists were simply dreaming in a self-created delusion when they posed the idea that magic would no longer be practiced and that myths would be outmoded in a world dominated by Science, or conversely that magic would be proven real "by the scientific method." Today's world is dominated by Science, yet myths and magic and the supra-rational abound. To be sure much of it is of the lowest quality and to be found on tabloid pages or cable television. But in fact today the appetite for the magical only seems to grow with the average person's level of education. Modernism failed to provide *meaning* for people's lives—and without meaning a culture can not long survive.

With the rejection of the idea that "progress" and "rationalism" are in and of themselves valuable things, the postmodernists open themselves to the exploration of the validity of past models or paradigms. Past, or perhaps better stated, timeless, models of human understanding are seen with fresh eyes. Their value is seen as something more than historical curiosities with relevance to the future limited to their roles as past foundations. Also, "legitimate" approaches to these paradigms are liberated from the purely rationalistic mode. The present academic sciences will become obsolete by their limited natures when it comes to unraveling the mysteries they were originally designed to "explain."

In these postmodern times magic remains tabu to a great extent. It remains tabu for all the same reasons it was tabu in medieval times (as an act of rebellion against the will of the Judeo-Christian God) and for modern reasons as well (as an act of rebellion against "Scientism").

Essential to the postmodern theory of magic is the idea of *communication*. This postmodern theory might also be called a semiotic theory of magic. Semiotics is the study of signs and symbols—the theory and practice of how meaning is conveyed from a sender to a receiver and back again. When these things happen communication takes place. This process is not without mysterious components when considering even the most "mundane" conversation between two human beings. Science can not answer the most basic and essential questions concerning the nature of the sender and receiver (their psyches) or of the system they use to communicate (language)—what is it, where did it come from, how does it work. It has been said by the wisest of men that nothing which has its origins in the human mind can be reduced to a set of logical, rational rules. The soul is not

a compilation of chemical reactions—otherwise its mysteries would
have long since been unraveled.

The semiotic theory of magic states that magic is a process of
inter-reality communication—when, in Hermetic terms, that which
is below is able to communicate its will to that which is above and
thereby bring about a modification in the configuration of that
which is above—the subtle paradigms of the cosmos—and thereby
receive a return message in the form of corresponding modifications
in the environment "below." That this should be so is not rational or
natural, it is not subject to objective experimentation—it is a non-
natural (rather than "supernatural") event. To be sure, magical communication may not seem to take place in exactly the same form as
mundane communication, but it does follow the analogous archetypal principles.

Even discussions of the type this chapter represents are preju-
diced in form toward the modernistic approach. When you started
this chapter you were hoping to have magic *explained* to you the way
Mr. Wizard used to explain how water boils at 212 degrees Fahrenheit (at sea-level, of course). But you see, such an explanation is impossible for magic—or for religion, or poetry, or love, or life, or any
of the things that are really important to human beings. These are
things of the soul, of the psyche, which are simply not subject to the
same kind of rules as physics, or chemistry, or geology.

Perhaps the most significant reason why magic can not be explained in the rational, predictable way some might wish is that the
magicians are all *different*. Magic is the exercise of the will of an individual, and as such it is dependent on the state of being of that individual at the moment the magical operation is executed. The
conditions for a magical operation can never be repeated. Ritual is
the attempt of the magician to create, as far as possible, the most similar conditions possible for the most reliable possible results

Postmodern magic explores the paradigms of the past and
gives them unprejudiced consideration, and rational approaches are
seen as springboards—not as explanations. Rationality in magic
must be rehabilitated. It must be restored to its rightful place as the
foundation of magical development, but not its essence. Modernism has split would-be magicians into two impotent camps—

those who have rejected rationality altogether (and have become so disoriented as to be virtually insane) and those who have embraced rationality totally (and have become virtually paralyzed as magicians).

The Hermetic magicians of fourth-century Alexandria and Thebes were in a position very similar to the one in which postmodern magicians find themselves—in a maelstrom of cultural influences in a world of rapidly shifting values and mental patterns. Their response, and the response of the postmodern magicians, can be seen to have much in common.

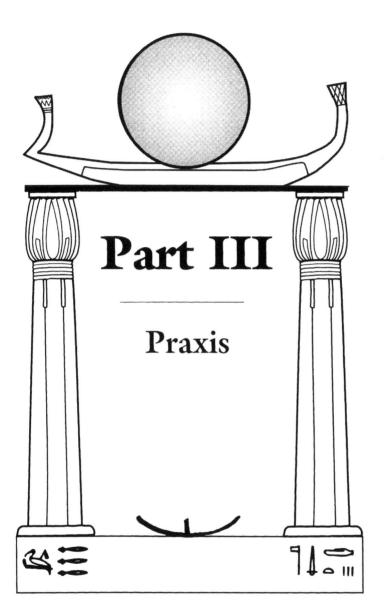

Part III

Praxis

TOOLS

There are a certain number of magical tools needed for the working of many operations of Hermetic magic. As a rule the originally highly pragmatic school of Hermetic magic is not as obsessed with elaborate paraphernalia as medieval and modern magicians. No more tools are needed than those necessary to do the work. Often items used for magical operations are ones also used for everyday purposes. This may seem unbelievable to modern magicians trained for the most part in medieval frameworks where each item must be specially consecrated for exclusively magical uses. The Hermetic tradition was more pragmatic, and should again be so today. Certain objects must be considered intrinsically sacred or holy, others are made so through magical operations, while others will merely serve a sacred or magical function for the time they are being used and return to their profane state thereafter.

Operations in this book that require special ingredients will have these listed at the beginning of each operation, but some standard items used in the frame rituals and in many of the operations themselves are presented here for the sake of clarity.

1. Altar

For a majority of operations the altar acts as a place to focus attention at the beginning of the working. Occasionally it will be directly involved in the mechanics of the operation, but usually it, along with the circle, robe, and other peripheral items, is part of the sacralized context which is necessary to construct before the holy work of Hermetic magic can continue. The altar itself may be elaborate or simple, large or small. Most will find it beneficial to have a small, portable altar, as often operations may be carried out in remote locations. The simplest kind of altar, and a traditional element in many altar de-

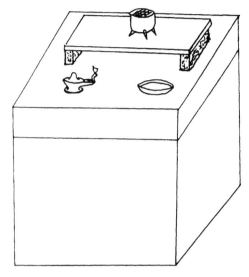

Figure 12. Postmodern Hermetic Altar.

signs, consists of two bricks spanned by a thin board upon which offerings can be placed.

In principle the altar is a table for the placement of offerings and objects used to focus the magician's attention during the operation. It should be large enough that it can hold a brazier, lamp and bowl, although all of these items do not have to be present for all workings.

A typical working altar of a postmodern Hermetic magician appears in figure 12.

2. Circle

The circle is an important element in the construction of sacred space in Hermetic magic. It continued to be important in the medieval tradition, where its principal function seems to have been protection. To a limited extent this is also true of the ancient Hermetic magical cir-

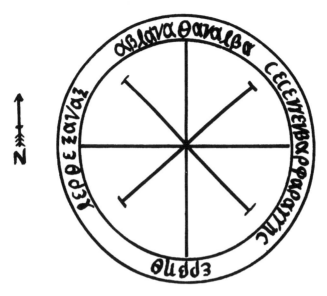

Figure 13.   Inscribed Magic Circle.

cle. "Encircling" a space was so essential in the performance of magic in ancient Egypt that the concept became synonymous with "working magic." Obviously the concept here implies a great deal more than mere "protection." The act of encircling the place of working (usually by pouring a solution of natron in a continuous circle around the area) first *purified* the area. In this purified state the area is made ready for the infusing of sacred meaning and power. As a side benefit it is protected from detrimental entities or forces.

In later times the magic circle became more elaborate with inscriptions of holy names of power, and so on. Certainly nothing prevents the postmodern Hermetic from using this somewhat later medieval practice, especially in those places where a permanent working environment has been established.

An illustration of a magical circle of this kind, inscribed with the Greek forms of the names used in the opening formula outlined in the section called "Ritual Structure," is shown in figure 13.

3. Robe

Often it seems in the pragmatic Hermetic tradition special garments are not necessary. However, we sometimes hear of the necessity of donning a new white garment or robe, especially after an initiatory experience. Also, it has been found to be generally beneficial to the workings of magic for the magician to put on some special garment for the performance of magical workings. This is basically a ritual act which separates the magicians workaday life from magical life and work. It is therefore advisable from a practical perspective for the Hermetic magician to design and wear a special garment for magical activity. The garment should, to be traditional, be a pure white. This color stresses the necessity for "ritual purity." Those following the Typhonian tradition would wear robes of dark color—red or black.

4. Black (Isis) Eye Band

Originally the black Isis eye band was made from a strip of black cloth taken from the material used to drape a sacred statue of Isis in an Egyptian temple. Today, as there are no such temples in existence, it is sufficient to use a strip of black cloth consecrated to the goddess Isis. The function of the black eye band, which is tied as a blindfold around the magician's head, is simply to deprive the magician of the sense of sight for a specified period. This early recognition of the power of sensory deprivation in magic is interesting in its own right, and provides an avenue for further pragmatic experimentation.

5. Tripod

The tripod is a brazier affixed to three long legs in such a way that the brazier is brought up to about chest level. This is for making certain offerings of incense in areas of the working space other than the altar. The tripod is only occasionally found in specific workings in the Hermetic corpus of operations, but was a part of the magician's set of tools from even more ancient times in the eastern Mediterranean region.

6. Lamp

The magical lamp is simply an oil-burning lamp with a wick used in more archaic times to illuminate an area for work at night.

Lamps have long exercised a degree of fascination in magical traditions of the East. Everyone remembers the "magic lamp" of Aladdin in the *Tales of Sheherazade* or the *Thousand and One Nights*. In the Hermetic tradition the lamp is actively used for divinatory purposes, although it may be used for general illumination as well. Sometimes the old papyrus texts say that the lamp should be one the magician uses for ordinary purposes. It is also often noted that the lamp should "not be painted red." Apparently this refers to the practice of treating brass lamps with red ochre, which caused them to have a red color. But as red is the liturgical color of Set-Typhôn, often a divine force to be avoided by magicians of antiquity, the prohibition against using red lamps was a way of banishing Typhonian influence in the working. This particular aspect seems clearly drawn from the Egyptian root of practical Hermeticism.

An example of a typical lamp used for magical purposes is shown in figure 14.

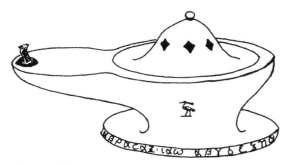

Figure 14.   Magical Lamp.

7. Bowl

For some acts of divination a bowl or saucer is used. This vessel is usually filled with a mixture of water and olive oil, or in some cases with ink. In operation number 20 in this collection (*PGM* IV 3209–3254) a white bowl inscribed with magical formulas is specified, but more often a brass bowl or vessel is mentioned. Pragmatically, an experimental attitude can be taken toward some of these material requirements. The most important thing is that you have a bowl of shallow liquid that forms a semi-reflective surface, and that you are able to position this vessel in such a way that you can look into it at the right time during the working.

8. Brazier

The brazier needs to be made of metal in which a fire can be ignited and items can be burned. It is usually either brass or some kind of earthenware. Some operations call for a specific kind of brazier. The most usual sort would be made of brass. It does not need to be any more than about four inches across.

9. Stylus

A stylus is a sharp instrument used to inscribe hard objects such as pots, shells, stones, or bones with magical formulas. The sharper this object is, the better. In original versions of the operations found in this book, the stylus is often identified as being made of either brass or copper. If you can not obtain one in these metals, one made of steel (or iron) may be substituted. The important thing here is to have a tool that you can reliably use to inscribe fairly small characters on hard surfaces.

The design of a typical stylus is shown in figure 15.

Figure 15. Design of the Stylus.

10. Papyrus

Papyrus is the oldest known type of paper. It is made from the plant of the same name which is native to the banks of the Nile river. Papyrus is available through importers throughout the world and was quite popular as a medium for Egyptian style paintings which were somewhat faddish in the 1980s.

To write on the papyrus it is best to use black India ink when special sacred inks are not called for. The pen used should be a medium nibbed calligraphy pen. The characters written on the papyrus should be made with quick light strokes of the pen, as the papyrus may often tend to absorb too much of the ink. One way to minimize this tendency was once used by all scribes in ancient Egypt. They would spend some time with a metal burnisher rubbing the surface of the papyrus to make its fibers more compact and less absorbent.

From a sacred perspective, the papyrus has a certain "time traveling" effect. Working with this substance, identical to that used by the original Nilotic Hermetics has its intrinsic value. Æsthetically it is quite pleasing. Also, it has been found to be an effective substitute for other writing surfaces for magical formulas. Papyrus, as rare as it might seem, is more available and easier to use than the "hide of a black ass." Information on how to obtain genuine papyrus can be received from Runa-Raven, P.O. Box 557, Smithville, TX 78957.

Consecration of Tools and Phylacteries

Many objects or tools used in magical operations should be consecrated and dedicated to the performance of magical acts. This is especially true if you feel this to be a vital and necessary part of magical symbolism, or if your primary focus of working magic will be personal development or actual initiation.

A simple ritual should be devised for the consecration of such tools. The next chapter deals with the establishment of frame rituals used to formally begin and end a ceremony. These should be studied and practiced in their own right. They can act as fine initial exercises in the art and practice of Hermetic ritual.

Any object or tool that you wish to consecrate should be laid on the altar. If you are consecrating the altar itself, have nothing on it. After performing the opening ceremony with an invocation to a group of gods and/or goddesses which you feel represent your personal pantheon, lay your hands on the object and say, "I, who am the holy one standing for Thoth-Hermês, do now consecrate this object, [name the object], to the service of holy mageia. It is now set apart from other profane things, and has power over them, as the Aiôns, the Heavens, and the great elements rule over things of the Earth!" When saying these words, concentrate on the sense of separation between this object and physical objects of the terrestrial sphere. See it, and feel it, being filled with holy *dynamis*. Close the ritual of consecration in the usual way shown in the section on "Ritual Structure."

In principle the consecration of protective amulets, called phylacteries in the ancient tradition, is done in the same way as any other object. Some more complex rituals for this purpose are presented in the operational section (numbers 4–6), but if you feel the need for a provisional protective amulet, a simple one can be devised by drawing a pentagram (or hexagram) on a piece of papyrus, placing it in a leather pouch, and performing a rite of consecration over it. The words used to consecrate it could be something like:

I, who am the holy one standing for Thoth-Hermês, do now consecrate this phylactery to the service of protecting my soul, my heart, and the power in my belly in all places and at all times. Nothing can harm me while I wear this protective shield which protects me as the shield of Pallas Athêna did protect Perseus against all things evil and vile.

It should be noted that the word phylactery comes from the Greek φυλακτηριον, where it originally meant a guarded post in a castle and was also used to indicate protective amulets. In Hellenistic times the Jews took up the practice of putting on such protective amulets when they prayed. These were made with biblical verses inscribed on parchment and bound to various parts of the body and are still used today by Orthodox Jews. The Hebrew word for this is *tefflin* [t'viln].

RITUAL STRUCTURE

There are certain aspects of the structure of magical rituals that seem almost universal, while others are particular to certain historical cultures. Because the Hermetic tradition is so eclectic, often rituals draw from various cultural spheres for differing rites, and even within a given ritual, structural elements from different traditions will be manifest.

An almost universal basic structure for a magical ritual involves an opening sequence, which prepares the elements of the operation—the magician, the site, and any tools—to undertake the working itself. Then there is the working, which may be as simple as a prayer and petition to a divinity, or so elaborate that it requires several days to complete. The operation will then generally be concluded with a standard closing formula.

The opening functions as a preparatory phase in which the magician engages a magical frame of mind. It is important for all magicians to be able to evoke this mental state. This is one of the beneficial functions of religious kinds of workings which are really only intended to create this sense of engagement with the numinous world.

Workings themselves may have a variety of internal structures. One is the prayer and petition. A divinity is called upon, and then the magician speaks directly to the entity, petitioning that the desire of the magician will be fulfilled. An alternate approach to this is seen when magicians actually "attach themselves" to a god—often Hêlios—and then act in the persona or identity of that god. In the latter case the operation to make the divine linkage may be the most complex part of the overall working.

Often the workings seem to presuppose the divine character of the magician. Those workings in which the words of the magician are to function on a causal level are examples of these. Once a *magos* has established a divine presence of self, that *magos* may, if the right *knowledge* is present, virtually "speak events into existence" with the divine formulas known technically as *voces magicae* in the scholarly literature. Quite often we see the pattern where the magician first writes or inscribes the formula on an object, then speaks it or another oral formula over the inscribed object to activate the formula objectified in the inscription.

One of the functions of the closing ritual is to put an "official" end to the working. This concentrates the magical will in a definite space and time. The main operative benefit of this is that the *dynamis* of the magician can be freed from the limitations placed on it by mental constraints—such as anxiety over the success of the rite, or desire for the result. Once the working is done it is already successful.

Frame Rituals

In the operational part of this book most of the instructions indicate that the magician should perform some version of an opening purification rite to begin an operation and some closing rite to conclude it. Such opening and closing operations have always been customary, yet are rarely, if ever given in the old papyri. Often magicians develop their own versions of such operations, or have been taught versions of this type of ritual through some tradition. The following operations have been gleaned from references to these kinds of workings made in the papyri themselves. Either full or abbreviated forms of such operations should be performed before beginning any general operation and at its conclusion. Such operations frame the greater working, setting apart, and thus sanctifying, the time and space in which it is carried out

The whole idea of "purification" is one that many modernists, and some postmodernists, have problems understanding. Often "purification" is just another way of saying "concentration of essence." When a person or area is "purified" it is dedicated to a single, pure, and simple purpose—that of the working. This involves two things. The exclusion of things detrimental to the concentrated purpose and the concentration of essence on the purpose of the operation. This is how *purification* is best considered. Even the often repeated injunctions to abstain from sexual activity for a period of days is hardly a moral judgment on sexuality—which is made clear by the fact that it most often appears as a prerequisite in operations for attracting lovers! Rather, the injunction is meant either to cause a build-up of sexual energy for the operation itself, or to make magicians more attractive to the goddesses or gods they may be trying to attract for the operation.

Opening Operation of Purification

1. *Purifying:* The magician should be purified for working in some way. This may be done through fasting for several hours before the working, or by abstaining from sexual activity for a specified time (24 hours being one standard), or by bathing in cold water (below about 40° Fahrenheit). Pragmatically any kind of ritual or procedure that makes you feel concentrated in purpose and open to the forces you intend to call upon in the working will be effective.

2. *Dressing:* Historically the usual dress for Hermetic magicians was a white robe or garment. This was the traditional color worn by both Egyptian and Greek priests and symbolizes ritual purity. Therefore the robe is a sign of the purified condition of the magician. The characteristics of this garment have already been discussed on page 148.

3. *Encircling:* The area where the operation is to take place should be set apart by putting a circle around it. Traditionally the circle was made by sprinkling a fine solution of natron (see Appendix A) around the perimeter of the area. Of course, a regular area of working can be set apart with a permanent circle drawn on the floor or made on the ground with either chalk or, better yet, a dry natron powder.

4. *Ritual of the Heptagram:* This is an invocation to the powers of the seven vocalic elements. Face east and stretch out both your right and left hands to your left side and intone the sound "A." Now turn to the north, and putting forward only your right fist, make the sound "E." Then turn to the west and extend both hands in front of

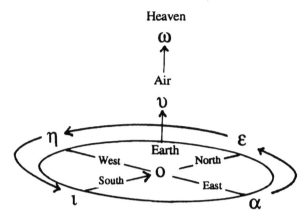

Figure 16. Spatial Model of the Ritual of the Heptagram.

you, and intone "Ê." Now turn to the south and lay both hands
across your stomach, and make the sound "I." To the earth, bend
over and touch your toes and intone the sound "O." Then look into
the air and place your right hand on your heart and intone "Y."
Now look into the sky, and with both hands on your head, make the
sound "Ô."[1] (See figure 16.)

[The following items 5 and 6 are optional. That is, if the rite you are
performing already contains an invocation or a sacrificial component, you do not need to do these twice, or in ways which might
conflict with one another. But if the operations in question are given
in only a basic form, an invocation and offering may prove to be
beneficial.]

5. *Invocation:* To invoke general magical powers, return to the east
and visualize a winged serpent rising over the horizon, and say the

---

[1]This instruction for the Heptagram ritual is based on *PGM* XIII.824–841. There
it is called the Heptagram, although no two dimensional representation of a seven
pointed figure appears. The true and real Heptagram is present in extradimensional
space. Sounds are to be pronounced for several seconds with qualities as indicated in
Appendix F.

name "ERBÊTH," then you turn to the north, visualize an infant child sitting on a lotus blossom, and say "**SESENGENBARPHA-RANGÊS.**" Now turn to the west and visualize a crocodile emerging from the waters, his tail in the shape of a serpent, and say "**ABLANATHANALBA.**" Then turn to the south and visualize a falcon with its wings outstretched, and say, "**LERTHEXANAX.**" Finally, visualize yourself enveloped in a cool flame, as the phoenix rises from your feet to your head you have become the magician able to perform all the magic you are capable of performing.[2]

Now deliver an invocation to the god or goddess most suitable to the operation you are performing. This should come from your heart. If no such god or goddess is apparent to you, deliver a general invocation of the kind given in the practical section of the text, or one to Hermês-Thoth, Hêlios-Phre, ABRASAX (or ABRAXAS) [= 365] who is also known to some as MEITHRAS or, for those who know it, to the great name, the number of which is 9,999. ABRASAX is the god of the microcosm, of the year and cyclical nature, while the Great Name is the god of Eternity itself.

6. *Offering.* The best form of offering is made by burning incense of frankincense and myrrh. Burn the offering in the brazier while saying:

To thee [name the divinity] I make this offering that thou wilt open thy ears to me and hear these, my holy words.

After you feel that a firm sense of connection with the elements of the Cosmos and the divinity you wish to invoke have been established, proceed on to the central working phase of the operation.

Closing Operation | To close any operation after the completion of the working phase, a customary ritual should be developed by every magician. It is important to signal the end of the working so that the mag-

---

[2]This arrangement of divine figures in an invocation for magical power is based on formulas contained in *PGM* II.104ff., III.153ff., XII.87ff., and on many amuletic gemstones.

ical effects which you have set into motion can begin to work independently of your own concentrated will. In order to have this happen you must give all forces gathered for the working leave to depart and you must break the encircling surrounding the place of operation. These ends are most easily reached by uttering a verbal formula, such as:

Depart now, Master of the World, Forefather, return to thine own thrones, and to thine own vaults and chambers, that the order of the universe be maintained. Keep me from harm. *Hêlios hemin, kyrie!* **(Be gracious to us, lord!)**[3]

Then simply step outside the area purified and sanctified for the working and put the events of the operation out of your mind.

---

[3] The closing formula is inspired by dismissals found in *PGM* IV.3120–3124 and V.41–52.

SELF-INITIATION

Postmodern Hermetics will, for the most part, be forced to take a path of pure self-initiation. This is because there are no true Hermetic *schools*—those with actual Hermetic qualities no longer use the designation "Hermetic." There are individual teachers who are capable of aiding other individuals in Hermetic initiation, but most of their identities remain hidden. Therefore, the best advice is to proceed with work on the self and wait for possible doors to open based on the success of your inner level work. In any event the true *initiator* is not any teacher you might find, but rather your own indwelling daimôn or genius—the pinnacle of your own soul. All any teacher can do is point you in the right direction, and keep pointing you there.

True teachers in the tradition of Abaris will be able to tell you the meaning of the formula: ΜΗΘΩΠΙΞΚΕΝ ΚΑΒΑΗ ΚΑΒΙΜ ΛΟΡΣΕΠΗΙΟ (MÊTHÔPIXKEN KABAÊ KABIM LORSEPÊIO), and will be able to tell you how the formula relates to the Hyperborean tradition of Hermeticism.

Hermetic initiation is not a matter of undergoing a set of pre-programmed external rituals or ceremonies. Rather it is a progression of true "rites of passage" from one state of understanding, or state of being, to another. It has been noted that to understand something at a certain level, one must *be* on that level. One arrives at that level of being through a combination of knowledge and experience. Experience must be gained both interiorly (in the realm of the psychê) and exteriorly (in the physical universe).

True initiation is not the kind of thing a member of the elect might choose to do in the same way one might choose to go to the movies on Saturday night. It is not simply a matter of desire, but of Necessity. The Necessity for initiation is governed by the Goddess Anankê. She determines that the initiate simply *must* seek *gnôsis* and *dynamis*. It is a matter of pure survival for one who is truly elect.

Initiation is not something that happens in a single ritual. It is the cumulative effect of conscious and willed life experience, and moments in which understanding of that experience are assimilated. Moments of initiation will come at the oddest moments to those who are open to them and ready to receive them. The ancient Hermetic word for such a moment was *kairos.* The old Hermetics knew well that true initiation could come when reading a text of philosophy as easily (or perhaps more so) than when involved in a complicated ritual. Rituals tend to be able to formalize changes that have already taken place, or set such changes into motion in a dramatic way. Rarely is true initiation coincidental with ceremonial activity.

For the Hermetic, eventually all of life becomes a great working of *mageia.* The more advanced the initiate, the more this is true. The more advanced the initiate, the more likely the initiatory stimulus will come in the form of what appear to the profane to be mundane events. This is why the most advanced initiates never seem to *do* magic. This is because they have *become magic.* For the beginner or even intermediate Hermetic magician the greatest danger, however, lies in the tendency to stop doing intense magical work before the process is complete (usually in order to lay claim to some "advanced" status in a group). This is perhaps one reason that the Hermetic school eschews degrees and formal recognitions of levels of initiation. Those who possess the Secret *know* it, and to them it is unimportant whether the world acknowledges it or not. Others with *knowledge* will recognize them immediately.

But Hermetic initiation is aided, if not actually *effected,* by operations of practical magic. The first three operations in the last part of this book are directed toward initiatory experience—toward the realization of some transformed state of being. This can be done in terms of a pure transformation or empowerment (through a growth in, or acquisition of *dynamis*) or through the acquisition of an "auxiliary spirit," a *genius* or daimôn—a *paredros,* as it is known technically in the old tradition. The act of coagulating your present spirit with that of the *paredros* would obviously be one of profound self-transformation.

Although it is traditional for the initiatory rites to appear at the beginning of the old papyri, and we continued that tradition here by placing them first in the collection of operations, this does not mean that they are to be performed first. They are usually the most difficult operations in the book. Work in the papyrus non-linearly. Undertake workings as you *need* them. At some point there will be a clear indication to you that it is time to attempt one of the initiatory rites. After you have successfully performed an initiatory rite, you will find it much easier to be successful with all sorts of magical rites. You will also more readily be able to make changes and innovations in the operations—as you move toward creating your own magical book or record.

The preliminary rite of self-initiation should be undertaken alone. It should not be done before you are thoroughly familiar with the frame rituals and have studied the Hermetic philosophy for at least one month.

Preliminary Rite of Self-Initiation

1. *Purify yourself.* Bathe or shower in cold water (below about 40 degrees Fahrenheit). Concentrate on all impurities being withdrawn from your being and drained away with the water.

2. *Dress yourself.* Put on a new white robe or other loose-fitting garment.

3. *Encircle the area of working.* Sprinkle the area with a natron solution.

4. *Perform the Ritual of the Heptagram of the seven vowel sounds* (as indicated in the Opening Operation of Purification on p. 155).

5. *Invoke general magical powers* by means of the names ERBÊTH, SESENGENBARPHARAGGÊS, ABLANATHANALBA and LERTHEXANAX. Visualize yourself enveloped in a cool flame. As the phoenix rises from your feet to your head, you have become the magician able to perform all the magic you are capable of performing.

Now deliver an invocation to the god or goddess most relevant to your present state of initiation. This should come from your heart, and be a "sacrifice in the form of words."

6. *Offer frankincense and myrrh* in the brazier, while saying:

To thee [name the divinity] I make this offering that thou wilt open thy mouth to me that I may hear thy holy words.

7. *Listen in your heart* for the words of the god in silence. Once you have heard the word of the god or goddess, express your thanks for that word and also express your need for further initiation. All such expressions are to be made interiorly within your heart.

8. *Close the rite* by giving the invoked divinity leave to depart with the words:

Depart now, [name divinity], return to thine own throne, and to thine own vault and chamber that the order of the universe be maintained. Keep me from harm, and hear me always. *Hêlios moi, kyrie!* ("Be gracious to me, lord!")

9. *Step outside the area* purified and sanctified for the working and put the events of the operation out of your mind.

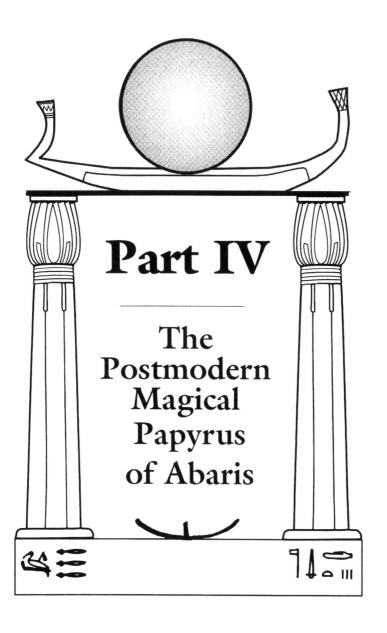

Part IV

The
Postmodern
Magical
Papyrus
of Abaris

INTRODUCTION
TO THE OPERATIONS

The texts of the magical operations you will read here are closely based on original ancient papyri. The exact papyrological source text is noted at the head of each operation along with an approximate date for the original papyrus. What you see here are not, however, intended as *translations* of the original texts. They have been rewritten and revised for clarity, and sometimes notes of explanation are added to reduce the possibilities of misunderstanding. Anyone who wishes to read straightforward translations of the texts in question can find all of them in *The Greek Magical Papyri in Translation* edited by Hans Dieter Betz.[1]

These operations remain true to the original intent of each source text. Operations were intentionally chosen that would be workable in today's social and cultural environment. It should also be pointed out that in ancient times these practical operations were part of a vast philosophical and cultural matrix. That context is the subject of the first half of this book. The theoretical and cultural matrix is important not only to the understanding of the ancient world in which these formulas have their roots, but is also fundamental for those interested in experimenting with the "modernizing" of the formulas. If the basic *principles* are understood, it becomes possible to modify in a meaningful fashion formulas based on those principles.

If the instruction tells the magician to inscribe a formula on a jar used for smoked *fish* (as in Operation number 47 on p. 243), and we realize that fish were tabu for Egyptians due to their correspondence to the Egyptian god of discord and rebellion, Set-Typhôn, then we understand that we can either use such a vessel and be traditional or we can substitute another container for other tabu substances (either as determined by your own culture or by personal [dis-]taste).

[1]Hans Dieter Betz, ed., *The Greek Magical Papyri in Translation* (Chicago: University of Chicago Press, 1986).

Examples of instances where this type of substitution would be possible are endless. Doing this kind of work with the formulas must be considered experimental, and at the same time it presupposes an advanced understanding of the original Helleno-Egyptian culture of the first few centuries of the common era.

The actual working of the operations contained in the Post-Modern Papyrus of Abaris are essential to the underlying purpose of the book. That purpose is the *experience* of inner and outer states of awareness particular to a certain time and place in the history of the human psyche. Knowledge must be made experiential before the being and understanding of the individual can be raised. This elevation of being and understanding is the essence of true μαγεια.

INITIATIONS

Often the more lengthy of the various magical papyri, the ones that are virtual manuals of magical practice, begin with a rite designed to help the recipient of the book to get an "assistant," that is an auxiliary divine, or semi-divine (daimônic) spirit which would facilitate the operator's magical will much more efficiently than the magician could ever do alone. The "assistant" was called a παραδρος in Greek. Such auxiliary spirits were *permanently* attached to the magician after certain rites were performed, not just for the duration of the operation, but for life. In such an instance, the magician is thought to gain a certain kind of union with that entity—to become a "son" of that god or daimôn. The essence of the magician and that of the entity have become, or are becoming, one. This is why the magician can himself be worshiped as god or daimôn. It is this type of magician that Jesus was, and which Simon the μαγος became after him.

Although these operations are presented first in this collection, they should only be undertaken after a great deal of experience has been gained in the other types of (goetic) operations. True success in an operation of initiatory μαγεια makes all other operations of γοητεια superfluous.

1. The Operation of Pnouthis the Sacred Scribe
(*PGM* I.42–195, ca. 400 c.e.)

This operation for obtaining an auxiliary spirit with which the magician can perform direct acts of will is found in the form of a letter from a master magician named Pnouthis to an advanced student named Keryx. Pnouthis characterizes himself as "one who knows." He prescribes this operation for acquiring an assistant to Keryx to prevent his failing as he undertakes the other rites contained in the papyrus book (*PGM* I) attached to it.

Pnouthis' operation is complex and requires several days to perform. Besides the standard tools, the following are needed for the completion of the entire rite: a staff carved with a falcon's head, a black Isis band (blindfold), uncut frankincense, rose oil, a tripod, an earthen censer with ashes from the plant heliotrope, myrrh troglitis, a branch of myrtle, wine, and festive foods.

The original papyrus version of this working says of the entity to be invoked that it is a god, and an aerial spirit—in fact "the only lord of the air." The papyrus further tells us that if a command is given to the god he will perform the task at once: He can send dreams, bring women or men without having to use magical material substances, he can kill or destroy anything and can stir up winds from the earth. He can acquire for you gold, silver, bronze and give them to you whenever the need arises. He can free you from bonds if you are "chained in prison," he can open any door, and even cause invisibility. He can provide fire and water as well as food of any kind. (Here the original text adds that he will not provide fish or pork.[2]) But outside of these limitations the Paredros is capable of fulfilling anything the magician wills, whether it is for protection or for the provision of material or spiritual gifts—"for without him nothing happens."

The recipient of the rite is exhorted not to share this great mystery with anyone else, but rather to conceal it, as the recipient has been thought of as worthy by the lord god.

---

[2]This is because both the fish and the pig were thought to be manifestations of Set-Typhôn by the Osirian Egyptians.

The Rite for Obtaining a *Paredros*

1. You should abstain from animal food and from all forms of un-cleanliness, as you have determined them, for 24 hours prior to the beginning of your operation.

2. Just before sunset, on any night you wish, perform a version of your rite for preliminary purification.

3. Clothe yourself in a pure white robe or other garment which has never before been worn.

4. Go up onto a roof, tower, or other high place where you have your altar set up. The place should overlook the roofs of a town or a broad landscape. Take with you the falcon staff, the black Isis band, frankincense, a brazier, rose oil, an earthen censer, ashes from the plant heliotrope, and an oblong stone.

5. As the sun's orb is disappearing say this formula seven times seven to Hêlios as an adjuration of the assistant:

ÔRI PITETMI AMOUNTE AINTHYPH PICHAROUR RAIAL KARPHIOUTH YMOU ROTHIRBAN OCHANAU MOUN-AICHANAPTA ZÔ ZÔN TAZÔTAZÔ PTAZÔ MAUIAS SOUÔRI SOUÔ ÔOUS SARAPTOUMI SARACHTHI AYÔI RICHAMCHÔ BIRATHAU ÔPHAU PHAUÔ DAUA AUANTÔ ZOUZÔ ARROUZÔ ZÔTOUAR THÔMNAÔRI AYÔI PTAUCHARÊBI AÔUOSÔBIAU PTBAIN AAAAAAA AEÊIOYÔYÔOIÊEA CHACHACH CHACHACH CHAR-CHARACHACH AMOUN Ô EI IAEÔBAPHREN-EMOUNOTHILARIKRIPHIAEYEAIPHIRKIRALITHON OMENERPHABÔEAI CHATHACH PHNESCHÊR PHICHRÔ PHNYRÔ PHÔCHÔCHOCH IARBATHA GRAMMÊ PHIBAÔCHNEMEÔ.

6. Once this adjuration is complete, put a black Isis band on your eyes, and in your right hand grasp your falcon's head staff and hold an all-night vigil, remaining in darkness, but fully awake the entire night.

7. When the sun rises, remove the black Isis band and greet the sun by shaking the falcon staff and reciting the sacred formula above as you make a sacrifice by burning uncut frankincense in your brazier and by pouring rose oil in an earthen censer on ashes from the plant heliotrope. As your are reciting the formula visualize a falcon flying down and spreading its wings out in front of you as it flaps its wings in midair. Visualize it in front of you and that, after flapping its wings in mid-air, it drops an oblong stone at your feet and immediately takes flight, ascending back to heaven.

8. Pick up the stone, which you will now turn into an amulet, and carve the inscription: ACHA ACHACHA CHACH CHARCHARA CHACH on the back side of the stone at the bottom so that it will be concealed when you wear it.

9. Come down from your high place during the day and spend your time engraving an image of Helioros[3] as a lion-faced figure, holding in the left hand a celestial globe and in his right hand a whip. Around him in a circle engrave a serpent biting its tail—the Ouroboros. Once you have engraved the stone, bore a hole in it, and run a black leather thong (or Anubian string) through it and wear it around your neck during subsequent operations.

10. Prepare a room below your high place in a fitting manner by providing all types of food and wine[4] to offer the god. Also prepare a suitable shrine on an altar in your room where the god can rest when he is with you.

11. Just before the sun goes down, go back up to your high place and, facing the light of the moon goddess Selênê, address this hymn to her as you again sacrifice myrrh troglitis in the censer. As you light the fire, hold a branch of myrtle and shake it, as you salute the goddess:

INOUTHÔ PTOUAUMI ANCHARICH CHARAPTOUMI ANOCHA ABITHROU ACHARABAUBAU BARATHIAN

---

[3]This is a combination of the names Hêlios and Horus.
[4]The original specifies "Mendesian wine," which is a wine from the city of Mendes in the Nile delta.

ATEB DOUANANOU APTYR PANOR PAURACH SOUMI
PHORBA PHORIPHORBARABAUÔÊTH AZA PHOR RIM
MIRPHAR ZAURA PTAUZOU CHÔTHARPARACHTHIZOU
ZAITH ATIAU IBAU KANTANTOUMI BATHARA CHTHIBI
ANOCH.

12. Now visualize a blazing star gradually freeing itself from
heaven coming down from the sky and hovering before you. Watch
as the light of the star dissipates before your eyes. As this happens
you will behold the god you summoned and who has been sent to
you.

13. Approach the god and visualize yourself taking him by the right
hand. Kiss him and speak this formula to the angel:

ÔPTAUMI NAPHTHAUBI MAIOUTHMOU MÊTROBAL
RACHÊPTOUMI AMMÔCHARI AUTHEI APHANTO
TAMARA CHIÔBITAM TRIBÔMIS ARACHO ISARI RACHI
IAKOUBI TAURABERÔMI ANTABI TAUBI.

14. When you have spoken this, he will acknowledge your formula.
But you say to him:

What is your divine name? Reveal it to me freely, so that I may call
upon it. (It will consist of 15 Greek letters: SOUESOLYR PHTHÊ
MÔTH.)

Adjure him with this oath so that he will speak and will obey your
commands in every respect.

15. Next address the god and say: Come to me, King, I call thee
god of gods, mighty, limitless, undefiled, beyond description,
strongly established Aiôn. From this day forth art thou inseparable
from me through the entire time of my life. SOUESOLYR
PHTHÊ MÔTH.

16. Once he has definitely accepted your oath to obey you and be
inseparable from you, again take him by the hand and bring him into
your living quarters or a room below the high place where you called
upon him. Have the god assume his place in the shrine you have prepared for him. Set the food and wine before him. (The original pa-

pyrus version says that an "uncorrupted boy" should serve the food and drinks and that he should maintain silence until the angel departs.)

17. Address these words to the god: **I shall have thou as a friendly assistant, a beneficent god who serves me whenever I say: "Quickly, by thy power now appear on earth to me, yea verily, god!"**[5]

18. While in a relaxed position before the god you should speak freely about any purpose you have. Test the power of your oath however you wish.

19. After three hours have passed, the god will immediately ascend to leave. "Open the door" for him and make his way clear to return to heaven by saying:

Go, lord, blessed god, where thou livest eternally, as is thy will.[6]

After saying this the god will vanish.

20. After he has returned to heaven, eat the remainder of the food and wine as a sacrifice to him, and you will surely become a friend of the mighty angel.

21. Whenever it is your will to undertake some working, just speak his name into the air and say: **Come!** You will see him at once standing near you. Then tell him: **Perform this task**, and tell him what it is you want done and he will do it at once. After doing so he will say: "What else do you want? For I am eager to return to heaven."

22. If you have no immediate orders, tell him: **Go, lord**, and he will depart. Working in this way the god will be seen only by you, and no one will be able to hear him speaking to you.[7]

---

[5]The original Greek for this formula would be: Ταχος, τη ση δυναμει ηδη εγγαιος, ναι ναι, φαινη μοι, θεη!
[6]The original Greek for this formula would be: ᾽χωρει, κυριε, θεη μακαρ, ᾽οπου διενεκως συ εις, ως βουλει!
[7]The original papyrus adds the note that "the address to the sun requires nothing except the formula IAEÔBAPHRENEMOUN and the formula IARBATHA."

The original papyrus concludes by telling us what the god or angel will be able to do for the magician:

Whenever you go anywhere, he will go with you; if you become impoverished, he will give you money. He will foretell things to you—and will even be able to tell you the date and at what time of the night or day things will happen. If someone asks you: "What am I thinking about?" or "What has happened to me in the past?" or even "What is going to happen to me in the future?"—just ask your angel, and he will speak to you in the silence of your mind. But you will speak to the one who is asking you the questions as if it is you yourself who is answering.

He will also give you both wild herbs and the power to cure, and you will be worshipped as a god since you have a god—as a friend.

When you die, the angel will wrap up your body as is fitting for a god. He will take your spirit and ascend with it into the air. This is because no aerial spirit, which you have become, having been joined with a mighty assistant, will go to Hades. For he has mastery over all things.

2. The Mithraic Initiation
(*PGM* IV.475–829, ca. 350 c.e.)

Another powerful initiatory working has been called "the Mithras Liturgy" in the past. In fact it may not be a document of the Mithraic religion itself, but an eclectic initiatory Hermetic working which nevertheless makes use of some genuine Mithraic material. The recent work of David Ulansey on the astrological aspects of Mithraic symbolism indicates that the idea of shifting the pole—in the form of the precession of the equinoxes—is a seminal Mithraic element in this working.

This operation contains a marked sense of urgency. The magician who performs this rite should be at the point of some great crisis in life. Magical power is often evoked out of such emergency situations in which the stress is turned to strength by the force of *Ananke*—the goddess of Necessity.

In the introduction to this rite in the old papyrus, the writer prays to Pronoia (Providence) and Psychê (Soul) for immortality and exhorts the fellow members of the cult to which he belongs to make use of certain herbs, "which the great god Hêlios-Mithras ordered to be revealed to me by his archangel," and which are mentioned later in the operation. These are apparently to be used in his funeral rites, so that he "may ascend into heaven as an inquirer and behold the universe."

Phylacteries needed for the rite require that with myrrh ink you copy the formula PSINOTHER[8] NOPSITHER THERNOPSI onto a piece of papyrus and bind it to your right wrist with a black leather thong, and copy the formula PROSTHYMERI and tie it to your left wrist with a white leather thong.

1. Perform your opening rite as usual.

2. Sacrifice frankincense to Hêlios-Mithras.

3. Now speak the invocation of this operation as follows:

First origin of my origin—AEÊIOYÔ—first beginning of my beginning— PePePe SSS PHRE—spirit of my spirit, the principal spirit in me—MMM—fire given by god to the mixture of the mixtures in me, the first of the fire in me—ÊY ÊIA EÊ—water of water the first of the water in me—ÔÔÔ AAA EEE—earthy material, the first of the earthy material in me—YÊ YÔÊ—my whole body, I, [state your name], whose mother is [state your mother's name], which was formed by a noble arm and an incorruptible right hand in a world without light and yet radiant, without soul—and yet alive with soul: YÊI AYI EYÔIE. Now if it be thy will: METERTA PHÔTH IEREZATH—commend me to immortal birth and, following that, to my underlying nature, so that, after the present distress which is vexing me so severely, I may gaze upon the immortal beginning with immortal spirit: ANCHREPHRENESOUPHIRGCH—with immortal water: ERONOUI PARAKOUNÊTH—with the most steadfast air: EIOAÊ PSENABÔTH—that I may be born again in

---

[8]PSINÔTHER is Egyptian for "the sons of god."

thought: KRAOCHRAX R OIM ENARCHOMAI—and the sacred spirit may breathe in me: NECHTHEN APOTOU NECHTHIN ARPI Ê TH—so that I may wonder at the sacred fire: KYPHE—that I may gaze upon the incomprehensible and awesome water of the dawn: NYÔ THESÔ ECHÔ OUCHIECHÔA—and the vivifying and encircling aether may hear me: ARNOMÊTHPH. For today I am about to behold with my immortal eye the immortal Aiôn and master of fiery diadems!

I, born of mortal womb, but transformed by the tremendous power and an incorruptible right hand and with immortal spirit!

I, sanctified through holy consecrations—while there subsists within me, holy, for a short time, the power of my human soul, which I will again receive after the present bitter and relentless Necessity which is pressing down upon me—

I [repeat your name], whose mother is [repeat your mother's name], according to the immutable decree of god, EYÊ YIA EÊI AÔ EIAY IYA IEÔ. Since it is impossible for me, born mortal, to rise with the golden brightness of the immortal brilliance, ÔÊY AEÔ ÊYA EÔÊ YAE ÔIAE, stand O perishable nature of mortals, and at once receive me safe and sound after the inexorable and pressing Necessity. For I am the Son: PSYCHÔN DEMOU PROCHÔ PRÔA, I am MACHARPHON MOU PRÔPSYCHÔN PRÔE.

4. Visualize the seven spheres above you inhabited by the seven elements of the vowels. Then visualize rays coming from each of them into your mouth. Now draw in breath from the rays. Inhale as deeply as you can and feel the power of the vocalic, planetary elements entering your being. Then exhale. Do this three times. Now visualize yourself rising up through the seven spheres to a great height, so that you feel yourself to be in midair. Turn all your attention away from the earth and earthly things, and direct all your attention to the heavens and their orderings and contemplate immortality. Contemplate the divine order of the skies: the reigning gods rising into heaven, and others setting in the west. Contemplate the course of visible gods as they emerge from the disk of Hêlios, the

father. Also contemplate the so-called pipe, which hangs from the disk of Hêlios. This is the origin of the "ministering wind." The original text says: "You will see the outflow of this object toward the regions westward, boundless as an east wind, if it be assigned to the regions of the east—and toward the regions eastward, boundless as a west wind, if it be assigned to the regions of the west." After you have established this vision of Hêlios, visualize the visible, planetary gods staring intently at you and rushing toward the place where you are in the heights.

5. At that moment put your right forefinger on your mouth and say:

Silence, silence, silence! Symbol of the living incorruptible god! Guard me, Silence: NECHTHEIR THANMELOU!

6. Then make a long hissing sound—SSSSS—and then a popping sound—Pe-Pe-Pe—and say:

PROPROPHEGGÊ MORIOS PROPHYR PROPHEGGÊ NEMETHIRE ARPSENTEN PITÊTMI MEÔY ENARTH PHYRKECHÔ PSYRIDARIÔ TYRE PHILBA.

7. Then you will see the gods looking upon you with favor. They will no longer be rushing toward you, but rather they will go back to their ordered planetary courses.

8. So when you see that the realms above are clear and circling, and that none of the gods or angels appears to be threatening you, you may expect to hear a great crash of thunder, which may startle you. Then say:

Silence! Silence!
I am a star,
wandering about with thee,
and shining forth out of the deep—
OXY O XERTHEUTH.

9. Right after saying these things visualize the sun's disk expanding.

10. Now make a hissing sound twice and a popping sound twice: SSSSS—SSSSS—Pe-Pe. Visualize then a host of pentagrams swirling forth from the disk and filling the air.

11. Again say: **Silence! Silence!** The disk of Hêlios will then appear to open, and you will see the fireless circle within and a set of massive fiery doors which are shut tight.

12. Close your eyes at once and recite the following prayer while your heart is inflamed with fire and spirit:

Give ear to me and listen to me, [state your name], whose mother is [state your mother's name], O lord, thou who has bound the fiery bars of the fourfold root together with thy breath:

Walker upon Fire: PENTITEROUNI,
Encloser of All: SEMESILAM,
Fire-breather: PSYRINPHEU,
Feeler of Fire: IAÔ,
Breather of Light: ÔAI,
Rejoicer in Fire: ELOURE,
Beautiful light: AZAI,
Aiôn: ACHBA,
Master of Light: PEPPER PREPEMPIPI,
Body of Fire: PHNOUÊNIOCH,
Giver of Light: AÔI,
Sower of Fire: AREI EIKITA,
Driver of Fire: GALLABALBA,
Forcer of Light: AIÔ,
Whirler of Fire: PYRICHIBOOSÊIA,
Mover of Light: SANCHERÔB,
Shaker of Thunder: IÊ ÔÊ IÔEIÔ,
Light of Glory: BEEGENÊTE,
Increaser of Light: SOUSINEPHIEN,
Maintainer of the Fire-light: SOUSINEPHI ARENBARAZEI
    MARMARENTEU,
Star-tamer: ÔIA.

Open for me PROPROPHEGGÊ EMETHEIRE MORIOMO-
TYRÊPHILBA, because of pressing and bitter inexorable Necessity, I invoke the immortal names, living and honored, which are
forever passing into mortal nature but cannot be spoken in articu-
late speech by human tongue or mortal speech or mortal sound:

ÊEÔ OÊEÔ IÔÔ OÊ ÊEÔ ÊEÔ OÊ EÔ IÔÔ OÊÊE ÔÊE ÔOÊ
IÊ ÊÔ OÔ OÊ IEÔ OÊ ÔOÊ IEÔ OÊ IEEÔ EÊ IÔ OÊ IOÊ
ÔÊÔ EOÊ ÔIÊ ÔIÊ EÔ OI III ÊOÊ ÔYÊ ÊÔOÊE EÔ ÊIA AÊA
EÊA ÊEEÊ EEÊ IEÔ ÊEÔ OÊEEOÊ ÊEÔ ÊYÔ OÊ EIÔ ÊÔ ÔÊ
ÔÊ EE OOO YIÔÊ.

13. If after saying these things you hear thundering and shaking in
the air surrounding you, and you feel agitated and excited, repeat the
prayer:

Silence! Silence!
I am a star,
wandering about with thee,
and shining forth out of the deep:
OXY O XERTHEUTH.

14. Now, open your eyes, and you will see the fiery doors within the
disk of the Sun open, and you will also see the world of the gods
within the doors. Let yourself feel the ecstatic joy and pleasure that
comes with this vision, as you feel your spirit ascending and being
drawn toward the realm of Hêlios.

15. Now stand very still and inhale deeply while visualizing divine
force entering your body as you gaze straight ahead. When you feel
ready say:

Come lord: ARCHANDARA PHÔTAZA PYRIPHÔTA
ZABYTHIX ETIMENMERO PHORATHÊN ERIÊ PROTHRI
PHORATHI.

16. When you have said this, the rays around the Sun will turn toward you—gaze into the center of them. When you have done
this, you will see a youthful god, beautiful in appearance, with

fiery hair, wearing a white tunic, a scarlet cloak, and a fiery crown.
This is Mithras.

17. At once greet him with the fire-greeting:

**Hail, O lord, Great Power, Great Might, King, Greatest of Gods,
Hêlios, the Lord of heaven and earth, God of Gods, mighty is thy
power, O lord. If it be thy will, reveal to me the supreme god, the
one who has begotten and made thee: that a human—I, [state your
name], who was born from the mortal womb of [state your mother's
name] and from the fluid of semen, and who, since being born again
from thee today, is become immortal out of myriads in this hour according to the wish of the exceedingly good god—resolve to worship
thee, and pray with all his/her human power, that thou mayest take
along with thee the horoscope of this day and hour today, which has
the name THRAPSIARI MORIROK, that he may appear and give
revelation during the favorable hours: EÔRÔ RÔRE ÔRRI
ÔRIÔR RÔR RÔI ÔR REÔRÔRI EÔR EÔRE!**

18. After you have said these things, a god will appear at the celestial
pole, and you will see him walking down toward you as if on a road.
Gaze intently upon the vision, take a deep breath and make a long
bellowing sound like a horn. Release all your breath until you are
straining your sides.

19. Then kiss the phylacteries on your wrists—first the right, then
the left—and say toward the right: "Protect me, PROSYMÊRI!"

20. After saying this you will see the mysterious doors near the
Polestar open and there will be seven virgins coming from deep within
dressed in linen garments, and they will have the faces of serpents.
They are called the Fates of Heaven, and they wield golden wands.

21. When you see them greet them in this manner:

**Hail, O seven Fates of heaven, O noble and good virgins, O sa-
cred ones and companions of MINIMIRROPHOR, O most holy
guardians of the four pillars!**

Hail to thee, the first, CHREPSENTHAÊS!
Hail to thee, the second, MENESCHEÊS!
Hail to thee, the third, MECHRAN!
Hail to thee, the fourth, ARARMACHÊS!
Hail to thee, the fifth, ECHOMMIÊ!
Hail to thee, the sixth, TICHNONDAÊS!
Hail to thee, the seventh, EROU ROMBRIÊS!

22. There also come forth from that door another seven gods, who have the faces of black bulls. They will be in linen loincloths and will be wearing seven golden diadems. They are called Pole Lords of Heaven, each of whom you must greet in the same manner, and each with his own name:

Hail, O guardians of the pivot, O sacred and brave youths, who turn at one command the revolving axis of the vault of heaven, who send out thunder and lightning and shocks of earthquakes and thunderbolts against the nations of impious people, but to me, who is pious and god-fearing, ye send health and soundness of body and acuteness of hearing and seeing, and serenity in the present good hours of this day, O my lords and powerfully ruling gods!

Hail to thee, the first, AIERÔNTHI!
Hail to thee, the second, MERCHEIMEROS!
Hail to thee, the third, ACHRICHIOUR!
Hail to thee, the fourth, MESARGILTÔ!
Hail to thee, the fifth, CHICHRÔALITHÔ!
Hail to thee, the sixth, ERMICHTHATHÔPS!
Hail to thee, the seventh, EORASICHÊ!

23. After they have taken their places in their proper order in the form of the constellation of the Bear, look into the air and visualize lightning bolts coming down, lights flashing, the earth shaking, and a god descending—a god immensely great, having a bright appearance, youthful, golden-haired, with a white tunic and a golden crown and trousers, and holding in his right hand a golden shoulder of a

young bull.[9] Visualize lightning bolts flashing from his eyes and stars flying from his body.

24. Once this visualization is complete, make a long bellowing sound, strain your stomach muscles and excite all five of your senses—bellow long until out of breath. Then kiss the phylacteries on your wrists again, and say:

MOKRIMO PHERIMA PHERERI, life of me, [state your name]: Stay! Dwell in my soul! Do not abandon me, for ENTHO PHENN THROPIOTH commands you!

25. Continue to visualize the god and again bellow as before and greet the god with these words:

Hail, O Lord, O Master of the water! Hail, O Founder of the Earth! Hail, O Ruler of the Wind! O Bright Lightning Flasher: PROPROPHEGGÊ EMETHIRI ARTENTEPI THÊTH MIMEÔ YENARÔ PHYRCHECHÔ PSÊRI DARIÔ PHRÊ PHRÊLBA! Give revelation, O lord, concerning the [paraphrase your ritual purpose]. O lord, while being born again, I am passing away, while growing and having grown, I am dying; while being born from a life-generating birth, I am passing on, released to death—as you have ordained, as you have decreed, and as you have established the Mystery. I am PHEROURA MIOURI.

26. After you have said these things, he will respond with some revelation. While he is doing this you will probably feel weak in your soul and will not be yourself when he answers you. He may speak his revelation to you in verse, and after speaking he will depart. Remain silent as the revelation is made, as you will be able to understand these matters by yourself. Perhaps at a later time you will remember the things spoken by the great god perfectly and clearly, even if the oracle consisted of many verses.

---

[9]This is a description of the god Mithras.

27. Once the revelation is complete, and the god has departed, close the rite in the usual manner.

3. The Stêlê of Jeu the Hieroglyphist or The Rite of the Headless One[10]
(*PGM* V.96–172, 350 C.E.)

This is another general initiatory rite for encountering a great god or daimôn. The Rite of the Headless (or Infinite) One is much simpler than the first two initiatory rites. It is subtle in its power at first. Note that the body of the working is a summoning—but in the course of the summoning the magician is transformed from a summoner to the entity being summoned—and ultimately to the god himself.

1. Perform a version of your usual opening rite of purification.

2. Prepare for the ritual by writing the formula: *AÔTH ABRAÔTH BASYM ISAK SABAÔTH IAÔ* on a new strip of papyrus, also draw

the magical sign ⟩ on it.

3. Face north and stretch the strip of papyrus across your forehead from one of your temples to the other and recite the six names:

AÔTH ABRAÔTH BASYM ISAK SABAÔTH IAÔ.

4. Then recite:

Subject to me all daimôns so that every daimôn, whether heavenly or aerial, or earthly or subterranean, or terrestrial or aquatic, might be obedient to me, and every enchantment and scourge which is from god.

Thus will all daimôns be obedient to you.

5. Now recite the summoning of the god:

---

[10]This is based on the rite mistranslated as the "Bornless One" during the early phase of the reception of the papyrus materials among modern occultists.

I summon thee, Headless One, who created earth and heaven, who created night and day, thou art Osoronnophris[11] whom none hath ever seen; thou art Iabas, thou art Iapos,[12] thou hast provided for discrimination between that which is just and unjust; thou hast made female and male; thou hast revealed both the seed and fruit; thou hast made humans love each other and hate each other.

I am Moses thy prophet to whom thou hast transmitted thy mysteries celebrated by Israel; thou hast revealed the moist and the dry and all nourishment; hear me!

I am the messenger of Pharaoh Osoronnophris; this is thy true name which hath been transmitted to the prophets of Israel. Hear me, ARBATHIAÔ REIBET ATHELEBERSÊTH ARA BLATHA ALBEU EBENPHCHI CHITASGOÊ IBAÔTH IAÔ! Listen to me and turn away this daimôn!

I call upon thee, awesome and invisible god, with an empty spirit, AROGOGOROBRAÔ SOCHOU MODORIÔ PHALARCHAÔ OOO. Holy Headless One, deliver him/her [state your name] from the daimôn which restraineth him/her, ROUBRIAÔ MARI ÔDAM BAABNABAÔTH ASS ADÔNAI APHNIAÔ ITHÔLÊTH ABRASAX AÊÔÔY—mighty Headless One, deliver him/her [repeat the name inserted above] from the daimôn that restraineth him/her! MABARRAIÔ IOÊL KOTHA ATHORE-BALÔ ABRAÔTH, deliver him/her [again insert the personal name] AÔTH ABRAÔTH BASYM ISAK SABAÔTH IAÔ!

He is the lord of the gods; he is the lord of the inhabited world; he is the one whom the winds fear; he is the one who made all things by the command of his voice.

Lord, King, Master, Helper, empower my soul, IEOU PYR IOU PYR IAÔT IAÊÔ IOOU ABRASAX SABRIAM OO YY EY OO YY ADÔNAIE, immediately, immediately, messenger of god AN-LALA LAI GAIA APA DIACHANNA CHORYN.

---

[11] *Osoronnophris* is a Hermetic formula representing the Egyptian phrase: *wsir wn nfr*—"Osiris the Beautiful Being."

[12] *Iabas* and *Iapos* are Samaritan versions of the name of the Hebrew god *Iaô*.

I am the headless daimôn with sight in my feet; I am the mighty one who possesseth the immortal fire; I am the truth who hateth the fact that unjust deeds are done in the world; I am the one that maketh the lightning flash and the thunder roll; I am the one whose sweat is the heavy rain which falleth upon the earth that it might be inseminated; I am the one whose mouth is utterly aflame; I am the one who begeteth and destroyeth; I am the Favor of the Aiôn; my name is a heart encircled by a serpent; come forth and follow.

5. After allowing time for the god to become manifest in your soul, close the working in your usual manner. This operation may be repeated until success is gained.

PROTECTION

Magicians may often feel themselves to be in need of protection from forces that might interfere with their magical operations or from the very forces called upon to do the magical work. This is especially true in the goetic stages of magical development. Once the stage known as *mageia* has been reached special operations for protection become virtually unnecessary. The Greek term for protective operations and the amulets which might be created to support them is φυλακ-τηριον (phylactery).

4. A Powerful Phylactery
(*PGM* VII.579–590, 300 c.e.)

This is called a body-guard against daimôns, phantasms, and against every kind of sickness and suffering. It is to be inscribed on a strip of gold, silver, or tin with a bronze stylus or written on papyrus. It is to be carried on the person of the magician. The inscription reads: KMEPIS CHPHYRIS IAEÔ IAÔ AEÊ IAÔ ÔÔ AIÔN IAEÔBAPHRENE MOUNOTHILARIKRIPHIAE Y EAIPHIRKIRALITHONYOMENERPHABÔEAI.

The magical signs to be written inside the circle made by the Serpent biting its tail—the Ouroboros—are:

$$\wedge \; \restriction \; \mathbf{\text{ⅉ}} \; \mathit{ᴄ \mathcal{9}} \; \mathbf{\text{Ƶ}} \cdot \mathbf{\text{Ƨ}} \; \mathbf{\text{ᗄ}}$$

After the magical form has been created, it is to be sanctified in the same way magical tools are sanctified and by speaking the following formula over it:

Protect my body and the entire soul of me, [insert your name].

The completed form would look like the figure below.

5. Another Phylactery
(*PGM* LXXI.1–8, 300 c.e.)

1. Perform your usual opening rite of purification.

2. Recite the following prayer:

Great god in heaven, who causes the world to revolve, the true god: IAÔ! Lord and ruler of all: ABLANATHANALBA, grant me this favor: Let me have the name of the great god in this phylactery, and protect me, whom [insert your mother's given name] bore, and whom [insert your father's given name] begot, from every evil thing!

This prayer can be used at any time.

3. Close the rite in your customary manner.

6. Another Phylactery
(*PGM* VII.317–318, 300 c.e.)

This is a protective operation to be addressed to the Moon when she is full.

1. Go to a place where the Moon can be seen.

2. Perform a version of your usual opening rite of purification.

3. Make this incantation to the Moon:

ACHTHIÔPHIPH ERESCHIGAL[13] NEBOUGOSOUALÊTH SATHÔTH SABAÔTH SABRÔTH.

4. After this add whatever you want to the incantation to make it specific to your protective purposes.

5. Close the working in your usual manner.

---

[13]Ereschigal is the Mesopotamian goddess of the underworld.

DIVINE INVOCATIONS

To the Hermetic, the gods and goddesses are understood as representing living beings, but at the same time they are archetypes, representatives of certain principles embodied in the sub-stellar realms. For this reason, the invocation of gods or goddesses into the presence or life of an individual is tantamount to drawing the influences or principles which they represent into the very essence of the individual. Changes or transformations will occur in accordance with the nature of the divinity invoked. Postmodern Hermetics should experiment with such invocations widely in order to experience their effects. Here are some ancient examples.

7. An Invocation to Apollo
(*PGM* I.262–347, 350 c.e.)

Needed for the rite: a seven-leafed sprig of laurel, a lamp, a strip of linen cloth, rose oil (or oil of spikenard), a robe of pure white, an ebony staff, an image of a wolf's head, a chair to serve as the throne of the god, a large piece of white cloth, a block of unfired potter's clay, wine, milk, honey, rainwater, and wheat flour.

Prepare yourself for the rite by refraining from all unclean things, and from eating fish, and from all sexual intercourse. This is done, as the original says, "so that you will make yourself most desired by the god."

The altar should be fitted with a lamp, a block of unfired potter's clay upon which you have laid an image of a wolf's head, and a brazier for the burnt offering. A chair should be set up north of the altar to serve as the resting place of the god when he arrives.

1. Dressed in a pure white garment, perform your customary opening rite of purification.

2. Take a seven-leafed sprig of laurel and hold it in your right hand as you summon the heavenly gods and chthonic daimôns.

Write the seven characters for deliverance on the sprig of laurel:

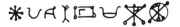

Write the first character onto the first leaf, the second one onto the second leaf and so on until the seven characters and the seven leaves match up. But be careful not to lose a leaf and in so doing run the risk of harming yourself. For this is said to be the body's greatest protective charm, and that all things are made subject to it. Seas and rocks will tremble, and malicious daimôns will avoid the powers of these characters—powers which you are about to have. This is the greatest protective charm for the rite, so there is nothing you have to fear.

3. Now write these names on a strip of linen cloth: ABERAMEN-THTHÔOULERTHEXANAXETHRENLYOÔTHEN-MARAIBAI AEMINNAEBARÔTHERRETHÔBABEANIMEA.

4. Then roll the cloth up so it can be used as a wick in your lamp, which should not be red in color. Pour either rose oil or oil of spikenard into the lamp and light it. Then set it on the image of the wolf's head resting on the block of unfired clay.

5. Cover the throne with a cloth of linen and return to your place before the altar facing the throne.

6. Sacrifice to the god by a burnt offering of storax gum, cassia, balsam gum, and other valuable spices. Also pour out a libation of wine, honey, milk, and rainwater to the north of the altar before the throne.

7. Now make seven flat cakes and seven round cakes from a mixture of wheat flour, honey, and rainwater. Lay them upon the altar.

8. Now take up the ebony staff in your left hand and the protective charm made of laurel in your right.

9. Now summon the god with this invocation:

O lord Apollo, come with Paian. Give prophecy concerning those things I desire, lord. O master leave Mount Parnassos and the Delphic Pytho whenever my priestly mouth gives voice to secret words, foremost angel of the god, great Zeus. IAÔ! I call thee MICHAÊL, who holdeth heaven's realm, I call thee, archangel GABRIÊL. Come down from Olympos, ABRASAX, who delighteth in the dawn, come with favor, who vieweth the sunset from the dawn: ADÔNAI. Father of the world, all nature trembles in fear before thee: PAKERBÊTH!

I adjure the head of God, for there is Olympos;
I adjure the seal of God, which is prophetic vision;
I adjure the right hand thou didst hold over the world;
I adjure the bowl of God which contains wealth;
I adjure the eternal God of all: AIÔN;
I adjure self-evolving nature, mighty ADÔNAIOS;
I adjure the ascending and descending ELÔAIOS;
I adjure these holy and divine names so that they may send me a divine spirit and that it may fulfill all that is in my heart and mind. Hear blessed one, I call thee who rules in Heaven and Earth and in Chaos and Hades where dwell the daimôns of men who once gazed upon the light. Send me this daimôn in response to my sacred chants, a daimôn who moveth by night by orders subject to thy force, from whose enclosure this formula is come, and let him tell me everything my mind conceives of according to absolute truth, and send him being gentle, gracious, and thoughtful, with no thoughts against me. And mayest thou not be angry at my sacred chants. But ensure that my whole body comes to light intact, for thou thyself hast arranged for these things among humankind for them to learn. I call upon thy name, in number equal to the Moirai:
ACHAIPHÔTHOTHOAIÊIAÊIA
AIÊAIÊIAOTHÔTHÔPHIACHA.

10. And when he comes, ask him whatever you wish about the art of prophecy, about divination with epic verses, about the sending of

dreams, about obtaining revelations in dreams, about interpretations of dreams, about causing disease, about everything that is a part of magical knowledge.

11. And after the inquiry, if you wish to release the god, shift the ebony staff from your left hand to your right hand; and shift the sprig of laurel from your right hand to your left hand. Then extinguish the burning lamp; and use the same burnt offerings while saying:

Be gracious to me, O primal father, O elder-born, self-generating god. I adjure the fire which first shone in the abyss; I adjure thy power which is greatest over all; I adjure him who destroyeth right down into Hades, that thou wilt depart, returning to thy ship, do me no harm, but be kind to me forever.

12. Close the working in your usual manner.

8. A General Prayer
(*PGM* XII.182–189, 350 c.e.)

1. Perform a version of your usual opening rite of purification.

2. Speak the following prayer:

Greetings, O Lord, thou who art the way to receive favor for the universe and for the world in which we dwell.

Heaven is become a place of dancing for thee: ARSENOPHRÊ, O King of the Heavenly Gods: ABLANATHANALBA, thou who possesses righteousness: AKRAMMACHAMAREI, Gracious God: SANKANATHARA, Ruler of Nature: SATRAPERKMÊPH, origin of the heavenly realm: ATHTHANNOU ATHTHANNOU ASTRAPHAI IASTRAPHAI PAKERTÔTH SABAÔTH ÊRINTASKLIOUTH ÊPHIÔ MARMARAÔTH.

Let my ability to speak not leave me. Let every soul pay attention to me, for I am PERTAÔ MÊCH CHACH MNÊCH SAKMÊPH

IAÔOYEÊ ÔÊÔ ÔÊÔ IEOYÔÊIÊIAÊA IÊÔYOEI! Grant to me that which be thy will!

3. Close the working in your usual manner.

9. Moon Prayer
(*PGM* IV.2241–2358, 350 C.E.)

To be carried out at the time of the Waning Moon. This and the next prayer formula contain numerous, often obscure, mythic formulas rooted in the Greek and Egyptian traditions. The names and references have been retained from the original formula and should be used, even if full understanding is lacking—their mysterious effects will be felt. However, the more one has learned of the references, the more powerful the prayers can become.

1. Perform a version of your usual opening rite of purification.

2. Speak the following prayer:

Hail, Holy Light, Ruler of Tartaros, who striketh with rays of light; hail Holy Beam, who whirleth up out of darkness and confuseth all things with aimless counsel. I shall call, and may thou hear my holy words—since awesome destiny is forever subject to thee. Thrice-bound goddess, set thyself free. For Klôthô will spin out her threads for thee. Assent to me, O blessed one, before I consider thee as hateful, before thou raisest thy sword-armed fists against me, and before thou becomest enraged, O god in maiden form, thou shalt [characterize your purpose in your own words].

For I know thy lights in their most refined points, and I am a mystagoge of thy beautiful services, and thy fellow witness, O Maid. Thou canst not escape what must take place. Thou must do what must be done. Thou shalt [repeat your purpose].

I now adjure thee by this mighty night,
in which thy light is last to fade away,

in which the hound openeth but closeth not, its mouth,
in which the stronghold of Tartaros is opened,
in which Kerberos rageth forth, armed with a thunderbolt.

Bestir thyself, Mênê, who needeth to nurse upon the Sun, guardian of the dead, thee I implore, hospitable, shining Maid, thee I implore, O artful, lofty, swift, O crested one, who draweth swords, courageous, Healer, foresighted, far-famed, encourager; fleet-footed, strong, blood-red, Darkness, Brimô, Immortal One, who listens to everything—Daughter of the Persian, who belongs to the flock, Alkyonê, gold-crowned, eldritch goddess, Shining, sea-goddess, ghostly and beautiful, The one who shows the way, barque-commander, aiming well, Self-generated one who wears the headband, virile, leader of the armies, O goddess of Dôdôna, of Ida, forever stricken with new sorrows, wolf-formed, denounced as infamous, destroyer, high-dwelling, whose gaze is fruitful, high-screaming, Thasian, Mênê, O nethermost one, beam-embracer, savior, world-wide, hound-shaped, Spinner of Fate, all-provider, eternally running, glorious, helper, queen, bright, far-aimer, vigorous, holy, kindly, immortal, high-voiced, thou with glossy locks, blooming, divine, with a golden face, who delights all mortals, Minoan, goddess of childbirth, Theban, long-suffering one, cunning, maleficent. Thou who hath a mane of rays, shooter of arrows, maid and savior from all terrors, I know thee well.

As Hermês the Elder, chief of all magicians, I am father of Isis. Hear me: EÔ PHORBA BRIÔ SACHMI NEBOUTO SOUALÊTH. For I have hidden this magic symbol of thine, thy sandal, and hold fast thy key. I opened the gates of Kerberos, the guardian of Tartaros, and I plunged the premature night into darkness. I turn the wheel for thee; I touch not the cymbals.

Gaze upon thyself—Behold! As thou seest thyself, thou wilt wonder at the mirror, at the beauty of Isis until thou castest the dark light from thine eyes. This thou must do, this thou must not escape. Thou shalt do this task for me: Mare, Maiden, dragoness, torch, bolt of lightning, Star, lion, she-wolf: AÊÔ ÊÊ.

A sieve, an old utensil, is my symbol, and one morsel of bread, a piece of coral, blood of a turtle dove, hoof of a camel, hair of a virgin cow, the seed of Pan, fire from the sun's rays, colt's foot, spindle tree, boy love, a bow drill, a woman's body blue-shimmering with thighs outspread, a black sphinx-ape's pierced vagina—all of these things are symbols of my power.

The bond of all Necessity will be loosened, and Hêlios will hide thy light at noon, and the Sea will overflow the world, which thou dost inhabit. Aiôn doth quake; heaven will be set in motion; Kronos, in terror at thy pole overpowered by force, hath fled to Hades as overseer of the dead below. The Moirai throw away thy thread, until now inviolate, unless thou canst stop the wingéd shaft of my magic, swiftest to reach the mark. For escape from the fate of my words is impossible: Happen it must. Do not force thyself to hear the symbols, from the beginning and then back again.

Thou shalt do whatever is needed. To prevent useless light becoming thy fate, do what I command, O Maid—ruler of Tartaros. I have bound thy pole with the chains of Kronos and with awesome compulsion I hold fast thy thumb. Tomorrow shall not come unless my will be done. To Hermês, leader of the gods, thou hast promised to lend force to this rite. I hold thee in my power. Hear, thou who watchest and who art watched. I gaze upon thee, thou gazest upon me. Then I shall also speak the sign to thee:
Bronze sandal of her who ruleth Tartaros, her fillet, key, wand, iron wheel, black dog, her thrice-locked door, her burning hearth, her shadow, depth, fire, the governess of Tartaros, fearing the Furies, those mighty daimôns, art thou come? art thou here? Be angry, O Maid, at all the foes of heaven's gods, of Hêlios-Osiris and of Isis his bedmate. As I instruct thee, hurl them thy ill-will because, Korê, I know thy good and great majestic names, by which heaven is illuminated, and earth drinketh dew and becomes pregnant; from all these the universe will increase and decrease:

EUPHORBA PHORBA PHORBOREOU PHORBA PHORBOR
PHORBOR PHORBORBORBORPHA ÊRPHOR PHORBAIÔ
PHORBOR PHORBOR BOROPH PHORPHOR BORPHOR-

BOR AÔ IÔÊ PHORBORPHOR EUPHOR BOPHOR EUOIEÔ
PHÔTH IÔPHÔTH IÔPHÔTH PHBTHIÔPH AÔÔÔTHÔ
ÔAI IÔEÔÔIÔ HAHAHA ÊÊ IOYY ÔÔÔ OYYYY AEÊIOUÔ
YYY—Mistress.

4. Close the rite in your customary manner.

10. Prayer to Mênê (Moon)
(*PGM* VII.756–794, 300 c.e.)

1. Perform your customary opening rite of purification.

2. Sacrifice frankincense to Mênê.

3. Recite this prayer:

I call upon thee who hast every form and many names, double-horned goddess, Mênê, whose form no one knows except him who fashioned the entire world—IAÔ! The one who shaped thee into the 28 shapes[14] of the world so that they might perfect and provide breath to every animal and plant, that it might thrive, thou who growest from darkness into light and leavest the light for darkness.

The first thing that accompanies thy name is silence, the second a popping sound, the third groaning, the fourth hissing, the fifth a cry of joy, the sixth moaning, the seventh barking, the eighth roaring, the ninth neighing, the tenth a musical sound, the eleventh the howl of the wind, the twelfth a wind-creating sound, the thirteenth a commanding sound, the fourteenth a commanding emanation from perfection.[15]

Ox, vulture, bull, beetle, falcon, crab, dog, wolf, serpent, horse, she-goat, asp, goat, he-goat, baboon, cat, lion, leopard, fieldmouse, deer, multiform, virgin, torch, lightning, garland, a herald's wand, child key.

---

[14]A reference to the 28 "mansions of the moon."

[15]These should be taken as clues to the correct performance of the *voces magicae*.

I have spoken thy signs and the symbols of thy name so that thou mightest hear me, for I am praying to thee, mistress of the whole world. Hear me, thou, the constant one, the mighty one:

APHEIBOÊÔ MINTÊR OCHAÔ PIZEPHYDÔR CHANTHAR CHADÊROZO MOCHTHION EOTNEU PHÊRZON AINDÊS LACHABOÔ PITTÔ RIPHTHAMER ZMOMOCHÔLEIE TIÊDRANTEIA OISOZOCHABÊDÔPHRA.

[Add whatever other magical effects you wish.]

4. Close the rite in your customary manner.

11. General Magical Invocation
(*PGM* V.459–489, 350 c.e.)

The ancient source says of this invocation that it is good for liberation, invisibility, the sending of dreams (psychic communication), or for gaining favor of any kind.

1. Perform your customary opening rite of purification.

2. Sacrifice frankincense to Abrasax or Aiôn, or another cosmic god.

3. Recite this prayer:

I call upon thee who hath created earth and bones and all flesh and all spirit and who hath established the sea and nailed the heavens, who separated the light from the darkness, the Supreme Intelligence, who lawfully governs all things, Eternal Eye, daimôn of daimôns, god of gods, the lord of the spirits, the unerring AIÔN IAÔ OYEI—hear my voice:

I call upon thee, master of the gods, high-thundering Zeus, sovereign Zeus, ADÔNAI, lord IAÔ OYÊE: I am he who calleth upon thee, great god, in Syrian: ZAALAÊRIPHPHOU! Thou must not leave my voice unheard, in Hebrew: ABLANATHANALBA ABRASILÔA! For I am SILTHACHÔOUCH LAILAL

BLASALÔTH IAÔ IEÔ NEBOUTH SABIOTH ARBÔTH AR-
BATHIAÔ IAÔTH SABAÔTH PATOURÊ ZAGOURÊ
BAROUCH ADÔNAI ELÔAI ABRAAM[16] BARBARAUÔ
NAUSIPH, high-minded one, immortal, who possesseth the crown
of the whole world:

SIEPÊ SAKTIETÊ BIOU BIOU SPHÊ SPHÊ NOUSI NOUSI
SIETHO SIETHO CHTHETHÔNI RIGCH ÔÊA Ê ÊÔA AÔÊ
IAÔ ASIAL SARAPI OLSÔ ETHOURÊSINI SEM LAU LOU
LOURIGCH.

[Now speak what is in your heart on the magical effects you wish.]

4. Close the rite in your customary manner.

12. Another General Invocation
(*PGM* VII.490–504, 300 c.e.)

This operation is to be carried out at the time of the Full Moon.

1. Perform your customary opening rite of purification.

2. Sacrifice sulfur and the seed of Nile rushes by burning them in the
brazier.

3. Recite this invocation:

I call on thee, Lady Isis, whom Agathos Daimôn hath permitted to
rule the entire Black Land.[117] Thy name is LOU LOULOU
BATHARTHAR THARÊSIBATH ATHERNEKLÊSICH ATH-
ERNEBOUNI ÊICHOMÔ CHOÔTHI Isis Sothis,[18] SOUÊRI,
Boubastis, EURELIBAT CHAMARI NEBOUTOS OUÊRI[19] AIÊ

---

[16]This is a Hermetic form of a Hebrew blessing formula: "Blessed be Yahweh . . .
lord god of Abraham. . . ."
[17]In Egyptian *Khemet* = Egypt.
[18]Sothis = the Dog Star.
[19]QUERI = Egypt. *wer*, great one.

ÊOA ÔAI. Protect me, great and wondrous names of all the gods. [To this add in the names of other gods and goddesses you might wish to invoke.]

For I am the one established in Pelusium:[20] SERPHOUTH MOUISRÔ[21] STROMMÔ MOLÔTH MOLONTHÊR PHON Thoth. Protect me, great and marvelous name of the great god. [Again add the names of other gods and goddesses you might wish to invoke].

ASAÔ EIÔ NISAÔTH. Lady Isis, Nemesis, Adrasteia,[22] many-named, many-formed, glorify me, as I have glorified the name of your son, Horus—[add the magical effects you wish.].

Now speak what is in your heart on the magical effects you wish.

4. Close the rite in your customary manner.

13. The Hidden Stêlê
(PGM IV.1115–1166, 350 C.E.)

As a cosmic invocation this operation is most effective as a means to gain spiritual knowledge or to raise your level of being. The names used here are formulas which contain mysteries within themselves.

1. Perform your customary opening rite of purification.

2. Sacrifice frankincense to Aiôn.

3. Recite this prayer:

Hail to thee, entire system of ærial spirit: PHOGÔLÔA!

---

[20]The one established in Pelusium is the god Amen (Ammôn).

[21]Magical rendition of Egypt. *serpet, mahy, ser* = "Lotus, Lion, Ram" (symbols of Ammôn-Rê).

[22]A nymph who nurtured young Zeus, but also an alternate name of Nemesis meaning "the Inevitable."

Hail to thee, spirit who extendeth from heaven to earth: ERDÊNEU, and who extendeth from the earth—which is in the middle chamber of the cosmos—unto the very borders of the abyss: MEREMÔGGA!

Hail to thee, spirit who cometh into me, who seizeth me, and who graciously departeth from me according to the will of god: IÔÊ ZANÔPHIE!

Hail to thee, beginning and end of invariable nature: DÔRYSLAOPHÔN!

Hail to thee, revolution of the elements[23] full of inexhaustible service: RÔGYEU ANAMI PELÊGEÔN ADARA EIÔPH!

Hail to thee, radiance of the universe, who art subordinate to the ray of the Sun: IEO YÊÔ IAÊAI ÊÔY OEI!

Hail to thee, orb of the Moon, who shineth nocturnally, and who illuminateth unequally: AIÔ REMA RÔDOUÔPIA!

Hail to all you spirits of ærial images: RÔMIDOUÊ AGANASOU ÔTHAUA.

Hail to those to whom the blessed greeting is given—to brothers and sisters—to holy men and holy women!

O great, greatest spherical and incomprehensible schema of the ordered universe, heavenly ENRÔCHESÊL:

In heaven, PELÊTHEU,
Ætherial-one, IÔGARAA,
In the æther: THÔPYLEO DARDY,
Shaper of Water: IÔÊDES,
Shaper of Earth: PERÊPHIA,
Shaper of Fire: APPHTHALYA,
Shaper of the Winds: IÔIE ÊÔAYA,
Shaper of Light: ALAPIE,
Shaper of Darkness: IEPSERIA,

---

[23]Here the Greek word *stoicheia*, "elements; letters," is used in the original version.

who shineth with heavenly light: ADAMALÔR—
moist, fiery, and cold spirit.

I glorify thee, god of gods,
who ordered the universe: AREÔ PIEUA;
who gathered together the depths upon the invisible foundation of
   their fixed position: PERÔ MYSÊL O PENTÔNAX;
who separated heaven and earth and covered heaven with eternal
   golden wings: RÔDÊRY OYÔA;
who fixed the earth upon its eternal foundations: ALÊIOÔA;
who hung the æther high above the earth: AIE IOYA;
who sowed the air with self-moving winds: AIE ÔÊ IOYA;
who placed the waters all around: ÔRÊPÊLYA;
who raiseth up storms: ÔRISTHAUA;
who thundereth: THEPHICHYÔNÊL;
who hurleth bolts of lightning: OURÊNES;
who raineth: OSIÔRNI PHEUGALGA;
who doth generate living creatures: ARESIGYLOA;
god of the Aiôns—thou art great, lord, god, ruler of the All:
   ARCHIZÔ NYON THÊNAR METHÔR PARY PHEZÊR
   THAPSAMYDÔ MARÔMI CHÊLÔPSA.

Now speak what is in your heart on the magical effects you wish.

4. Close the rite in your customary manner.

14. Bear Working To Arktos
(PGM VII.686–702, 300 c.e.)

One of the least discussed, yet most powerful aspects of astral
mythology and star-magic is that which surrounds the Polar region of
the night sky—dominated by the Bears and Draco—with the Pole
Star in their midst. For the earliest Egyptians this was the region of
immortality, the stars that "knew no death," although in later times
these constellations became more associated with Set-Typhôn as the
Solar cult came to predominate. For the Greeks, and kindred Indo-
European peoples, the northern sky was more symbolic of their spir-

itual homeland at the Pole—Hyperboric. Invocations to the northern stars are among the most powerful in any tradition.

On any clear night, go to a place where the stars of the northern sky are plainly visible.

1. Perform your customary opening ritual.

2. Now address the following prayer to the constellation of the Bear:

Arktos, Arktos! Thou who ruleth over heaven, over the stars and over the whole of the world! Thou who causeth the axis to turn and governeth the system of the cosmos by force and through Anankê! I appeal to thee, imploring and supplicating that thou may [briefly state the purpose of your appeal], because I call upon thee in thy holy names at which thy deity rejoiceth, names which thou art unable to ignore:

BRIMÔ: subduer of the earth, great huntress!

BAUBÔ LAUMORI AUMÔR AMÔR AMÔRES IÊA: [shooter] of deer!

AMAMAMAR APHROUMATHAMA: universal queen of wishes!

AMAMA: whose bed is good, Dardanian, who can see all, who wandereth through the night, attacker of man, subduer of man, summoner of man, conqueror of man!

LICHRISSA PHAESSA: O ærial one, O goddess of Erymna, O strong one, thou art the song and the dance, guardian, spy, gracious, delicate, guardian, uncompromising, inflexible, O Damnameneia!

BREXERIKANDARA: Highest of All, Taurine, unutterable, fiery bodied, light-giving, sharply armed!

Now speak what is in your heart on the magical effects you wish.

3. Close the rite in your customary manner.

A Ring Charm

Although this is given as an operation to consecrate a magical ring, the basic formula can be used to consecrate any talismanic object. As the original text itself reads: "Here is truly written out, with all brevity, the rite by which all modeled images and engravings and carved stones are made alive."

Once a magical ring has been made and consecrated, it can become the chief magical tool of the Hermetic magician. But it is not necessary to have one from the beginning of your work in Hermetic magic. It is rather a sign of the advanced initiate.

15. A Magical Ring
(*PGM* XII.270–350, 350 c.e.)

The original papyrus source for this operation says that this ring is for success, favor, and victory. It is reputed to be able to make men famous, great, admired, and wealthy. It can also make friendships with other powerful individuals possible.

The original goes on to say that the world has never had a formula greater than this one. For when you have it with you, you will always get whatever you ask from anybody. Besides, it calms the angers of masters and kings. Wearing it, you will be believed, no matter what you say to anyone, and everyone will like you. Anyone can open doors and break chains and rocks if he touches them with the [gem-]stone . . . and says the name written below.

First the form of the ring must be manufactured, then consecrated. For the creation of the ring, if you are not a trained jeweler, have a heliotrope stone, that is a bloodstone, carved with these designs which represent Hêlios-Rê: On the base of the front side of a cabochon stone a thick bodied serpent biting its tail (an Ouroboros) should be carved. Inside the circle formed by the serpent, in the center of the stone, there should be a sacred scarab beetle, surrounded by

Left: obverse side;
right: reverse side.

rays of the Sun. On the reverse side of the stone, have the name inscribed "in hieroglyphics, as the prophets pronounce it." Once the
stone is carved, have it set in a ring of gold, where the reverse side is
invisible.

Do not wear the ring until you have consecrated it with the following series of operations which will require a fortnight to complete.
The whole cycle of operations should commence when the Moon en-
ters her third quarter. It is also best if, at the time the operations
begin, the goddess, the Moon, is rising in the zodiacal sign of Taurus,
Virgo, Scorpio, Aquarius, or Pisces.

1. At dawn stand facing the sun, while holding the divine and holy
stone, perform your usual opening rites. As an offering, burn all
kinds of perfumes *except* frankincense.

2. Now repeat this entire formula three times:

Greatest of the gods, who exceedeth all power, I call upon thee,
IAÔ SABAÔTH ADÔNAI EILÔEIN[24] SEBÔEIN TALLAM
CHAUNAÔN SAGÊNAM ELEMMEDÔR CHAPSOUTHI
SETTÔRA SAPHTHA NOUCHITHA ABRAAN ISAK
IAKKOBI[25] CHATHATHICH ZEUPAIN NÊPHYGOR
ASTAPHAIOS KATAKERKNÊPH KONTEOS KATOUT
KÊRIDEU MARMARIÔTH LIKYXANTA BESSOUM
SYMEKONTEU KATATOUTHOITH[26] MASKELLI

---

[24]A Hermetic form of Heb. *Elohim* = god(s).
[25]ABRAAN ISAK IAKKOBI = Abraham, Isaac, and Jacob.
[26]KATATOUTHOITH = Gk. κατα του Θοιθ = "the opponent of Thoth."

MASKELÔTH PHNOU KENTABÔATH OREOBAZAGRA
HIPPOCHTHÔN RÊSICHTHÔN PYRIPÊGANYX NYXIÔ
ABRÔROKORE KODÊRE NOUISDRÔ, King, THATH
PHATH CHATH XEUZÊN ZEUZEI SOUSÊNÊ ELATHATH
MELASIÔ KOUKÔR NEUSÔÔ PACHIÔ XIPHNÔ THEMEL
NAUTH BIOKLÊTH SESSÔR CHAMEL CHASINEU XÔCHÔ
IALLINÔI SEISENGPHARAGGÊS MASICHIÔR IÔTABAAS
CHENOUCHI CHAAM PHACHIARATH NEEGÔTHARA
IAM ZEÔCH AKRAMMACHAMAREI CHEROUBEIM
BAINCHÔÔCH EIOPHALEON ICHNAÔTH PÔE
XEPHITHÔTH XOUTHOUTH THOÔTHIOU XERIPHÔ-
NAR EPHINARASÔR CHANIZARA ANAMEGAR IÔO
XTOURORIAM IÔK NIÔR CHETTAIOS ELOUMAIOS
NÔIÔ DAMNAMENEU AXIÔTHÔPH PSTHAIAKKLÔPS
SISAGETA NEORIPHRÔR HIPPOKELEPHOKLÔPS
ZEINACHA IAPHETHANA A E Ê I O Y Ô.

I have called upon thee, greatest god, and through thee upon all
things, so that thou may give divine and supreme strength to this
image and may be able to make it effective and powerful against all
opponents and be able to call back souls, move spirits, subject legal
opponents, strengthen friendships, produce all kinds of profits,
bring dreams, give prophecies, cause psychological passions and
bodily sufferings and incapacitating illnesses, and perfect all erotic
philters. Please, lord, bring to fulfillment a complete consecration.

Each time you recite the formula pour out a libation made of a mixture of wine, honey, milk, and saffron to the east of the altar.

This formula is to be repeated three times each time the operation is performed, and the operation itself must be repeated three
times each day, in the third, sixth, and ninth hour of the day for four-
teen days running. In the ninth hour of the night take the ring out and
put it away in a holy place until the series of operations is complete.

As the final operation, perform your opening rite as usual and
use this invocation of the god to bring the stone alive:

The gates of heaven have been opened. The gates of the earth have
been opened. The pathway of the sea hath been opened. The path-

ways of the rivers have been opened. My spirit hath been heard by
all gods and daimôns. My spirit hath been heard by the spirit in
heaven. My spirit hath been heard by the spirit of the earth. My
spirit hath been heard by the spirit of the sea. My spirit hath been
heard by the spirit of the rivers. Therefore give spirit to the mystery
which I have made ready, O ye gods whom I have named and have
called upon. Give the breath[27] of life to the mystery which I have
prepared:

ÊI IEOU[28] MAREITH
ÊI IEOU MONTHEATHI MONGITH
ÊI IEOU CHAREÔTH MONKÊB
ÊI IEOU SÔCHOU SÔRSÔÊ
ÊI IEOU TIÔTIÔ OUIÊR
ÊI IEOU CHARÔCHSI CHARMIÔTH
ÊI IEOU SATHIMÔOYÊEOY
ÊI IEOU RAIRAI MOURIRAI
ÊI IEOU AMOUN ÊEI OUSIRI[29]
ÊI IEOU PHIRIMNOUN[30]
ÊI IEOU ANMORCHATHI OUÊR
ÊI IEOU ANCHEREPHRENEPSOUPHIRINGCH
Ê I IEOU ORCHIMORÔIPOUGTH
ÊI IEOU MACHPSACHATHANTH
ÊI IEOU MOROTH

Now you have completely consecrated the ring and made it alive. To
command the god, all you need do is call on his name, OUPHÔR,
while you are wearing the ring. You now have the formula to secure
the highest divine action. Here has been accurately written out, as
succinctly as possible, the rite by means of which all modeled images
and engravings and carved stones can be made alive. Therefore keep
it in a secret place as a great mystery. Hide it!

---

[27]In this passage in the original papyrus the Greek word πνευμα (*pneuma*) is used
for "spirit" and the related word πνοη (*pnoê*) is used for "breath of life."
[28]EI IEOU = Egypt. *i iaw* = "O, hail!"
[29]AMOUN = Ammôn/Amen; OUSIRI = Osiris
[30]PHIRIMNOUN = Egypt. "He who comes forth from the abyss (= Nun)."

CONTROLLING THE SHADOW

The *shadow* is an important soul concept in the ancient world. The Egyptians called it the *khaibit*, and it is necessary to good fortune and health. It can also be a great aid in magical operations.

16. Controlling the Shadow
(*PGM* III.502–536; 612–632, 350 c.e.)

Portions of the original papyrus version upon which this operation is based are defective or the papyrus itself is disintegrated. Reconstructions of those portions have been placed in square brackets here.

This rite should be performed some time in the summer months when the sun rises during the sixth hour of the day. Prepare yourself by dressing in dark clothing. Tie a red cord around your head as a headband and put feathers behind each of your ears. The original source says these should be a hawk feather behind your right ear and an ibis feather behind your left ear.

At the sixth hour of the day, just before the sun rises, go to a deserted place. When you get there begin your rite.

1. Perform your customary opening rite of purification. The original papyrus says that you should "make an offering of wheaten meal and ripe mulberries and unsoftened sesame and uncooked *thrion*[31] and throw into this a beet" in order to "gain control of your own shadow so that it will serve you."

2. Now lie down on your stomach and stretch out your hands, and speak this formula:

---

[31] *Thrion* is a Greek word for "fig-leaf," but here it means the mixture of eggs, milk, lard, flour, honey, and cheese popular among the Greeks. This is cooked and wrapped in a fig-leaf—hence the name.

Cause now my shadow to serve me, because I know thy sacred names and thy signs and thy symbols, and who thou art at each hour, and what thy name is.

3. Stand up and speak these formulas:[32]

In the first hour thou hast the form and character of a young monkey, the tree thou dost produce is the silver fir, the stone, the *aphanos*, the bird, the owl; on land, the ram—thy name is PHROUER.[33]

In the second hour thou hast the form of a unicorn, the tree thou dost produce is the persea, the stone, the pottery stone; the bird, the halouchakon; on land, the ichneumon—thy name is BAZE-TOPHOTH.

In the third hour thou hast the form of a cat, the tree thou dost produce is the fig tree, the stone, the *samouchos;* the bird, the parrot; on land, the frog—thy name is AKRAMMACHAMMAREI.

In the fourth hour thou hast the form of a bull, the tree thou dost produce is the olive, the stone, the amethyst; the bird, the turtle-dove; on land, the bull—thy name is DAMNAMENEUS.

In the fifth hour thou hast the form of a lion, the tree thou dost produce is the prickly shrub, the stone, the loadstone; the bird, [the hawk]; on land, the crocodile—thy name is PHO-KENGEPSEUARETATHOUMISONKTAIKT.

In the sixth hour thou hast the form of a donkey, the tree thou dost produce is the thorn tree, the stone, the lapis lazuli; in the sea, the jellyfish; on land, the white-faced cow—thy name is EIAU AKRI LYX IAÔ.

In the seventh hour thou hast the form of a crayfish, the tree thou dost produce is the poplar, the stone, the sun opal; the bird, the eagle; on land, the cat—thy name is [MAIUEOR.]

---

[32]The remainder of the rite is derived from the fragmentary *PGM* III.502–536.
[33]"The great Sun."

In the eighth hour thou hast the form of an elephant, the tree thou dost produce is the aloe, the stone, the emerald; the bird, [the great sparrow]; on land, the hippopotamus—thy name is [APETEPA.]

In the ninth hour thou hast the form of an ibis, the plant thou dost produce is the lotus, the stone, the aquamarine; the bird, the eagle; on land, the chameleon—thy name is [THECHOMACHEI.]

In the tenth hour thou hast the form of a scorpion, the tree thou dost produce is [the acacia], the stone, the snakestone; the bird, [the phoenix]; on land, the beetle—thy name is [SERKACHEP-HAREUS.]

In the eleventh hour thou hast the form of a jackal, the [plant thou dost produce is the papyrus], the stone, [granite]; the bird, the [vulture]; on land, the [ibis]—thy name is [ANAPTHEOUTA].

In the twelfth hour thou hast the form of a [dog], the tree thou dost produce is the [palm], the stone, the [crystal]; the bird, [the little swallow]; on land, the [bull]—thy name is [OUCHERACHEP-HES].

4. If you feel there seems to be no response, say:

I have uttered thy sacred names and thy signs and thy symbols, wherefore, O lord, cause my shadow to serve me.

5. In the seventh hour your shadow will come to you and appear before you. Speak to it and say: **Follow me everywhere!**

6. Close the rite in your customary manner.

OPERATIONS
FOR PICKING HERBS

On occasion, for some operations, the magician will need to pick
some herbs or plants. It is important to do this in a sacred way. The
life of the plant must not be threatened, and in some way you want
the plant to co*operate* in the purpose of your working(s). This can
even be modified for buying herbs commercially. Just say the formula
as soon after leaving the store as possible. Your words will surely flow
back to the time and place the herb was harvested.

17. To Pick a Plant
(*PGM* IV.286–295, 350 c.e.)

This formula is to be used for picking herbs that are to be gathered
before sunrise:

1. Go to the place where the herb is to be picked.

2. Perform your customary rite of purification.

3. Recite the following formula:

I am picking thee, [name the type of plant or herb you are picking],
with my five-fingered hand, I, [insert your own name or magical
name]—and I am bringing thee home so that thou mayest work for
me for a certain purpose. I command thee by the undefiled name of
the god: if thou payest no heed to me the earth which produced
thee will no longer be watered for thee—ever in thy life, if I were to
fail in my operation:

> MOUTHABAR NACH BARNACHOCHA BRAEÔ
> MENDA LAUBRAASSE PHASPHA BENDEÔ

Fulfill for me this, the most perfect of incantations.

4. Pick the herb.

5. Close the rite in your customary manner.

18. Plant Picking
(*PGM* IV.2967–3006, 350 c.e.)

The ancients report that among the Egyptians herbs were always picked like this: the herbalist would first purify his own body. Then the area around where the herb was to be picked would be sprinkled with natron and fumigated with pine resin—circumambulating the area three times. Then *kyphi*[34] would be burned and a libation of milk poured out near the plant.

During these ritual actions, just before picking the plant, which is to be dug up by its roots, the following invocation is spoken:

Thou wert sown by Kronos, thou wert conceived by Hera, thou wert maintained by Ammôn, thou wert given birth by Isis, thou wert nourished by Zeus the god of the rain, thou wert given growth by Hêlios and the dew. Thou art the dew of all the gods, thou art the eye of Hêlios, thou art the light of Selênê, thou art the majesty of Osiris, thou art the beauty and glory of Ouranos, thou art the soul of the daimôn of Osiris which revels in every place, thou art the spirit of Ammôn. As thou hast exalted Osiris, so exalt thyself and rise just as Hêlios riseth each day. Thy size is equal to the zenith of Hêlios, thy roots come from the depths, but thy powers are in the heart of Hermês, thy fibers are the bones of Mnevis,[35] and thy flowers are the eye of Horus, thy seed is the seed of Pan. I am washing thee in resin as I also wash the gods even as I do this for my own health. Thou art also cleansed by prayer and give us power, as Arês and Athêna do. I am Hermês. I am taking thee with Tychê[36] and

---

[34]An Egyptian compound incense.
[35]Hellenized form of the Egyptian god-name *Mr-wr*: the divine bull of Heliopolis, which is a manifestation of the sun-god Pre.
[36]Good Fortune.

Agathadaimôn,[37] both at a propitious hour and on a propitious day which is effective for all things.

Then while repeatedly calling on the name of the daimôn to whom the plant is to be dedicated, pull up the plant. Then add a paraphrase of the purpose of the magical rite for which the plant is being picked.

Now roll the harvested herb up in a pure linen cloth. Pour a mixture of seven seeds of wheat and seven of barley, and honey into the ground where the herb was dug up. This is an offering of repayment to the earth. Depart in silence.

---

[37]Good Daimôn.

BOWL DIVINATIONS

The bowl or saucer was an important magical tool in ancient Hermetic magic. It was used mainly as a divinatory tool, but the idea of a vessel used for eating or drinking being the principle magical symbol for the divine *magos* is also essential. Here we see the eastern root of the idea of the "holy grail," or the importance of the cup in the myth of the Christ.

As the first operation here shows, the bowl divination is something more than mere "fortune telling." It involves a whole technology of self-deification and must be counted as one of the major forms of self-initiation in the Hermetic tradition.

19. Bowl Divination
(*PGM* IV.154–285, 350 c.e.)

The ancient source for this operation is in the form of a letter from a certain Nephotes to Psammetichos. Nephotes seems to have been the pupil of Psammetichos, but the student wants to show the teacher what magical skill he has acquired.

With this operation of bowl divination the operator will be able to see the god in the water of the bowl and hear the words of the god—who can be questioned on any matter. This operation comes in two parts to be treated separately.

1. First Part:

To begin with the magician must attach himself to Hêlios. To accomplish this go together with a fellow initiate to the highest part of a building at sunrise of the third day of any month. There spread a linen garment on the floor. You should be naked. Crown yourself with dark ivy when the sun is at midheaven and lie down on the linen. Have your fellow initiate cover your eyes with a black Isis band and have yourself

wrapped in the linen like a corpse. Close your eyes, and have yourself
directed toward the sun and recite this prayer three times in succession:

Mighty Typhôn, wielder of the scepter!
Ruler of the scepter-power on high!
God of gods, O lord: ABERAMENTHÔOU!
O disturber in darkness, bringer of thunder and storms,
Who flasheth through the night,
And who doth breathe forth hot and cold,
Shaker of rocks, who maketh the walls quake,
Stirrer of waves, who maketh the depths shake:
IÔ ERBÊT AU TAUI MÊNI!
I am the one who searched the whole world with thee and
Found great Osiris, whom I led to thee in chains.
I am the one who joined thee in war against the gods.
I am the one who closed the double gates of heaven
And caused to slumber the serpent which must not be seen,
Who stopped the seas, the streams, the river currents
Until thou didst come to rule this realm.
I, as thy soldier, have been conquered by the gods,
I have been thrown upon my face because of their vain wrath.
Raise thy friend up, I bid thee—I implore;
Do not throw me down upon the earth,
O lord of gods:
AEMINAEBARÔTHERRETHÔABEANIMEA!
Grant me power, I bid, and give to me
This favor, so that, whensoever I tell
One of the gods to come, he will be seen coming
Quickly to me in answer to my invocations:

NAINE BASANAPTATOU EAPTOU MÊNÔPHAESÊ PAPTOU
    MÊNÔPH AESIMÊ
TRAUAPTI PEUCHRÊ TRAUARA PTOUMÊPH MOURAI
    ANCHOUCHAPHAPTA
MOURSA ARAMEI IAÔ ATHTHARAUI MÊNOKER BOROP-
    TOUMÊTH AT TAUI
MÊNI   CHARCHARA   PTOUMAU   LALAPSA   TRAUI
    TRAUEPSE MAMÔ

PHORTOUCHA AEÊIO IOY OÊÔA EAI AEÊI ÔI IAÔ AÊI AI IAÔ.

Repeat this formula three times. After this there will be a sign of your encounter with the god. You will see a falcon fly down and strike you on the body with its wings. Because you are armed with a magical soul, you need have no fear of this. After this, rise up and have yourself unwrapped; clothe yourself in a white robe and burn frankincense in an earthen censer. While doing this say:

I have been linked to thy holy form.
I have been given strength by thy holy name.
I have taken part in thy emanation of riches,
Lord, god of gods, master, daimôn:
ATHTHOUIN THOUTHOUI TAUANTI LAÔ APTATÔ!

Once this operation has been truly completed, you will be yourself a lord of god-like nature.

2. Second Part:

Before beginning the following ritual you should put on the great protective charm. To make this, you should ceremonially create the talisman by inscribing the name of 100 letters on a silver sheet or plate of silver using a bronze stylus. Wear it strung on a leather thong.[38]

ACHCHÔR   ACHCHÔR   ACHACHACH   PTOUMI
CHACHCHÔ   CHARACHÔCH   CHAPTOUMÊ
CHÔRACHARACHÔCH APTOUMI MÊCHÔCHAPTOU
CHARACHPTOU   CHACHACHÔ   CHARACHÔ   PTE-
NACHÔCHEU.[39]

---

[38]The original version has it that this should be strung on a thong made of the hide of an ass—identified as the Typhonian animal.
[39]This formula has 100 letters in the Greek alphabet:
ΑΧΧΩΡ ΑΧΧΩΡ ΑΧΑΧΑΧ ΠΤΟΥΜΙ ΧΑΧΧΩ ΧΑΡΑΧΩΧ ΧΑΠΤΟΥΜΗ
ΧΩΡΑΧΑΡΑΧΩΧ ΑΠΤΟΥΜΙ ΜΗΧΩΧΑΠΤΟΥ ΧΑΡΑΧΠΤΟΥ ΧΑΧΧΩ
ΧΑΡΑΧΩ ΠΤΕΝΑΧΩΧΕΥ.

Inquiry of bowl divination and necromancy: Whenever you wish to ask the god about anything take a bronze vessel, either a bowl or a saucer, fill it with water and set it on your knees. The water you put in the bowl should be rain water if a heavenly god is being called upon, sea water for gods of the earth, river water for Osiris or Serapis, and spring water for the dead. Then pour some green olive oil out into the bowl with the water and speak this incantation over the bowl:

AMOUN AUANTAU LAIMOUTAU RIPTOU MANTAUI IMANTOU LANTOU LAPTOUMI ANCHÔMACH ARAP-TOUMI—come to me, O [name the god you are invoking]! Appear to me and do not frighten my eyes. Come to me, O [repeat the name of the god you are invoking], be attentive to me because he wishes and commands this ACHCHÔR ACHCHÔR ACHACHACH PTOUMI CHACHCHÔ CHARACHÔCH CHAPTOUMÊ CHÔRACHARACHÔCH APTOUMI MÊCHÔCHAPTOU CHARACHPTOU CHACHACHÔ CHARACHÔ PTENACHÔCHEU.

You should know that this is the chief name of Typhôn at whom the ground, the depths of the sea, Hades, heaven, the sun, the moon, the visible chorus of stars, the whole universe all tremble—the name which, when uttered, forcibly brings the gods and daimôns to it. This is the name that consists of 100 letters. Finally, when you have called, whomever you called will appear, god or dead man, and he will give an answer about anything you ask. And when you have learned what you want to know, dismiss the god by merely uttering the powerful name of 100 letters as you say:

Depart, master, for the great god, IAÔ, wishes and commands this of thee.

Then speak the name of 100 letters and he will depart.

An operative formula which can be used after your first summoning of Typhôn should be spoken to the rising sun, and goes like this:

I call thee who first controlled the wrath of the gods, thou who holdest the royal scepter above the heavens, thou who art the mid-point of the stars above, thou, master Typhôn, thee I call, who art the dreaded sovereign over the firmament. Thou who art fearful, awesome and threatening, thou who art dark and invincible and hater of the wicked, thee I call, Typhôn, in hours without law and without measure, thou who didst walk across unquenched, crackling fire, thou who hast sovereign power over the Moirai, I invoke thee in prayer, I call, almighty one. That thou wouldst perform for me whatever I ask of thee, and that thou nod in assent at once to me and grant that what I ask be mine! [Put your magical will into your own words.] Because I adjure thee:

GAR THALA BAUZAU THÔRTHÔR KATHAUKATH IATHIN NA BORKAKAR BORBA KARBORBOCH MÔ ZAU OUZÔNZ ÔN YABITH mighty Typhôn, hear me, [state your name], and perform for me this [paraphrase your magical will]! For I speak thy true name: IÔ ERBÊTH IÔ PAKERBÊTH IÔ BOL-CHOSÊTH OEN TYPHÔN ASBARABÔ BIEAISÊ ME NERÔ MARAMÔ TAUÊR CHTHENTHÔNIE ALAM BÊTÔR MENKECHRA SAUEIÔR RÊSEIODÔTA ABRÊSIOA PHOTHÊR THERTHÔNAX NERDÔMEU AMÔRÊS MEEME ÔIÊS SYSCHIE ANTÔNIE PHRA. Listen to me and [again paraphrase your magical will].

20. Bowl Divination of Aphroditê
(*PGM* IV.3209–3254, 350 C.E.)

Keep yourself pure, have no sexual activity for seven days so that you may make yourself more attractive to the goddess.

Prepare a white saucer or shallow bowl by writing ÊIOCH CHIPHA ELAMPSÊR ZÊL A E Ê I O Y Ô[40] on the inside bottom of the vessel with myrrh ink. This should be waxed over to make it waterproof. Beneath the base on the outside write: TACHIÊL CHTHONIÊ DRAXÔ.[41] On the outside of the rim at the top, write IERMI PHILÔ S' ERIKÔMA DERKÔ MALÔK GAULÊ

---

[40]This formula has 25 letters in Greek.
[41]This formula has 18 letters in Greek.

APHRIÊL *EROTÔ*.[42] After writing this latter formula it should be vocally repeated three times. Now fill the vessel with water and olive oil and let it rest on the floor. Looking at it with great concentration say:

I call upon thee, the mother of the nymphs: ILAOUCH OBRIÊ LOUCHTLOR—come in, holy light, and give me answers showing thy beautiful form.

Then concentrate intently at the surface of the liquid in the vessel. When you see her, welcome her and say:

Hail, glorious goddess: ILARA OUCH. If thou wilt give me a response, extend thy hand.

And when she extends it, expect answers from your inquiry. But if she does not listen, say:

I call upon ILAOUCH who hath begotten Himeros,[43] the lovely Horai and you Graces; I also call upon Zeus-sprung Physis of all things, two-formed, indivisible, quick, foam-beautiful Aphroditê. Reveal to me thy beautiful light and thy beautiful face, O mistress ILAOUCH. I conjure thee, giver of fire, by ELGINAL and by the great names OBRIÊTYCH KERDYNOUCHILÊPSIN NIOU NAUNIN IOUTHOU THRIGX TATIOUTH GERTIATH GERGERIS GERGERIÊ THEITHI. I also ask thee by the wondrous names, OISIA EI EI AÔ ÊY AAÔ IÔIAIAIÔ SÔTHOU BERBROI AKTEROBORE GERIE IÊOYA; bring me light and thy beautiful face and the true bowl-divination, thou who art shining with fire and who art surrounded all around with fire, and who stirrest the land from afar: IÔ IÔ PHTHAIÊ THOUTHOI PHAEPHI!

Now let the goddess reveal what she has to reveal to you.

---

[42]ερoτω is Greek for "I ask."

[43]Personification of "yearning for love."

DREAM ORACLES

In ancient Greece the practice of dream interpretation was widespread. Priests would often give those who would inquire a special meal and/or drink and have them sleep inside a temple complex. The dreams of the night would then be interpreted. In the practice of μαγεια, however, the magician is his or her own priest or priestess.

21. Dream Oracle
(*PGM* VII.250–254, 300 c.e.)

Before going to bed speak this formula to your magical lamp:

NAIENCHRÊ NAIENCHRÊ, Mother of Fire and Water, thou art the one who riseth before ARCHENTECHTHA, reveal unto me what I desire about [say what you want revealed to you]. If the answer is yes, show me a plant and water, if no, fire and iron. *Êdê, êdê—tachy, tachy!* [= Now, now—quick, quick in Greek]

22. Dream Oracle
(*PGM* VII.255–259, 300 c.e.)

Here is another version of the previous working. If you have a question on your mind to which you desire a yes or no answer, ask it firmly and in a well thought out manner, and then speak this formula to your magical lamp before going to bed:

Hail, Lord, lamp—thou who shinest beside Osiris and shinest beside Osirchentechtha, and my Lord, Archangel Michaêl. If it is not advantageous for me to do this, show me a plant and water, but if not, show me fire and iron. Ηδη ηδη ταχυ ταχυ *Êdê, êdê—tachy, tachy!* [Now, now—quick, quick].

If you dream of a plant or of water then the answer to your question is "no."

23. Dream Oracle
(*PGM* VII.359–369, 300 C.E.)

Just before you go to bed in the evening, take a strip of clean linen
and write this name on it:

HARIOUTH LAILAM CHÔOUCH[44] ARSENOPHRÊ PHRÊU
PHTHA HARCHENTECHTHA

Roll it up tightly into a wick, pour olive oil on it, put it in your lamp
and light it. As it is burning say these words seven times over the
lamp:

SACHMOUNE[45] PAÊMALIGOTÊRÊNCH, the one who
shaketh, who thundereth, who hath swallowed the serpent, encir-
cleth the moon, and hour by hour raiseth the disk of the sun—
CHTHETHONI is thy name. I ask you lords of the gods: SÊTH
CHRÊPS: Reveal to me things concerning that which I desire!

Go then immediately to bed and to sleep to await the dreams which
will come to you.

24. Dream Revelations
(*PGM* VII.664–685, 300 C.E.)

Take a linen strip and, with myrrh ink, write on it a paraphrase of the
matter about which you want a revelation. Wrap an olive branch
with the linen strip and place it beside your head on the left side as
you go to sleep. The ancient source advises the magician to sleep on
the ground on a mat made of rushes.

    Before going to sleep, speak the following formula over your oil
lamp seven times:

Hermês, lord of the All, who dwelleth in the heart, O orb of Selênê,
spherical and square, founder of the words of speech, pleader of the
cause of justice, who art clothed in a mantle, wearing golden san-

---

[44]This seems to be the Egyptian word for "darkness."
[45]This is a Hermetic form of the name of the Egyptian Lion-Goddess, Sekhmet.

dals, turning thy ærial course down beneath earth's depths, who holdeth the reins of the spirit and the Sun, and who by means of the lamps of the immortal gods giveth joy to mortals beneath earth's depths, those who've finished life. The Moirai's fatal thread, and a divine dream art thou said to be, who sendeth forth oracles by day and night. Thou curest the pains of all mortals with healing arts. Hither, O blessed one, O mighty son of the Goddess who doth bring full mental powers, by thine own form and gracious mind:

OIOSENMIGADÔN ORTHÔ BAUBÔ NIOÊRÊ KODÊRETH DOSÊRE SYRE SUROE SANKISTÊ DÔDEKAKISTÊ AKOUROBORE[46] KODERE RINOTON KOUMETANA ROUBITHA NOUMILA PERPHEROU AROUÔRÊR AROUÊR.[47]

To this add whatever other words that express your magical will.

---

[46]AKOUROBORE is part of the YESSIMMIGADON AKROUROBORE formula and is from an original Greek phrase meaning "eater of the tip of your tail" and is as such a veiled reference to the Ouroboros—the cosmic serpent at the outer borders of the world, cf. Heb. Leviathan.

[47]AROUÊR = Egypt. *Hr-wr* (Har-Wer), "Horus the Great."

To Appear in Dreams

The ability to appear in the dreams of other people was a frequent aim of magical operations in ancient times. The main purpose for this seems to have been a kind of erotic magic, to cause the other person to dream about, and hence erotically desire, the magician in her or his waking state. This can be undertaken today in the spirit of experimentation.

25. To Appear in Dreams
(*PGM* VII.407–410, 300 c.e.)

If you wish to appear to someone at night in his or her dreams, magically address your lamp on a nightly basis with this invocation:

CHEIANÔPSEI ERPEÔTH, let him/her [insert the name of the person to whom you wish to appear], whom [insert his/her mother's name] bore, see me in his/his dreams. *Êdê, êdê—tachy, tachy*! [Now, now—quick, quick!]

You can also add other things about how you wish to appear to the person if you wish.

VISION

Of paramount importance to ancient Hermetics was the obtaining of visions or revelations from the world of the gods. To be in regular spiritual contact with the world of the divine was the great aim and accomplishment of the ancients, and one step away from entering that realm themselves. The following rites demonstrate the close linkage between the aims and methods of the philosophical and practical, or operative, Hermetics and the Hermetica which they wrote.

26. Vision
(*PGM* VI.1–47, 200 c.e.)

This operation is designed to obtain visions from the Sun, Hêlios and from the Moon, Selênê.

Needed for the rite is a sprig of laurel leaf.

At sunrise on the second and/or fourth day of the Moon from the ground floor of a building, perform your invocation to Hêlios. After each of the invocations, you should remain at the altar for at least twenty to thirty minutes to await a special vision.

1. Perform your usual opening rite of purification.

2. While holding a sprig of seven-leafed laurel, speak this invocation to the rising Sun:

Laurel, Apollo's holy plant of presage, which Phoebus tasted once and with the fresh cut branches wreathed his holy head, adorned with tresses long and golden. In his hands he hath shaken a scepter on the peaks of Mount Parnassos—high and with many valleys— and gave to all the gods responses and prophesied to mortals. For in the throes of grievous love, it was Apollo who himself gaveth thee, a nymph, dread virgin, the power to utter prophecies. Come

quickly hither to me beseeching thee in holy measures and in my hands holding a laurel leaf. Send me divine responses and a holy prophetic sign. In clear words, O priestess, reveal all things: when these will occur and how they will come to pass. Give me a prediction, so that with it I may perform a test on something. Subduer, humankind's force, come blessed Paian, most supreme, help me; come hither to me, O Phoebus, who hath many names. O Phoebus Apollo, Lêtô's son, who worketh from afar, hither, come hither, hither come; respond with prophesies, give presage in this hour of the night.

3. Then intone this sacred formula: EÊ IE IE ÊI IÔ IÔ IAÔIE IYE IA IAÔ ÊE AEÊIOUÔ.

4. Do not close the rite, but return to your altar at sunset and speak the following formula:

Hear me, god of the silver bow, who standeth as protector of Chryse and holy Cilla and are the mighty lord of Tenedos, goldshining, storm-wind, and dragon-slayer: MESEGKRIPHI, Lêtô's son: SIAÔTH, SABAÔTH, MELIOUCHOS, ruler, PEUCHRÊ, night-wanderer, SESEGGEN BARPHARAGGÊS, ARBÊTHÔ, god of many forms, O thou who art fond of chariots, AR-BATHIAÔ, Smintheus, if ever I have placed a roof over a pleasing shrine for thee, or if I have ever burned fat thighs of bulls or goats for thee, grant my prayer.[48]

5. At night, when the Moon is full, speak this formula to the goddess, Selênê:

Laurel, Apollo's holy plant of presage, O virgin, Laurel, Laurel, Phoebus' mistress, SABAÔTH IAÔAÔO IAGCHÔTHIPYLA MOUSIARCHA OTONYPON, come my way quickly; hurry to sing Divine precepts to me and to proclaim pure words and in dark night bring me true sayings. RÊSABAAN AANANAANANA

---

[48]From Homer, *The Iliad,* lines 39–41. Numerous references to Homeric literature in the magical papyri demonstrate the fact that the writers of the papyri were well versed in Greek cultural material.

AANANAANANALAAA AAA AAA. It is for thee, O Delios, O Nomios, o son of Lêtô and Zeus, to give persuasive oracles at night as you proclaim the truth through dream oracles.

6. Close the rite in your usual manner after the encounter with Selênê.

27. Revelation
(*PGM* XII.153–160, 350 c.e.)

This is an operation for revelations from a divine source. The operation should only be used in times of great personal stress or crisis, or at some other powerful moment. The ancients say that this formula will cause the Serpent-faced God to appear and reveal the whole of the truth.

1. Perform your usual opening rite of purification.

2. Call out the name IAÔ three times, then recite this, the Great Name of God:

I call upon thee: PHTHA RA PHTHA IÊ PHTHA OUN EMÊCHA ERÔCHTH BARÔCH THORCHTHA THÔM CHAIEOUCH ARCHANDABAR ÔEAEÔ YNÊOCH ÊRA ÔN ÊLÔPH BOM PHTHA ATHABRASIA ABRIASÔTH BARBAR-BELÔCHA BARBAIAÔCH.

Let there be depth, breadth, length, and light: ABLANA-THANALBA ABRASIAOUA AKRAMMACHAMAREI THÔTH HÔR ATHÔÔPÔ. Enter Lord, and reveal!

3. Await the revelation from the god, who will speak to you in your heart.

4. Once the revelation has been made, and when you are ready to dismiss the Serpent-faced one, you may make an offering of papyrus or a snake's skin. (But do not cause the death of a serpent!) Otherwise, dismiss the god in the usual manner and close the rite.

28. Direct Vision
(*PGM* VII.319–334, 300 c.e.)

As a preliminary preparation for this operation the ancient source says the magician should keep himself or herself pure for three days.

1. Perform your usual opening rite of purification.

2. Take a copper vessel, pour rainwater into it, and make an offering of frankincense in your brazier on the altar.

3. Now speak the formula:

Let the earth be still, let the air be still, let the sea be still, let the winds also be still, and not disturb me during this, my divination— no sound, no loud cry, no whistling. For I am a prophet, and since I am about to call a terrible fearful name: KOLLA OLPHILOGE- MALA ACHERÔIO, open up the holy temple, which is the cosmic order, constructed over the earth—and give welcome to Osiris, for I am MANCHNÔBISÊ CHOLCHOBÊ MALASÊT IAT THANNOUITA KERTÔMENOU PAKEROAÔ KRAN- NASIRAT MOMOMO MELASOUT PEU PHRÊ. Open my ears so that thou canst reveal to me what I desire about those matters I ask thee about! Come forth, come forth—*Êdê, êdê—tachy, tachy*! And speak to me concerning those things about which I questioned thee. Appear to me, lord Anubis, I command thee, for I am IEO BELPHENO, who is inquiring about this matter.

4. Wait in silence for the god to speak to you within your heart and mind. If he does not speak, repeat the formula above.

5. Once he has spoken, and you are satisfied with his revelation, close the rite in your usual way and dismiss the god by saying:

Go away, Anubis, to thine own thrones, for the sake of my health and well-being.

A Working for Memory

The development and maintenance of a prodigious memory is not only important for the obvious purpose of being able to remember the words of incantations for the sake of performance, but it is also important because magicians must be able to internalize totally the initiatory and magical formulas they have learned in life, so that they will be of use to them in the existence after death.

29. Memory
(*PGM* I.232–247, 400 c.e.)

The original source tells the magician to take some papyrus and with Hermetic myrrh ink (see Appendix A) write these names:

KAMBRÊ CHAMBRE SIXIÔPHI HARPON CHNOUPHI BRINTATÊNÔPHRIBRISKYLMA AROUAZAR BAMESEN KRIPHI NIPTOUMI CHMOUMAOPH AKTIÔPHI ARTÔSE BIBIOU BIBIOU SPHÊ SPHÊ NOUSI NOUSI SIEGÔ SIEGÔ NOUCHA NOUCHA LINOUCHA LINOUCHA CHYCHBA CHYCHBA KAXIÔ CHYCHBA DÊTOPHÔTH AA OO YY ÊÊ EE ÔÔ.

Now speak the whole formula out loud over the papyrus, then wash the formulas off into spring water. This water should be taken from seven different springs. Collect the water in an air-tight vessel and drink some of the water on an empty stomach for seven days as the Moon is rising in the east. At least a few ounces of water should be drunk each time.

WORKINGS FOR LIBERATION

Workings designed to liberate or deliver a captive from bondage are ideal means for gaining release from any and all situations in life which restrict or bind the free exercise of your will. Bonds are not only physical, but have their origins in the upper worlds. Before you can be released in the Kingdom, you must be released in the celestial and/or infernal regions. Situations have their genesis in subtle realms and eventually become manifest in the Kingdom. Through *mageia* the magician is able to release the bonds in heaven, that they may be loosened here on earth.

> Verily I say unto you, Whatsoever ye shall bind on earth shall be bound in heaven: and whatsoever ye shall loose on earth shall be loosed in heaven (Matthew 18:18).

30. Release from Bonds
(*PGM* XII.160–178, 350 c.e.)

To release someone from bonds of any kind, and to open any door, stand outside a door and repeat seven times:

I call upon you gods with a loud voice:
AISAR AIÔTH OUAISNÔRMARSABÔOUTÔRTHE LABATH ERMOU CHOÔRTHEN MANACHTHORPH PECHRÊPH TAÔPHPÔTHTHOCHO THARÔCH BALETHAN CHE-BRÔOUTHAST ADÔNAI HARMIÔTH.

This will release the inner bonds; to cause the doors to open for him or her, say:

OCHLOBARACHÔ LAILAM DARIDAM DARDA DARD-ARAMPTOU IARTHA IERBA DIERBA BARÔTHA THIARBA AKBITHÔ Ô MAAR SEMESILAM MARMARACHNEU MANE THOTH—**holy one, enter and release him/her [insert**

his/her name], and give him/her a way to escape—SESENGEN-
BARPHARAGGÊS, thou who wilt loosen all bonds and thou who
wilt loosen the fetter of iron placed on him/her, [insert his/her
name]—because the great, unutterable, awesome, powerful, un-
speakable, fearful, and not-to-be-despised daimôn of the great god
commands thee: SOROERMER PHERGAR BAX AMPHRI
OURIXG!

When the bonds have been broken give thanks saying:

Thank thee lord, because the holy spirit, the unique one, the living
one, hath released me!

31. Deliverance
(*PGM* I.195–222, 400 c.e.)

The original source calls this the prayer for deliverance of the first-be-
gotten and first-born god, identified as Hêlios, and says the magician
should address the prayer to him "whenever you are forced to do so."

1. Perform your customary rite of purification.

2. Recite this prayer to Hêlios:

I call upon thee, lord. Hear me, holy god who abideth among the
holy ones, beside whom the renowned spirits stand forever. I call
upon thee, primal father and I pray to thee, eternal one, and ruler
of the Sun's rays and of the cosmic Pole, standing within the seven
part realm:[49] CHAÔ CHAÔ CHA OUPH CHTHETHÔN-
IMEETHÊCHRINIA MEROUMI ALDA ZAÔ BLATHAM-
MACHÔTH PHRIXA ÊKE EPIDREI PHYÊIDRYMEO
PHERPHRITHÔ IACHTHÔ PSYCHEÔ PHIRITHMEÔ
ROSERÔTH THAMASTRA PHATIRI TAÔCH IALTHE-
MAECHE; thou who holdest the root fast to its appointed place,
who possesses the powerful name which hath been consecrated by
all the angels. Hear me, thou who hast established the mighty de-

---

[49]This is a reference to the seven planetary spheres.

cans and archangels, and beside whom stands an infinity angels. Thou who hast been exalted unto heaven, and the lord hath borne witness to thy wisdom and hath praised thy power highly and hath said that thou hast strength in the same way as he, and as much power as hath he himself.

I call upon thee, Lord of the All, in my hour of need; hear me, for my soul is distressed, and I am lacking in everything, and I am perplexed. Therefore, come to me, thou who art lord over all angels; hold thy shield over me against all manner of assault by the magical power of ærial daimôns and of Heimarmenê.[50] Verily, Lord, because I call upon thy secret name, which extendeth from the firmament of heaven into the earth:

ATHÊZOPHÔIM ZADÊAGÊÔBEPHIATHEAA AMBRAMI ABRAAM THALCHILTHOE ELKÔTHÔÔÊÊ ACHTHÔNÔN SA ISAK CHÔÊIOURTHASIÔ IÔSIA ICHÊMEÔÔÔÔ AÔAEI,[51]

Rescue me in this hour of need!

3. Close the rite in your customary manner.

---

[50]Personification of Greek word for "fate."
[51] This formula contains the Hebrew names Abraham (ABRAAM), Isaac (ISAK), and Hosea (IOSIA). See also operations 3 and 15 in this collection.

Operations to Gain Favor

One of the most general types of magical operations is designed to gain the favor of entities, human or super-human, which might be able to help the magician in various areas of life. Depending on the entities involved, these favors could range from the acquisition of wealth, to security, to the gaining of wisdom, and to the winning of love.

32. Stêlê of Aphroditê for Favor
(*PGM* VII.215–218, 300 c.e.)

This amulet, or stêlê, is used to gain friendship, favor, success, and friends. Take a strip of tin and engrave this formula on it with a bronze stylus.

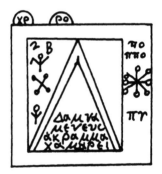

After engraving it, make it sacred by offering frankincense to it and pray to Aphroditê in your own words for what you want from the stêlê. Put the stêlê in a pouch of white linen and wear it on your person.

33. To Win the Favor of Crowds
(*PGM* XXXVI.275–283, 350 c.e.)

1. Perform a version of your customary opening rite of purification.

2. Offer a sacrifice of aromatic woods (frankincense).

3. Then inscribe these characters on a silver tablet:

ℓ Ρ𝟾☙☍ + ʊ ssss ⊞ ☞

⊐ℓ𝕵° 𝟊 ɤℓ𝕵 Χ ⊠ ΒΖ𝚮

Now, sing this incantational formula over the tablet:

ERÊKISIPHTHÊARARCHARAÊPHTHISIKÊRE
[er-ayk-izif-thay-ahr-ahr-kharah-ayf-thizi-kay-reh].

4. Then coat the tablet with a paste of frankincense.

5. Put the tablet in a pouch of linen and wear it as an amulet concealed under your clothing. It will serve you well.

The ancients also believed this charm would work beneficially on someone afflicted by a maleficent daimôn (*kakodaimôn*).

WORKINGS FOR THE GAINING OF LOVE

Historically there have been few magical aims or purposes more popular than winning the love of a sexual partner. The Hermetic magicians seem to have been especially interested in this magical goal. It should be born in mind that although a human partner is usually intended, there is also an erotic component to philosophy and to the religion of the Hermetics that is often overlooked. The loved one—with whom one desires union—could be a goddess or god, or even one's own soul: Psychê.

34. For Love
(*PGM* IV.1265–1274, 350 c.e.)

The name of Aphroditê, which the magician can only learn after some time, is NEPHERIÊRI. This means "the one beautiful to the eye" in Egyptian. If you want to win the love of a beautiful woman, abstain from sexual activity for three days, make an offering of frankincense and sing the name NEPHERIÊRI over it. When you see the woman say it seven times in your heart while gazing upon her. Do this for seven days. On the seventh day your purpose will have been accomplished. Go and talk to her and she will be receptive to your approach.

35. For Love
(*PGM* VII.300a–310, 300 c.e.)

The ancients say this charm will work in the same hour it is used. It should be made when the Moon is waxing and in the sign of Aries or Taurus.

1. Perform your usual opening rite of purification.

2. Take a large sea shell and write upon it in red (Typhonian) ink or paint:

I adjure thee, o shell, by bitter Anankê—Goddess of Necessity: MASKELLI MASKELLÔ PHNOUKENTABAÔ OREOBAZA-GRA RHÊXICHTHÔN HIPPOCHTHÔN PYRIPÊGANYX and by those given dominion over all Punishments: LAKI LAKIÔ LAKIMOU MOUKILA KILAMOU IÔR MOUÔR MOUDRA MAXTHA MOUSATHA.

Attract him/her [state the name of the beloved], whom [state name of the mother of the beloved] bore! [Here you can add any other particulars or limitations you wish.]

Do not be stubborn, but attract him/her: OUCH OUCH CHAUNA MOUCHLIMALCHA MANTÔR MOURKANA MOULITHA MALTHALI MOUI ÊIÊI YYY AÊ AIÊ YOÔ AÊI AÊI AÊI AÔA AÔA AÔA IAÔ ÔAI ÔAI AIÔ ÔIA IÔA IAÔ ÔAI: Attract him/her, [repeat the name of the beloved].

3. Close the rite in your customary manner.

36. For Love
(*PGM* VII.405–406 300 C.E.)

While kissing your lover passionately say in your heart:

I am[52] THAZI N EPIBATHA CHEOUCH CHA *I am I am* CHARIEMOUTH LAILAM [add what ever else you want].

37. For Love
(*PGM* XXXVI.187–210, 350 C.E.)

This working is best undertaken when the Moon is in the sign of Aries.

1. Perform your customary opening rite of purification.

---

[52]The word *anok* means "I am" in Coptic, and may be substituted here for that phrase.

2. Take a sharp bronze stylus and before your personal altar inscribe the following formula on an unbaked piece of pottery:

Hekatê, thou, O Hekatê! Triple-Formed Goddess! As every form of the magical signs is complete, I call upon thee, by the great name of ABLANATHANALBA and by the power of AGRAM-MACHAMARI, for I invoke thee who possesseth the fire of ONYR, and by all those who dwell within it, that [insert the name of the lover you wish to attract] be set aflame and that she [or he] come in pursuit of me [insert your own name] for I hold in my right hand the twin serpents and the victory of IAÔ SABAÔTH and the great–name BILKATRI MOPHECHE who brandisheth the fire STOUTOUKATOUTOU, so that she [or he] will love me completely and be aflame and on fire for me, yes and tortured too! I am SYNKOUTOUEL.

Then write the formula: Grant me, indeed, the favor of all, ADÔ-NAI.[53] Followed by these eight additional characters:

3. Perform the song of the seven vowels and write the following magical square on the reverse side of the piece of pottery.

$$
\begin{array}{ccccccc}
\alpha & \alpha & \alpha & \alpha & \alpha & \alpha & \alpha \\
\varepsilon & \varepsilon & \varepsilon & \varepsilon & \varepsilon & \varepsilon & \varepsilon \\
\eta & \eta & \eta & \eta & \eta & \eta & \eta \\
o & o & o & o & o & o & o \\
\upsilon & \upsilon & \upsilon & \upsilon & \upsilon & \upsilon & \upsilon \\
\omega & \omega & \omega & \omega & \omega & \omega & \omega
\end{array}
$$

4. After the piece of pottery has been properly inscribed, have it fired in a kiln. While it is being fired, concentrate on the purpose of the working and repeat the verbal portions of the formula.

5. Close the rite in your customary way.

---

[53]In Greek this would appear: μοι την χαριν Αδωναι

Leave the fired piece of pottery on your personal magical altar until the lover comes to you. (Remember, Hekatê and all the other gods and goddesses will help those who themselves are active.)

38. Love
(*PGM* VII.462–466, 300 c.e.)

The ancients called this an excellent love-charm.

1. Perform your customary opening rite of purification.

2. Take a thin sheet of tin and scratch the following characters and formulas on it with a copper stylus:

ICHANARMENTHO CHASAR, cause him/her, [write the name of the beloved] to love me. [Add whatever else you wish.]

3. Then sanctify it with some *usia*,[54] magical material, for example a hair or some bodily fluid from the beloved mixed with frankincense paste or rose oil.

39. For Love and Attraction
(*PGM* XXXVI.69–101, 350 c.e.)

The original source says that this is an "excellent divination by fire, than which none is greater. It attracts men to women, and women to men and makes virgins rush out of their homes."

1. Perform your customary rite of purification.

---

[54]The Greek word used here, ουσια, means "substance" or "essence" and is used for sympathetic purposes.

2. Take a piece of papyrus and with Typhonian ink write this formula:

Come Typhôn, who sitteth high atop the gate: IÔ ERBÊTH IÔ PAKERBÊTH IÔ BALCHOSÊTH IÔ APOMPS IO SESENRÔ IÔ BIMAT IAKOUMBIAI ABERRAMENTHÔ OULERTHEXANAX ETHRELUOÔTH MEMAREBA TOU SÊTH,[55] as thou art aflame and on fire, so also is the heart and soul of him/her, [name the one you wish to attract], whom [name his/her mother] bore, until he/she cometh loving me, [insert your own name], and bind his/her sexual essence to mine—*Êdê, êdê—tachy, tachy!*

3. Now draw this figure on the papyrus in the same Typhonian ink:

4. Now glue some magical material (ουσια) from the one you desire onto the papyrus. This could be one of his/her hairs, nail parings, or any other part of his/her person.

---

[55]BALCHO-SÊTH and TOU SÊTH record original Egyptian forms of the name of Set-Typhôn.

5. Affix this piece of papyrus to the wall of your bathroom where showers are taken regularly. The desired one will soon come to you.

6. Close the rite in your customary way.

40. To Gain Friendship
(*PGM* XII.397–400, 350 c.e.)

This operation is to be used if you want to gain the favor and friendship of others forever.

1. Perform your customary rite of purification.

2. Take the root of pasitha or wormwood and write this name in a sacred manner on it:

$$ \mathcal{F} \Upsilon \lambda \llcorner \int \neg 3 \, \text{m} \, \text{m} \, \text{L} $$

Wear this on your person and you will be the object of admiration for those who meet you.

If you can not obtain a root of pasitha or wormwood, the name can be written with a special ink[56] on a strip of papyrus or paper.

---

[56]The formula for this ink is given here as: 1 dram of myrrh, 4 drams of truffle, 2 drams of blue vitriol, 2 drams of oak gall, 3 drams of gum arabic.

RESTRAINING OPERATIONS

The universe abounds in psychoid beings—either human beings or entities whose constitution makes them seem as if they have wills to either help or harm us. Restraining operations are designed to prevent harm from coming to you from these beings, be they human or non-human. If the magician believes that his or her lack of success is due to the activities of others, a "restraining spell" is perhaps the key ingredient to success.

41. To Restrain Anger and Gain Success
(*PGM* XXXVI.161–177, 350 c.e.)

The ancient source claims that no operation is greater than this one, and that it is to be performed by means of "words alone." Hold your thumbs inside your fists as tightly as you can and repeat this incantation seven times:

ERMALLÔTH ARCHIMALLÔTH, stop any mouths that speak against me—for I glorify thy sacred and honored names which are in heaven.

To act as an anchor for the spoken formula and to aid it in its working, you should take papyrus and write these words with myrrh ink:

"I am CHPHYRIS! I must be successful. MICHAÊL RAPHAÊL ROUBÊL NARIÊL KATTIÊL ROUNBOUTHIÊL AZARIÊL IOÊL IOUÊL EZRIÊL SOURIÊL NARIÊL METMOURIÊL AZAÊL AZIÊL SAOUMIÊL ROUBOUTHIÊL RABIEÊL RABIEÊL RABCHLOU ENAEZRAÊL, angels protect me from any bad situation that might come upon me."

42. To Restrain Anger
(*PGM* LXXX.1–5, 350 c.e.)

To restrain the anger of another, repeat this incantation three times:

I am the soul of darkness,[57] ABRASAX, the eternal one, MICHAÊL, but my true name is THÔOUTH, THÔOUTH. Restrain the anger and wrath of him/her, [here name the person whose anger you wish to restrain], toward me, [here insert your name], by the authority of the great god NEOUPHNEIÔTH!

43. Cease Anger
(*PGM* XII.179–181, 350 c.e.)

If someone is angry with you and you want to make them stop, write the name of anger, CHNEOM,[58] on pure white linen with myrrh ink. Hold the linen in your left hand and say:

I restrain the anger of all, especially that of him/her [name the one whose anger you want to restrain] which is CHNEOM.

44. Restraining Operation
(*PGM* VII.417–422, 300 c.e.)

This entire operation should take place in the morning, in the hours before sunrise.

1. Perform your customary rite of purification.

2. Take a tin lamella (a thin sheet of tin) and with a bronze stylus, write the names: CHRÊMILLON MOULOCH KAMPY CHRÊ OPHTHO MASKELLI MASKELLÔ PHNOUKENTABAÔ OREOBAZAGRA RHÊXICHTHON HIPPOCHTHON

---

[57]In the original papyrus this and the rest of this sentence is written in Coptic, but in Greek letters: *Bainchôôôch* = "soul of darkness" in Coptic.

[58]CHNEOM is a Hermetic magical form of the Egyptian god-name Khnum.

PYRIPÊGANYX and the formula: ERÊKISIPHTHÊ IABEZE-BYTH. Also inscribe the lamella with these magical characters:

⊗ Ⅎ Ƶ 𝆑 ⌐ Χ Ε

After these characters write the phrase: θεοι κραταιοι κατεχετε (Mighty gods, restrain!). To this you can add whatever you will.

3. Now go to the shore of a large body of water and throw the lamella into the water, a river or the sea.

4. Close the rite in your customary manner.

The entire rite is best done at the shore of the body of water into which you are going to throw the lamella.

45. Restraining Operation
(*PGM* VII.429–458, 300 C.E.)

The ancient source says this works on anything—"even chariots." It is also said to be able to cause enmity and sickness, cut down, destroy, or overturn anything. The operation conjures daimôns and makes them enter objects or people.

1. Perform your customary opening rite of purification.

2. Take a lead plate, preferably one from a cold-water pipe, and with a headless bronze needle or stylus engrave the following formula on it:

I conjure thee, O lord Osiris, by thy holy names: OUCHICÔCH OUSENARATH, Osiris, OUSERRANNOUPHTHI OS-ORNOUPHÊ[59] Osiris-Mnevis, OUSERSETEMENTH AMARA MACHI CHOMASO EMMAI SERBÔNIEMER Isis ARATÔPHI ERACHAX ESEOIÔTH ARBIÔTH ARBIÔTHI AMEN CHNOUM MONMONT OUZATHI PÊR OUN-

---

[59]From the Egyptian *wsir nefer.* "Osiris the good."

NEPHER EN ÔÔÔ: Lord Osiris, I commend to thee, and deposit with thee, this matter: [Add the magical effects you wish]

3. Now consecrate the plate with bitter smelling incense such as myrrh, bdellium, styrax, and aloes, and thyme, and anoint it with river mud.

4. Drill a hole in the plate and tie a sturdy cord several feet in length to it.

5. Late in the evening or in the middle of the night go to some body of water—a stream or drainage ditch, or even to the sea. Tie the loose end of the cord to a stable object on the bank and throw the plate into the water so it will be carried along by the current.

6. Now vocally perform the formula seven times "and you will see something wonderful."

7. Then leave the water without turning back or speaking to anyone. Return to your dwelling and there wash and immerse yourself in water. Rest and eat only vegetable food.

To undo the formula untie the plate from its anchor.

An alternate to this formula is to be used if you want to bury the plate in the ground or put it in a coffin, or sink it in a river or at sea, or in a well. This is called the Orphic formula: ASKEI KAI TASKEI. It is to be inscribed on the plate as in the instructions above. Then take a black thread and make 365 knots in it and wrap the thread around the outside of the plate. Repeat the ASKEI KAI TASKEI formula, and add: "**Keep him/her who is held**" [or "**bound**"], or whatever else you wish. And thus the plate is to be buried or otherwise deposited.

The original papyrus tells us that when Selênê goes through the underworld, she breaks whatever spell she finds there. But as long as this rite has been performed properly, the formula will remain in force as long as you repeat the formula every night at the place where you deposited the plate. The ancient source adds that you should not be anxious to share the methods of this operation with anyone, because you will not easily find another like it.

46. Restrain Anger
(*PGM* X.24–35 400 c.e.)

The ancients claimed that this amulet worked against the anger and hatred of all kinds of people and entities—against enemies, bandits, accusers, phobias, and even nightmares. The operation should be performed when the Moon is in the sign of Cancer.

1. Perform your customary opening rite of purification.

2. Take a gold or silver sheet of metal—a lamella—and engrave the following characters on it:

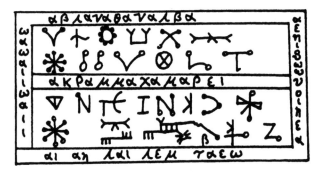

The names are: ABLANATHANALBA AEÊIOYÔÔYOIÊEA ÔAÔAIIÔAII AKRAMMACHAMAREI AI AE LAI LEM TAEÔ.

3. Intone these names over the lamella while it is lying on the altar.

4. Offer incense to the lamella.

5. Close the rite in your customary manner.

Incense should continue to be offered to the lamella whenever the Moon is in the sign of Cancer.

AN OPERATION TO
CAUSE SEPARATION

Although the operation here is intended to cause a human and an erotically attached pair to separate, the formula can be used for other purposes as well. If you think of the formulas of alchemy, you will perhaps see into some of the other uses of the formula.

47. To Cause Separation
(*PGM* XII.365–375, 350 c.e.)

1. Perform your usual opening rite of purification.

2. On a pot for smoked fish[60] inscribe this formula with a bronze stylus and then recite it orally:

I call upon thee, god, thou who art in the void of ærial space, thou who art awesome, invisible, and great, thou who shakest the earth and causest the universe to tremble, thou who lovest disturbances and hatest stability and scatterest the clouds one from the other: IAIA IAKOUBIAI IÔ ERBÊTH IÔ PAKERBÊTH IÔ BOL-CHOSÊTH BASDOUMA PATATHNAX APOPSS OSESRÔ ATAPH THABRAOU ÊÔ THATHTHABRA BÔRARA ARO-BREITHA BOLCHOSÊTH KOKKOLOIPTOLÊ RAMBITH-NIPS. Give to him/her, [name of the first person], the son/daughter of her, [name the mother of the first person], strife and war; and to him/her, [name the second person], son/daughter of her, [name the mother of the second person], odiousness, enmity, just as Typhôn and Osiris had. [But if it is a man and woman say: "Just as Typhôn

---

[60]Fish are associated with Set-Typhôn, hence they were tabu for members of Osirian cults.

and Isis had."] Strong Typhôn, almighty one, complete thy mighty deeds!

3. Take the talismanic object and put it in a place near where those who you wish to separate live, or near the way by which they usually return home, and while you are doing this repeat the formula given above.

VICTORY AND
SUCCESS OPERATIONS

Operations for victory or success have always been popular among magicians. They can be adapted easily to all kinds of purposes and aims in which the magician wishes to be successful.

48. Victory
(*PGM* XCVIII.1–7, 250 c.e.)

Write the following formula in myrrh ink on a piece of papyrus:

A		α
E E		ε ε
Ê Ê Ê		η η η
I I I I	with Greek *stoicheia*	ι ι ι ι
O O O O O		o o o o o
Y Y Y Y Y Y		υ υ υ υ υ υ
Ô Ô Ô Ô Ô Ô Ô		ω ω ω ω ω ω ω

Make the papyrus sacred by sacrificing incense to it in the brazier on your altar. Recite the prayer:

Victorious in all things is the one who nourisheth the whole inhabited world—Lord Serapis: make [here insert the name of the one who is to have the victory or success] victorious.

49. Victory
(*PGM* VII.528–539, 300 c.e.)

1. Perform your customary opening rite of purification.

2. Make an offering of sacred incense mixed with wheat germ over oak charcoal.

3. Recite this formula:

Hêlios, Hêlios, hear me [state your name], Hêlios, lord, great god, thou who maintaineth all things and who giveth life and who ruleth over the world, toward whom all things go, from whom all things also came—inexhaustible one:

ÊIE ELÊIE IEÔA ROUBA ANAMAÔ MERMAÔ CHADAMATHA ARDAMATHA
PEPHRE ANAMALAZÔ PHECHEIDEU ENEDEREU SIMA-TOI MERMEREÔ
AMALAXIPHIA MERSIPHIA EREME THASTEU PAPIE PHEREDÔNAX
ANAIE GELEÔ AMARA MATÔR MÔMARÊSIO NE-OUTHÔN ALAÔ AGELAÔ
AMAR AMATÔR MÔRMASI SOUTHÔN ANAMAÔ GALA-MARARMA.

Hear me, lord Hêlios, and let the [paraphrase your magical will] take place on time.

4. Close the rite in your customary manner.

50. Hermês' Victory Working
(*PGM* VII.919–924, 300 c.e.)

1. Perform your customary opening rite of purification.

2. Offer cassia incense in the brazier on your altar.

3. Execute the following inscription on a thin gold tablet or plate, or even on a gold covered piece of parchment or papyrus.

⊓ ✕ ⋎ 33～ H ✳ ⋏⋏. ⌐⌐⌐ ♂ K ⋺⋺K

THÔOUTH, give victory, strength, influence to the wearer. [Θωουθ, δος νικην, ισχυν, δυναμιν τω φορουντι, as the Greek appears in the original.]

4. After it has been fashioned sanctify it in the fumes of the incense and speak the words of the inscription over it.

5. Close the rite in your usual manner.

Keep the inscription with you always in your shoe. It can be placed on a vehicle or any other object. The ancients report that you will be amazed with its effectiveness.

51. For Victory and Success in All Things
(*PGM* VII.1017–1026, 300 c.e.)

1. Perform your customary opening rite of purification.

2. Recite this formula:

Hail Hêlios! Hail Hêlios! Hail Gabriêl! Hail Raphaêl! Hail Michaêl! Hail the whole cosmos! Give me the power and authority of SABAÔTH, the strength of IAÔ, the success of ABLANATHANALBA, and the might of AKRAM-MACHAMAREI! Grant that I gain the victory for which I summoned thee!

3. Now write the 59-letter IAEÔ-formula on a strip of papyrus:

IAEÔBAPHRENEMOUNOTHILARIKRIPHIAE
YEAIPHIRKIRALITHONOMENERPHABÔEAI

[In Greek *stoicheia* this would appear:]

ιαεωβαφρενεμουνοθιλαρικριφιαε
υεαιπιρκιραλιθονυομενερφαβωεαι

4. Then continue with the prayer formula:

Give me victory for I know the names of the Agathodaimôn, the Good Daimôn: HARPON CHNOUPHI BRITATÊNOPHRI BRISAROUAZAR   BASEN   KRIPHI   NIPTOUMI CHMOUMAÔPHI. [At this time add the things you want to happen.] **Accomplish all this for me!**

5. Close the rite in your customary manner.

After you have done the work, speak to no one for twelve hours. Keep the papyrus with you at all times.

WINNING AT GAMES OF CHANCE

Games of chance have always been closely related to magic. Some games evolved from divinatory rites, such as the casting or drawing of lots, and so continued to have a magical aura about them. Since ancient times, magicians have tried to influence the outcome of such games for their own benefit. The old papyri contain a few of these attempts. Such formulas can also be adopted for any purpose in which chance or probabilities are involved.

52. To Win at Dice
(*PGM* VII.423–428, 300 c.e.)

If it is your will to win at dice, or at any game of chance, silently repeat in your mind this formula:

THERTHENITHÔR DYAGÔTHERE THERTHENITHÔR SYAPOTHEREUO KÔDOCHÔR make me a winner at dice [or whatever other game], O prevailing Adriêl!

If you are playing dice whisper into your hand holding the dice the following formula:

Let none be my equal, for I am THERTHENITHÔR ÊRÔTHORTHIN DOLOTHOR, and I throw what I will!

This should be repeated as long as you are playing.

53. To Catch a Thief
(*PGM* V.172–212, 350 c.e.)

In an age when there were no police and there was little personal security for persons of modest means, apprehending thieves and recovering lost articles was an important endeavor. Such formulas can also be turned to spiritual purposes to recover lost or stolen ideas. This would be a typical Greek linkage between Hermês and the magic found in the old papyri, as Hermês is the "god of thieves."

Prepare your tripod by writing this formula on a piece of papyrus and gluing it on the underside of the tripod:

δεσποτα Ιαω, φωσφορε, παραδος φωρ, 'οω ζητω

1. Perform your customary opening rite of purification.

2. Offer myrrh and frankincense to Hermês in the tripod while reciting this prayer twice:

In order to catch a thief I summon thee, Hermês, immortal god, who didst cut a furrow down Olympos and the holy barge, light-bearer IAÔ, the great eternally living one, terrifying to behold and terrifying to hear. Hand over the thief whom I seek: ABERAMEN-THÔOULERTHEXENAXONELYSÔTHNENAREBA.

3. Take a faience vessel, add water and myrrh. Wet a branch of laurel in the vessel and sprinkle around the altar.

4. Take 8 drams of winter wheat and 8 drams of goat-cheese and offer it into the tripod while reciting the following formula (which is the same as that inscribed on the papyrus under the tripod): **Master IAÔ, light-bearer, hand over the thief whom I see.**

5. Over a plate of bread and cheese laid upon your altar recite this formula:

Come to me: LISSOIN MATERNA MAUERTÊ PREPTEK-TIOUN INTIKIOUS OLOKOTOUS PERIKLYSAI, may you bring back to me what was lost and point out the thief this very day. I call upon Hermês, finder of thieves, Hêlios and the eye of Hêlios,[61] **the two who bring lawless deeds to light, and Themis,**[62]

---

[61]That is the Sun.
[62]Themis is the Greek personification of Justice.

Erinys,[63] Ammôn and ParAmmôn,[64] to take control of the thief's throat and to single him out in this day—in this hour!

6. Close the rite in your usual manner.

In the original papyrus it seems that suspects were to be given pieces of the sanctified bread and cheese and if one of them could not swallow it, he or she was shown to be the thief.

---

[63]Erinys is the Greek goddess of vengeance.

[64]Ammôn and ParAmmôn are probably designations of Zeus and Hermês respectively. Zeus was honored with the name Ammôn, with whom he was identified in Hellenistic times. ParAmmôn means "he who is beside Ammôn."

FORMULA OF THANKSGIVING

At the end of the path, which may have its beginnings in the realm of *goêteia*, lies the world of the purest form of *mageia*—in which the initiation of the magician is completed to the extent that operations in the objective universe become unnecessary. At that point, magicians need no longer indulge in ritual, for their magic has been entirely internalized. This is the *end*, not the beginning, of the journey. The following formula is closely based on one shared by three documents in the ancient Hermetic tradition: *PGM* III.591–610; *Nag Hammadi Codex* VI, 7; and the *Asclepius* 41.[65] It is to be spoken when one has reached the end of the path of goêtia.

We give thanks to thee! Every heart and soul is stretched out to thee, whose name is holy and whose name is god. Thou art blesséd with the name of the Father, for thou hast shown us fatherly goodwill, love, friendship, and the sweetest power, giving us intellect, speech, and knowledge:

> Intellect, that we might understand thee,
> Speech, that we might invoke thee,
> Knowledge, that we might know thee.

We rejoice for thou hast illuminated us with thy knowledge.
We rejoice for thou hast shown us thy self.
We rejoice for thou hast made us divine through thy knowledge.
We rejoice for thou hast done this while we still had bodies.
Our delight abideth in one thing: That we know thee.

> O intellectual light—we have known thee,
> O life of life—we have known thee,
> O womb of knowledge—we have known thee,

[65] For information on the *Nag Hammadi Codex VI, 7*, see James M. Robertson, *The Nag Hammaradi Library* (Leiden: Brill, 1977), pp. 298–299. For information on *Asclepius* 41, see Walter Scott, *Hermetics* (Boston: Shambhala, 1985), pp. 374–377.

O womb, pregnant with the Father's nature—we have known
    thee,
O eternal permanence of the generating Father—we have
    worshipped thy goodness.
There is but one petition we ask of thee:
    Preserve us in our illuminated knowledge.
There is but one protection we ask of thee:
    Preserve us in our present life.

AEHIOYΩ
IAΩ

Appendices

Appendix A
Recipes

1. Myrrh Ink (from *PGM* I.232–247)

4 drams of myrrh troglitis
3 karian figs
7 pits of Nikolaus dates
7 dried pinecones
7 piths of the single stemmed wormwood
7 wings of the Hermetic ibis (= 7 leaves of buckthorn)
spring water

Burn the ingredients to ashes. Prepare ingredients as an ink or paint.

2. Typhonian Ink

fiery red poppy
juice from an artichoke
seed of the Egyptian acacia
red ochre
asbestos
quicklime
wormwood
gum
rain water

Prepare ingredients as an ink or paint.

3. Natron (used for purification of the ritual area)

1 part powdered sodium carbonate
1 part powdered sodium bicarbonate

Grind together to a fine powder and mix with water to make a dilute solution.

4. For a General Offering

Take white frankincense and grind to a fine powder. Mix with fine wheat flour, egg, milk, (rose-)honey, and a little olive oil. Knead into a small ball of dough.

Offer by burning on charcoal in the brazier.

Appendix B
Days for Divination

(from *PGM* VII.155–167)

Here each day of the month is ascribed a number (1–30), and to each of these enumerated days is added the time of day most advantageous for divinatory purposes. Certain days are unsuitable for divinatory practices and are so noted.

1	at dawn	16	do not use
2	at noon	17	do not use
3	do not use	18	at dawn and in the afternoon
4	at dawn	19	at dawn
5	at dawn	20	at dawn
6	do not use	21	in the afternoon
7	at noon	22	in the afternoon
8	throughout the day	23	at dawn
9	do not use	24	at dawn
10	throughout the day	25	do not use
11	in the afternoon	26	in the afternoon
12	throughout the day	27	throughout the day
13	throughout the day	28	throughout the day
14	at dawn	29	throughout the day
15	throughout the day	30	in the afternoon

Appendix C
Lunar Positions
for Workings

(from *PGM* VII.284–299)

Another, fragmentary papyrus (*PGM* III.275–281) has some alternate uses for the Lunar positions. These are given in parentheses after the attributions in *PGM* VII.

Moon in Aries: Fire divination or love charm.

Moon in Taurus: Invocation to the lamp.

Moon in Gemini: For winning favor (or for binding).

Moon in Cancer: For protective spells (or ones for reconciliation or air divination).

Moon in Leo: Rings and bindings.

Moon in Virgo: Anything is rendered obtainable (also for bowl divinations).

Moon in Libra: Necromancy.

Moon in Scorpio: Inflicting evil.

Moon in Sagittarius: Invoking or making incantations to the Sun and Moon.

Moon in Capricorn: Say whatever you wish for best results.

Moon in Aquarius: For a love charm.

Moon in Pisces: For foreknowledge (or love charm).

APPENDIX D
MAGICO-POETIC
NAMES OF HERBS

It has long been supposed that many of the old magical spells and recipes calling for things like "eye of newt" were using a kind of code in which an herb or some other substance was being secretly indicated. But, of course, systematic lists of these coded references are hard to find. *PGM* XII:401–444 contains just such a list:

A snake's head: a leech.

A snake's "ball of thread": soapstone.

Blood of a snake: hematite.

Bone of ibis: buckthorn.

Blood of hyrax: actually hyrax.

Hamadryas baboon tears: dill juice.

Crocodile dung: Ethiopian soil.

Hamadryas baboon blood: blood of a spotted gecko.

Lion semen: human semen.

Blood of Hephaistos: wormwood.

Hamadryas baboon hairs: dill seed.

Semen of Hermês: dill.

Blood of Arês: purslane.

Blood of an eye: tamarisk gall.

Blood from a shoulder: bear's breach.

From the loins: camomile.

A man's bile: turnip sap.

A pig's tail: leopard's bane (*Boronicum*).

A physician's bone: sandstone.

Blood of Hestia: camomile.

An eagle: wild garlic.

Blood of a goose: sap of a mulberry tree.

Kronos' spice: piglet's milk.

A lion's hairs: "tongue" of turnip (leaves of its taproot).

Kronos' blood: [sap of] cedar.

Semen of Hêlios: white hellebore.

Semen of Heraklês: mustard-rocket (*Eruca sativa*).

A Titan's blood: wild lettuce.

Blood from a head: lupine.

A bull's semen: egg of a blister beetle.

A hawk's heart: heart of wormwood.

Semen of Hephaistos: fleabane.

Semen of Ammôn: houseleek.

Semen of Arês: clover.

Fat from the head: spurge.

From the belly: earth-apple.

From the foot: houseleek.

APPENDIX E
ON THE WRITING OF
GREEK LETTERS AND
THEIR TRANSCRIPTION

Some operations call for the magician to write formulas in Greek letters. Since most readers may be unfamiliar with the Greek language, it is necessary to say a few words about how the characters are actually made on paper and how to transcribe Roman-letter formulas (as are mostly seen in this book) into their Greek equivalents.

In the tradition of the papyri, the Greek letters used are almost exclusively the cursive, manuscript style letters, not the capitals. Also, the Egyptian tradition of writing the letters is slightly different from the style usually seen in printed versions of the *alphabeta*.

α β γ δ ε ζ η θ
A B G D E Z E TH

ι κ λ μ ν ξ ο π
I K L M N X O P

ρ ϲ τ υ φ χ ψ ω
R S T Y PH CH PS O

The letters are to be made by starting the pen stroke at the point shown by the asterisk *. Making the letters in the exact same way the ancients did not only makes them appear more authentic and æsthetically pleasing, it has the *magical* effect of ritually reenacting the motions of the ancients, and thereby remanifesting dormant atavisms otherwise untapped.

For the purpose of transliterating formulas, the Greek letters have the Roman equivalences shown here. Be careful to distinguish between E and Ê and O and Ô in the formulas. Note also that Greek ου combination is transcribed OU.

In the *voces magicae* formulas printed in Roman capitals in this book, as well as in most transcriptions of Greek words, I have kept the orthography as "conservative" as possible. The "classical" transcriptions of Greek words often found elsewhere have the following equivalences:

αι is transcribed ae;   for example: *daimôn* = daemon.

γγ is transcribed ng;   for example: *aggelos* = angelos.

γξ is transcribed nx;   for example: *sphigx*   = sphinx.

γκ is transcribed nc/k; for example: *Anagkê*   = Anankê.

ου is transcribed u;   for example: *Ouranos* = Uranos.

ει is transcribed i;   for example: *Eirênê*   = Irene.

υ is transcribed y;   for example: *psychê*   = psychê.

οι is transcribed oe;   for example: *phoinix* = phoenix.

Appendix F
On the Pronunciation
of Greek and
Hellenized Foreign Words

It is imperative that the working Hermetic magician be able to pronounce the vocal magical formulas, or *voces magicae* in the operations that call for such performance. The Index of Common Magical Formulas (pp. 275–276) provides some phonetic transcriptions of a selection of these words, but a more general set of rules for pronunciation will also be helpful.

The formulas are written in Greek letters because this writing system provides for a full range of phonetic possibilities. The original writers of the papyri used the Greek *alphabeta* as a system for the phonetic transcription of magical formulas, which could not be represented with the Egyptian or Hebrew systems. They are therefore to be pronounced as the Greek of the first half of the first millennium C.E. would have been pronounced:[1]

A = α as the "a" in "father."

AI = αι as the "ai" in "Isaiah."

AU = αυ as the "ow" in "grown."

B = β as the "b" in "bad."

G = γ as the "g" in "get."

GG = γγ as the "ng" in "anger."

GK = γκ as the "ngk" in "Chungking."

D = δ as the "d" in "day."

E = ε as the "e" in "fret."

---

[1] For the sake of completeness and accuracy, it must also be mentioned that the particularly *Egyptian* pronunciation of the Greek characters, which surfaces in the Coptic system should, or could, also be taken into account in the performance of *voces magicae*.

EU = ευ as the "ew" in "f<u>ew</u>."

Z = ζ   as the "z" in "<u>z</u>oo"
         —but in Classical Greek as the "zd" in "Ma<u>zd</u>a."

Ê = η   as the "a" in "m<u>a</u>te."

EI = ει as the "ey" in "gr<u>ey</u>" or "ee" in f<u>ee</u>d."

TH = θ   as "t + h" in "ho<u>th</u>ouse"
         —but later as "th" in "<u>th</u>in."[2]

I = ι   as the "ee" in "f<u>ee</u>d."

K = κ   as the "k" in "<u>k</u>ing."

L = λ   as the "l" in "<u>l</u>yre."

M = μ   as the "m" in "<u>m</u>use."

N = ν   as the "n" in "<u>n</u>ow."

X = ξ   as the "x" in "ne<u>x</u>t."

O = ο   as the "o" in "n<u>o</u>t."

OI = οι as the "oi" in "b<u>oi</u>l."

P = π   as the "p" in "<u>p</u>ie."

R = ρ   as the "r" in "<u>r</u>ich" (trilled).

S = σ   or (ς in final position) as the "s" in "<u>s</u>it"
         —but as a "z" before B, G, D or M.

T = τ   as the "t" in "<u>t</u>ap."

Y = υ   as in German "ü" or French "du" (that is as the "ee"
         sound with the lips rounded)

OU = ου as the "u" in "r<u>u</u>le."

---

[2]It is unclear as to when these developments in the sound system occurred.

PH = ϕ   as "p + h" in "up̲h̲ill"
        —but later as "ph" in "p̲h̲oto."[3]

CH = χ   as "k + h" in "bloc̲k̲h̲ead"
        —but later as "ch" in Scottish "loc̲h̲."

PS = ψ   as the "ps" in "lap̲s̲e."

O = ω   as the "o" in "h̲o̲me."

_____

[3]It is unclear as to when these developments in the sound system occurred.

APPENDIX G
THE SEMITIC WRITING SYSTEM

The Semitic writing system, with its named phonemes, apparently had its origins among the Semitic (Phoenician) population on the island of Crete around 1000 B.C.E., from where it spread to the mainland of Phoenicia. From Phoenicia, it then spread throughout the western Semitic world, where some form of it was eventually used by the Canaanites, Hebrews, and other Semitic peoples. It is from this system that the Hebrew *alef-bet* of 22 letters is derived.

A casual look at Table 1 on p. 269 will suffice to demonstrate the fact that the Hebrew letter names, inherited from the common Semitic lore and not actually specific or unique to Hebrew, are clearly illustrated in ideographic form in the original Cretan forms. The lore encoded in the Hebrew writing system is therefore particular to extremely archaic, but non-Judaic mythology of the Semites of the eastern Mediterranean. Some of this may have even been lore shared with the Mycenaean Greeks or Old Europeans on the island of Crete at the time of the genesis of the system.

Certain alterations in the system were made later by the Hebrews for theological reasons. For example, the name of the N-letter, *nehas* (= serpent) was changed to *nun* (= fish) because of the later association of the serpent with "evil" by the forces of orthodoxy. (Although the fish too was considered a "Typhonian creature," at least by the Egyptians.)

The importance of this lore for magical studies of the Hebrew *alef-bet* should be obvious. First, the system itself would be most attuned, not to the Biblical mythology of the Hebrews, but to the "pagan" magic and mythology of the Phoenicians or Ugaritic peoples. This may explain why so little use is made of these particular mysteries in the magical study of the Hebrew letters. They do not tend to reveal *orthodox* lore, but yield rather heterodox conclusions about certain passages contained in both the Hebrew and Christian Bibles.

Lore hidden in Table 1 on p. 269 can be used to decode a variety of texts found in the Judeo-Christian tradition. Knowledge of the

Table 1.   The Semitic Alef-bet

Number	Cretan Form	Old Semitic Form	Hebrew Form	Hebrew Name	Meaning	Phonetic Value
1	[glyph]	[glyph]	א	*alef*	ox	ʼ
2	[glyph]	[glyph]	ב	*bet*	house	b
3	[glyph]	[glyph]	ג	*gimel*	rope/camel	g
4	[glyph]	[glyph]	ד	*dalet*	door (=leaf)	d
5	[glyph]	[glyph]	ה	*he*	(latticed) window	h
6	[glyph]	[glyph]	ו	*waw*	nail/hook	w
7	[glyph]	[glyph]	ז	*zayn*	sword/ weapon	z
8	[glyph]	[glyph]	ח	*het*	fence	ḥ
9	[glyph]	[glyph]	ט	*tet*	coil? bundle?	ṭ
10	[glyph]	[glyph]	י	*yod*	hand	y
11	[glyph]	[glyph]	כ	*kaf*	palm (of the hand)	k
12	[glyph]	[glyph]	ל	*lamed*	(ox-)goad	l
13		[glyph]	מ	*mem*	water	m
14	[glyph]	[glyph]	נ	*nun/ nahas*	fish/ serpent	n
15	[glyph]	[glyph]	ס	*samekh*	prop/ support	s
16	[glyph]	[glyph]	ע	*ʼayin*	eye	ʻ
17	[glyph]	[glyph]	פ	*pe*	mouth	p/f
18	[glyph]	[glyph]	צ	*tzade*	(fish-) hook	tz
19	[glyph]	[glyph]	ק	*qof*	back of head	q
20	[glyph]	[glyph]	ר	*resh*	head	r
21	[glyph]	[glyph]	ש	*shin*	tooth	sh
22	[glyph]	[glyph]	ת	*taw*	sign	t

esoteric tradition, often contrary to orthodox exoteric teachings, was obviously preserved by certain schools, and it is to one of these that Jesus apparently belonged. Note how many times Jesus (as well as other teachers and prophets) used metaphors that make use of words translated by the Hebrew letter names.

The study of this lore could easily be the subject of another entire book.

Glossary of Divine Names

The numbers in parentheses refer to the operations in this book where the formula or name of the god or goddess can be found.

Abrasax: A numerical gematria formula which adds to 365—the cosmic god often identified with Mithras. Also spelled Abraxas (3, 7, 42).

Agathos Daimôn: Greek god-form meaning "good daimôn" (12, 51).

Aiôn: Greek word meaning an "age," a vast expanse of time and space. Often personified to be a god-form (1, 2, 3, 4, 7, 9, 11).

Ammôn: Egyptian god whose name means "the Hidden," usually appears in the papyri as AMOUN (12, 15, 18, 53).

Anankê: Abstract Greek goddess of necessity or compulsion. A personification of a principle (2, 14, 35).

Apollo: Highly complex Greek god of the arts, prophesy and wolves (7, 26).

Arês: Greek god of war = Roman Mars (18).

Athêna: Greek goddess of wisdom. Patroness of Athens (18).

Hekatê: Originally an Anatolian goddess, her Greek name means "the hundredth part," which refers to the portion of the grain crop returned to the ground for the next harvest. She is a chthonic goddess of the underworld associated with the Moon (37).

Helioros: Combination of the gods Hêlios-Horus (1).

Hêlios: Greek personification of the Sun (1, 2, 51).

Hermês: Greek god of intelligence and communication. Identified with the Egyptian Thoth (9, 18, 24, 50, 53).

Iaô: Heb. Yahweh. Creator god of the Hebrews, thought to be the Demiurge by Gnostics, and generally held to be a powerful god in Hermetic magic because of his association with the natural cosmos (2, 3, 4, 7, 10, 11, 15, 16, 19, 26, 27, 35, 37, 51, 53).

Khnum: Egyptian god of creation, shaper of gods and humanity. An ancient ram-god (43).

Kronos: Greek god of time = Roman Saturn (9, 18).

Isis: Egyptian goddess of life and creation. Identified with the star Sothis, the Dog Star (9, 12, 18, 19, 45, 47).

Mithras: An originally Iranian god (of law and war) who became the focus of a syncretic cult in late antique times throughout the Mediterranean and western Europe (2).

Mnevis: The Egyptian divine bull of the Moon (18, 45).

Nemesis: Greek goddess of the inexorable equilibrium of the human condition (12).

Osiris: Egyptian god of the dead. Often invoked for chthonic workings (3, 9, 15, 18, 19, 24, 28, 45, 47).

Ouranos: Greek god of the sky (18).

Pan: An ancient Greek divinity which by the time of the papyri had come to symbolize "the All" (9, 18).

Phre: Hellenized form of the name of the Egyptian sun god, Rê, with a definite article attached: "the Sun" (2, 28).

Sekhmet: Egyptian lion-goddess of war and plague (23).

Serapis: A Greco-Egyptian god-form derived from the Egyptian combination of Osiris and Apis (Asar-Hapi). In Ptolemaic times Serapis becomes a god of the Underworld (19, 48).

Set: Egyptian god of discord and disruption of the natural order. Greek form of the name: Sêth (19, 23, 39, 47).

Tychê: Greek goddess of fortune, Roman Fortuna (18).

Typhôn: Last and greatest of the pre-Olympian Titans. See also Set (1, 19, 35, 39, 47).

Zeus: Chief god of the Greeks. God of law and sovereign power (2, 7, 11, 18, 20, 26, 53).

Index of Common Magical Formulas

Formulas included in this index are either those that appear more than once in this collection of operations, or are clearly otherwise well-known formulas, or are based on names of divinities or concepts in other languages. The numbers in parentheses refer to the operations in this book where the formula or name of the god or goddess can be found.

ABERAMENTHTHÔ [ab-er-am-ENT'-t'oh]: A formula that stands alone (19, 39) and begins longer formulas as well (7, 53). It seems most often to be a Typhonian name.

ABLANATHANALBA [ab-lan-ah-t'an-AL-bah]: A palindromic name of the god of this world (5, 8, 11, 27, 37, 46, 51).

AIÔ [ah-ee-oh]: Light-Forcer Permutation of IAÔ (2, 13, 35).

BOLCHOSÊTH [boll-kho-SAYT']: A Typhonian name (19, 47).

BAINCHÔÔÔCH [bayn-k'oh'oh'oh-kh]: A Coptic word (from older Egyptian b_3 n khy), "soul of darkness."

CHNOUPHI [khnoo-p'ee]: A daimonic, lion-headed, serpentine entity, which is a syncretic combination of Chnoum, the Egyptian creator-god, the serpent Kneph, and the star called *Knm*. This occurs in conjunction with the name HARPON, which is a form of Horus (29, 51).

ERBÊTH [err-BAYT']: Typhonian name, almost always together with PAKERBÊTH (19, 39, 47).

ERESCHIGAL [err-ess-KHI-gal]: From the name of the Mesopotamian goddess of the underworld.

IAEÔBAPHRENEMOUN [ee-ah-eh-oh-bap'ren-eh-moon]: Formula often used to introduce a longer version of the sequence (1, 4, 51).

IAÔ [ee-ah-oh]: Hermetic form of the Hebrew divine name, Yahweh (the *Tetragrammaton*) (2, 3, 4, 5, 7, 10, 11, 15, 16, 19, 26, 27, 36, 37, 53).

IARBATHA [ee-ahr-baht'ah]: Common shorter form of a longer palindrome which contains the Egyptian phrase "the great lamb of Khnum the great." Occurs together with the IAEÔBAPHREN-EMOUN formula. Numerological evidence shows it to be a Typhonian name (1).

MASKELLI: (15, 35, 46) Often together with MASKELLÔ (35). A Typhonian formula.

NEOUPHNEIÔTH [nay-oop'-NAY-oht'] = name of the great god.

PAKERBÊTH [pak-err-BAYTh]: Typhonian, almost always together with ERBÊTH (7, 19, 39, 47).

PENTITEROUNI [pent-EETER-oonee] = Fire-Walker (2).

SABAÔTH [sab-ah-OHT']: From the Hebrew *Tzabaoth*, "armies." Often found together with IAÔ—thus representing the Hebraic *Yahweh Tzabaoth*, which literally means "god of the armies," the ancient Hebrew war god (3, 6, 11, 15, 26, 37, 51).

SESENGENBARPHARAGGÊS [ses-en-gen-bahr-p'arang-ays]: A Typhonian name which occurs in various forms and lengths in the papyri (26, 30).

THÔOUTH [thoh-ooth]: From the Egyptian *Djhuti*, "the god Thoth" (15, 19, 20, 27, 30, 42, 50).

Bibliography

Agrell, Sigurd. *Die pergamenische Zauberscheibe und das Tarockspiel* (Humanistiska vetnskapssanfundet Lund. Årsberättelse 1935–1936). Lund: Gleerup 1936.

Agrippa von Nettesheim, Heinrich Cornelius. *Three Books of Occult Philosophy* [1651]. London: Chthonios, 1986.

Armstrong, A. H. *The Cambridge History of Later Greek and Early Medieval Philosophy.* Cambridge: Cambridge University Press, 1967.

Aureleus, Marcus. *Meditations.* Maxwell Staniforth, trans. New York: Penguin, 1964.

Bonnet, Hans. *Reallexikon der ägyptischen Religionsgeschichte.* Berlin: De Gruyter, 1952.

Betz, Hans Dieter, ed. *The Greek Magical Papyri in Translation.* Chicago: University of Chicago Press, 1986.

Boyce, Mary. *Zoroastrians: Their Religious Beliefs and Practices.* London: Routledge & Kegan Paul, 1979.

Budge, E. A. Wallis. *Egyptian Language.* London: Routledge & Kegan Paul, 1958.

Burkert, Walter. *Ancient Mystery Cults.* Cambridge, MA: Harvard University Press, 1987.

Cassirer, Ernst, et al., eds. *The Renaissance Philosophy of Man.* Chicago: University of Chicago Press, 1948.

Cicero, *The Nature of the Gods.* London: Penguin, 1972.

Cohn, Norman. *Europe's Inner Demons.* New York: Basic Books, 1975.

―――. *In Pursuit of the Millennium.* 2nd ed. Oxford: Oxford University Press, 1961.

Cornford, Francis M., trans. and ed. *The Republic of Plato*. Oxford: Oxford University Press, 1941.

Cumont, Franz. *The Mysteries of Mithras*. New York: Dover, 1956.

Davies, Stevan, et al. "The Kabbalah of the Nations: Anglicization of Jewish Kabbalah," in *Studia Mystica* 3:3 (Fall, 1980), 34–47.

Dornseiff, Franz. *Das Alphabet in Mystik und Magie*. Leipzig: Teubner, 1922.

Doresse, Jean. *The Secret Books of the Egyptian Gnostics*. Rochester, VT: Inner Traditions, 1986.

Eliade, Mircea. *History of Religious Ideas*. 3 vols. W. Trask, A. Hiltebeitel, D. Apastolos-Cappadona, trans. Chicago: University of Chicago Press, 1978–1985.

―――. *Patterns in Comparative Religion*. R. Sheed, trans. New York: Meridian, 1963.

―――. *The Two and the One*. J. Cohen, trans. New York: Harper & Row, 1965.

Fontenrose, Python. *A Study of Delphic Myth and Its Origins*. Berkeley, CA: University of California Press, 1959.

Forsyth, *Old Enemy: Satan and the Combat Myth*. Princeton, NJ: Princeton University Press, 1989.

Fowden, Garth. *The Egyptian Hermes: A Historical Approach to the Late Pagan Mind*. 2nd ed. Princeton, NJ: Princeton University Press, 1993.

Frankfort, Henri. *Kingship and the Gods*. Chicago: University of Chicago Press, 1948.

Godwin, David. *Light in Extension*. St. Paul, MN: Llewellyn, 1992.

Guthrie, Kenneth S., ed. *The Pythagorean Sourcebook and Library*. Grand Rapids, MI: Phanes, 1987.

Guthrie, William K. C. *Orpheus and Greek Religion*. 2nd ed. New York: Norton, 1966.

Hamilton, Edith and Huntington Cairns. *Plato: The Collected Dialogues.* Princeton, NJ: Princeton University Press, 1963.

Helck, Wolfgang and Otto Eberhard, eds. *Lexikon der Ägyptologie.* Wiesbaden: O. Harrassowitz, 1972–.

Herodotus. *The Persian Wars.* George Rawlinson, ed. New York: Random House, 1945.

Hesiod. *Theogony.* N. O. Brown, trans. Indianapolis, IN: Bobbs-Merrill, 1953.

Hooke, S. H. *Middle Eastern Mythology.* London: Penguin, 1963.

Hornung, Erik. *Conceptions of God in Ancient Egypt: The One and the Many.* John Baines, trans. Ithica, NY: Cornell University Press, 1982.

Jacobsen, Thorkild. *The Treasures of Darkness.* New Haven, CT: Yale University Press, 1976.

Jordan, Paul. *Egypt: The Black Land.* Oxford: Phaidon, 1976.

Kaplan, Aryeh. *Sefer Yetzirah: The Book of Creation.* York Beach, ME: Samuel Weiser, 1990.

Kramer, Samuel N. *The Sumerians.* Chicago: University of Chicago Press, 1963.

Littleton, C. Scott. *The New Comparative Mythology.* Berkeley, CA: University of California Press, 1973.

Luck, Georg. *Arcana Mundi: Magic & the Occult in the Greek & Roman Worlds.* Baltimore, MD: Johns Hopkins University Press, 1985.

Lucretius. *On the Nature of the Universe.* R. Latham, trans. London: Penguin, 1951.

Mallory, J. P. *In Search of the Indo-Europeans.* London: Thames & Hudson, 1989.

Pausanias. *Description of Greece.* 4 vols. W. H. S. Jones, trans. London: Heinemann, 1918–1935.

Philo Judaeus. *The Works of Philo Judaeus.* C.D. Yonge, trans. London: George Bell, 1855, 4 vols.

Plotinus. *The Enneads.* Stephen MacKenna, trans. London: Penguin, 1991; Burdeth, NY: Larson, 1991.

Preisendanz, Karl, ed. and trans. *Papyri Graecae Magicae.* 2 vols. Stuttgart: Teubner, 1973–1974.

Pritchard, J. B. *Ancient Near Eastern Texts Relating to the Old Testament.* 2nd ed. Princeton, NJ: Princeton University Press, 1955.

Rhode, Erwin. *Psyche: The Cult of Souls and Belief in Immorality Among the Greeks.* W. B. Hillis, trans. Freeport, NY: Books for Libraries Press, 1972.

Robinson, James M., ed. *The Nag Hammadi Library.* Leiden: Brill, 1977.

Romer, John. *Ancient Lives: Daily Life in Egypt of the Pharaohs.* New York: Henry Holt, 1984.

Rudolph, Kurt. *Gnosis: The Nature and History of Gnosticism.* San Francisco: Harper, 1984.

Saunders, Jason L. *Greek and Roman Philosophy after Aristotle.* New York: Free Press, 1966.

Schmidt, C., ed. *Pistis Sophia.* V. MacDermot, trans. Leiden: Brill, 1978.

———, ed. *The Books of Jeu and the Untitled Text in the Bruce Codex.* V. MacDermot, trans. Leiden: Brill, 1978.

Scholem, Gershom. *Kabbalah.* New York: Meridian, 1974.

———, ed. *Zohar: The Book of Splendor.* New York: Schocken, 1949.

Scott, Walter. *Hermetica.* 4 vols. Boston: Shambhala, 1985.

Sethe, Kurt. *Die ägyptischen Pyramidentexte.* 4 vols. Hildesheim: Olms, 1960 [1908–22].

Settegast, Mary. *Plato Prehistorian.* Hudson, NY: Lindisfarne Press, 1990.

Seznec, Jean. *The Survival of the Pagan Gods.* B. Sessions, trans. New York: Harper & Row, 1953.

Smith, Morton. *Jesus the Magician.* San Francisco: HarperSanFrancisco, 1978.

Tacitus. *The Histories.* K. Wellesley, trans. London: Penguin, 1964.

Te Velde, H. *Seth: God of Confusion.* Leiden: Brill, 1967.

von Eschenbach, Wolfram. *Parzival.* A. T. Hatto, trans. New York: Viking Penguin, 1980.

Walker, Benjamin. *Gnosticism: Its History and Influence.* London: Aquarian Press, 1983.

Waterfield, Robin, trans. *Theology of Arithmetic.* Grand Rapids, MI: Phanes, 1988.

Widengren, Geo. *Die Religionen Irans.* Stuttgart: Kohlhammer, 1965.

Zoller, Robert, trans., Robert Hand, ed. *Liber Hermetis: Part I.* Berkeley Springs, WV: Golden Hind, 1993.

Index

Dyad, 131
dynamis, 152

E

Egyptian
  culture, 19
  gods and goddesses, 84
  roots, 5
Eight, 132
elemental letters, 118
Elements, 21, 126
Eliade, Mircea, 42
Elohim, 95
Emerald Tablet, 40
encircling, 155
Endlessness, 61
Ennead, 132
Ennoia, 29, 53
Ephesus, 15
Epicureanism, school of, 26
Epinoia, 53
Epistle from Abaris to Ammo-
    nius, 65
  second part, 79
Erebos, 55, 59
evil, 56

F

Fayyum, 3
fear, 77
Ficino, Marcilio, 12
Field of Reeds, 63
fish, 90
Five, 131
fixed stars, 54, 59

formulas, common magical, 275
Four, 131
Fowden, Garth, 7, 38, 48, 118
friendship, gaining, 237

G

Gabriêl, 99
Geb, 62
gematria, 119, 132
gnôsis, 40, 55, 57, 68
Goddess Anankê, 159
goês, 36
goêteia, 59, 101, 102
Gnostic
  cosmograph, 58
  stream, 26
Goodwin, Charles Wycliffe, 13,
    16
Great Wain, 32
Greek
  cultures, 20
  pronunciation, 265
  tradition, 119
  writing of letters, 263
Gyges, 6

H

Hadês, 55
heart, 75
Hebrew, 110
Hebrew Gods, 95
Hebrew tradition, 118
Heka, 60, 74, 77
Helen of Troy, 29
Helene, 28

Stephen Edred Flowers has been developing the methods outlined in this book since the early 1970s. In 1984 he received a Ph.D. for his work on runic magical formulas. It was during this research that the original work on the Greek Magical Papyri was begun.

Dr. Flowers lives with his wife, Crystal, and together they established Woodharrow, a center for initiatory work, in 1993.

Made in United States
Orlando, FL
20 August 2023

36271034R00193